A Cyclist's Guide to the Shenandoah Valley

Randy Porter and Nancy Sorrells

A CYCLIST'S GUIDE TO THE SHENANDOAH VALLEY

ISBN 0-9637819-0-1

FIRST EDITION

Designed by Michael Vayvada, Ace Graphics
Photography Credits: Page vii - Nancy Sorrells, Page 79 - Gary Bordeaux,
Page 233 - Dennis Sutton. All other photographs by Randy Porter

Contents

APPENDIXES

Here I am, in the centre of the magnificent valley of the Shenandoah, the great valley of Virginia. And a glorious valley it is — equal to the promised land for fertility, far superior to it for beauty and inhabited by an infinitely superior people...

Washington Irving, 1853

Contributors

Thanks to the following people for their input into the content of this book.

Mark Gatewood — *Pedaling Past Wildflowers*

Ann McCleary — *Pedaling Past Early Valley Architecture, Later Victorian Architecture,* and *Log Buildings*

Susanne Simmons — *Pedaling Past African-Americans*

John Taylor — *Pedaling Past Jackson's Valley Campaign* and *Civil War Destruction*

James Wilson — *Pedaling Past Ironworks*

Becky Witmer — *Pedaling Past Mennonites*

Andy Hunter, Lexington Bike Shop; Gerald Knicely, Mole Hill Bikes; and Dave Shipp — Route suggestions

Other thanks to Janet Downs and Betty Jo Hamilton

Dedications

Writing a book is like giving birth after a pregnancy that can last indefinitely. While the labor is plenty tough, so is that period preceding it as one tries to attend to the everyday stuff while keeping track of that seed of an idea that grows and grows inside, eventually acquiring a life of its own. Well, it's time to give out the cigars, but not without first thanking those folks who contributed in large and small ways.

Nancy Sorrells' thorough research and willingness to spend her spare time on the road knocking on the doors of interesting houses up and down the Shenandoah Valley, talking to strangers, and clarifying confusing route directions after driving 10 miles out of the way. And all the while she believed that these efforts would not be in vain. Well, they weren't!!!

Mike Vayvada of Ace Graphics in Staunton took a pile of computer printouts and the half-baked ideas of an aspiring writer/publisher and turned them into a real book.

My wife and life partner, Cindy provided love and support during my extended pregnancy to help bring this new life full-term. Thanks for attending to the details of life while I passed in and out on my way to work on "The Book." After 15 years of running together for better or worse, she jumped on board to become my business partner as well.

And of course my 6-year-old son, Chris, who hopefully understood that my love for him never faltered despite all the time I spent working on "the dumb old book."

R.P.

The only grandfather I ever knew was actually my great-grandfather, a time-worn character who passed away at the age of 97 when I was a freshman in college. Perhaps it is not a coincidence that within weeks of his death, I changed my major to history. Was it a subconscious effort to span the chasm separating the past from the present which his mind, clear until just weeks before his death, had bridged? Maybe. At any rate, my love of history was sparked at an early age by Andrew Vincent Griffith, and so I offer a belated thanks.

There is also a pair of Randys whom I would like to thank. The first is my husband who brings to our marriage a Shenandoah Valley heritage which I lack as well as a belief that I could be successful in my writing efforts. Thanks for doing the laundry, feeding the animals, and eating fast food while I was riding routes, knocking on doors, or hacking away at the computer. At the same time, thanks should also go to the rest of my family for believing me — or at least not openly disbelieving me — during the last 18 months when I repeatedly told them I was working on a book.

The second Randy is my co-author who called me out of the blue several years ago with an idea for a book. He'd read an article I'd written about bicycling for the *Staunton Daily News Leader* and wanted to compare notes with a kindred spirit and fellow writer. Little did I know that I would end up so involved in this project. Thanks for letting me take part in bringing this idea to fruition and for having the flexibility which allowed our creativity to flow as "The Book" took on a life of its own.

N.S.

Preface
By Nancy Sorrells

In the years since my transplant to the Shenandoah Valley more than two decades ago, I have worked hard to earn my status as a local. In the process I have come to appreciate the depth and complexity of the culture which has evolved here, nourished by the struggles of settling a rich frontier. My respect for the early settlers of the Valley, be they Native American, African-American or European, expands as my knowledge of their lives grows.

Although there were settlers hugging Virginia's shores in the early 1600s, it took more than 100 years for those immigrants to cast their eyes westward past the flat Tidewater and rolling Piedmont and across the mighty Blue Ridge Mountains. European explorers first penetrated the Great Valley of Virginia in the late 1600s, but settlers did not start wending their way here until the early 1700s. Those coming from the east traversed one of several passes through the Blue Ridge Mountains. The majority, however, came southwestward from Pennsylvania between the parallel ridges that define Virginia's Great Valley.

Ironically, the Native Americans who had actually lived in the Shenandoah Valley over the previous 10,000 years had virtually abandoned this region by the time of the first European settlements. As a result, the fertile lands of the Shenandoah River watershed were wide open for settlement.

And so they came. English settlers whose families had already established a firm foothold in America topped the mountains at places like Swift Run Gap and Rockfish Gap. They brought with them a language and the blueprint for a government to be transferred onto the New World. Pennsylvania had been the first stop for many German-speaking and Scots-Irish settlers who were interested in Virginia's frontier where available land was said to be abundant and could be had for literally pennies an acre. These multi-cultural pioneers brought an Old World heritage which included specific ways to build houses, cultivate farms, and cook meals.

The frontier west of the Blue Ridge Mountains was settled in a defined and orderly way. Initially tracts of around 100,000 acres were granted to individuals by the English monarch through Virginia's colonial government. These Crown Grants were given with the stipulation that at least one family would settle on every 1,000 acres within a two-year period. Men like William Beverley and Benjamin Borden became land speculators and even immigration agents as they attracted settlers onto newly acquired lands. For the most part, the routes that you'll pedal along in *A Cyclist's Guide to the Shenandoah Valley* pass through lands that were once included in the Beverley (Augusta and Rockingham Counties) or Borden Grant (Rockbridge and some of Augusta County).

As these New World pioneers forged ahead on muddy wagon roads and felled trees in an effort to clear land and build homes, they were casting the mold for a new culture on the American frontier using the raw materials from their Old World heritage. It is this sometimes hazy past which I have attempted to rediscover and piece together for this book. I've learned that local history is fascinating AND frustrating. National events, such as presidential elections and wars, are well documented in history books. However, there is a considerable scarcity of information about less noteworthy facts like who ran the general store in Zack, a small mountain community in Rockbridge County, or why there are two South Rivers within a few miles of each other, one running north and the other south.

It is certainly true that we may never know all the answers when attempting to find out what village once existed in what is now a patch of woods or how a particular creek got its name. More frustrating, however, is that often there are several answers, all or none of which may be true. For instance, the Rockingham County village of Mount Clinton reportedly got its name in the 1800s after a fierce campaign in which votes were bought with applejack brandy. That's one version. Another story tells of a flirtatious cavalry officer named Clinton. While passing through town, he struck up a conversation with the local ladies until he was told by a superior," Mount Clinton," and he left the village. His temporary charms are said to have left a permanent impact in terms of a name for this crossroads community. Which is true? Maybe the first. Probably not the second. It could be both or it could be neither. But both explanations are plausible and have been repeated enough to be a part of the local lore.

Little written documentation was left by people trying to work their land, raise a family, or carve out a subsistence living, and the details that I've tried to pull together are sometimes sketchy at best. I have concluded that the optimal recipe for unearthing local history is one part written documentation and two parts oral history mixed slowly over time. As a result, you'll find many explanations prefaced by "Tradition has it..." or "According to local legend..." That's okay. Folklore is defined as "unwritten traditional beliefs, legends, sayings, customs of a culture." Supposedly Winston Churchill once said of King Arthur and his legendary Knights of the Round Table, "It is all true, or it should be..." And that's the way I feel about Shenandoah Valley history.

While King Arthur was searching for the Holy Grail, I had less lofty goals in my quest for local lore. Along the way, I encountered dozens of unforgettable characters pointing me in some direction. The people of the Shenandoah Valley invited me into their homes and shared their lives. They opened creaky doors to attics and brushed cobwebs from both photograph albums and memories in an attempt to answer my questions. Through it all, it's been a rewarding experience.

There was a 95-year-old woman at Getz Corner who taught the "three R's" in a two-room Rockingham County schoolhouse. An Arbor Hill resident remembered the old tollroad which used to run from Staunton to Middlebrook. As I sat and chatted with furniture makers and clockmakers, I was able to piece together the past. The reader will not find a time machine to the past in these pages for even more scholarly tomes struggle with the inconsistencies of local history. Through my travels, readings, and conversations, I've tried to merely create a window through which cyclists can peek into the past as they pedal along the Valley's rural roads and perhaps more fully appreciate all that surrounds them.

My job as a historian was eased by many published historical works. The following list includes those which proved most helpful. They are recommended for anyone whose historical curiosity is piqued. Although some are out of print, they may still be available at the local libraries. Others are still in print or have been reprinted and can be purchased at area bookstores or through the historical societies whose phone numbers are in the back of this book.

Annals of Augusta County Virginia 1726-1871 by Joseph A. Waddell

A History of Rockbridge County by Oren F. Morton

Atlas of Rockingham County Virginia 1885 reprinted by the Harrisonburg-Rockingham Historical Society

A History of Rockingham County Virginia by John W. Wayland

Atlas of Rockingham County, Virginia (1939) by Noah D. Showalter

Augusta County Historical Bulletins published by the Augusta County Historical Society

Augusta County History 1865-1950 by Richard K. MacMaster

Civil War Virginia-Battleground for a Nation by James Robertson

History of Augusta County, Virginia by John Lewis Peyton

Illustrated Historical Atlas of Augusta County Virginia 1885 by Jedediah Hotchkiss and Joseph Waddell. Reprinted by the Augusta County Historical Society.

Life Under Four Flags in the North River Basin of Virginia by C.E. May

My Augusta: A Spot of Earth Not a Woman by C.E. May

Old Houses in Rockingham County 1750-1850 by Isaac Terrell

One Hundred Historic Sites and Structures in Rockbridge County and Lexington by The Association for the Preservation of Virginia Antiquities

Pedaling Through Time by B.C. Sheetz from *Curio*

Proceedings of the Rockbridge Historical Society published by the Rockbridge Historical Society

Shenandoah Sketches by Joe Nutt from *The Daily News Leader*

Study Unit: Historic Resources in Augusta County, Virginia Eighteenth Century to the Present by Ann McCleary

The Heartland: Rockingham County edited by Nancy Hess

The Tinkling Spring: Headwater of Freedom by Howard McKnight Wilson

Valley Patriots by Howard McKnight Wilson

Virginia Place Names, Derivations Historical Uses by Raus McDill

West of Suez by J. Flint Walker

Introduction
By Randy Porter

This book has been a long time coming. It really started in 1968 when I got a Schwinn Varsity to take with me as a freshman to the College of William and Mary. It got another push several years later with a lighter Gitane Gran Sport. Then there was starting up the Freewheeler Bike Shop in Williamsburg in '73, and a lot more bikes and riding over the years in various parts of Virginia. But in the course of setting up and running bike tours through Bike Virginia in the early Eighties, I came to discover the joys of riding in the Shenandoah Valley. And I knew that nothing could rival the geography, people, and quiet backroads that abound in this land between the Blue Ridge and Alleghenies. In the course of living and riding here for the last 14 years, I'm continually amazed that it only gets better.

Repeatedly, I've heard people say, "I'd like to ride but don't know where to go," or "I'd go riding if it weren't for the hills." And on and on. So now I get the opportunity to present *A Cyclist's Guide to the Shenandoah Valley.* Pedaling through the Valley is a great chance to put aside life's daily troubles, and focus on the rhythm of the ride. The sounds of a smoothly operating derailleur and chain, the crickets and warblers, and the burble of a nearby mountain stream may be your only companions. The sights will vary from well-kept farms to decrepit, run-down homeplaces. If you're hoping to escape subdivisions and mobile homes, I can't guarantee that. This is, after all, America, not a Currier and Ives print. However, the mountains are omnipresent, and they are eternal.

As cyclists, we may uncover beautiful places to ride and then find that our curiosity is aroused by a historic sign or building. This book is based on the premise that your two-wheel pleasure will be enhanced by a better understanding of the surroundings. And it is with this in mind that we've provided historical and narrative information along the way. This book is not intended to be a comprehensive historical guide. As Nancy Sorrells said in her Preface, this is merely intended to provide a window of knowledge and an enhanced perspective on the Shenandoah Valley.

We've taken some liberties with what we call the Shenandoah Valley. Technically, the southern boundary of the Valley is at the Dividing Ridge between the James and Shenandoah River watersheds. The northern terminus is somewhat blurred by the presence of the Massanutten Range which divides the Shenandoah Valley. So from the very beginning, we plead guilty to crossing the lines of absolute correctness under the guise of providing access to some of the best cycling to be found anywhere.

It should come as no surprise to anyone that there are a lot of hills in the Valley. However, what goes up also comes down. And besides, most folks would prefer to struggle up a hill with a definite beginning and end rather than battle a headwind *ad infinitum.* If you're not afraid of a few hills, the Shenandoah Valley offers some of the best road cycling to be found anywhere. The routes of choice are the ones that meander through rolling farmland with the least amount of vehicular traffic and offer spectacular views of the Blue Ridge and Allegheny Mountains. The other trick is to stay off gravel roads which may make the going a bit rough for skinny tire bikes.

Although the word seems to be getting out to the cycling public about the wealth of opportunities for two-wheel travel, the area has not been overrun. The Virginia Loop and Trans-America Bikecentennial trails both pass through the Shenandoah Valley. World class cyclists in the Tour de Trump and Tour Du Pont discovered the ecstasy of riding on the Blue Ridge Parkway and the agony of the 2,637-foot climb at Wintergreen resort. Several of the commercial bike touring companies have begun to incorporate local routes into their offerings.

Much has been written and said about the great views along the 105-mile Skyline Drive that runs from Front Royal south to Afton Mountain. From there the 470-mile Blue Ridge Parkway begins with its terminus in Cherokee, North Carolina. If you pick out a nice looking stretch from either of these roads and confine your riding to weekdays, especially during the magnificent autumn colors, you'll have some superb cycling experiences to remember for years to come. You can expect to share the road with a variety of four-wheelers, so always stay as far to the right as possible. If you're especially interested in riding the Parkway or the Skyline Drive, *Bicycling the Blue Ridge* by Elizabeth and Charlie Skinner is required reading.

Down in the Valley to the west of the Blue Ridge Mountains, there's a different kind of cycling that incorporates mountain views as well as the vast tracts of farmland which give this area its distinctive "down home" flavor. Often the quiet and relative lack of traffic lulls cyclists, especially in groups, into a false sense of security. Keep an eye out for cars, trucks, and farm equipment. Anyone who's interested in bicycle travel on quiet country roads off the beaten path will find that the Shenandoah Valley has it all. So if you've got the inclination, pack your bike and gear and head out to the place where the road meets the sky. You won't leave disappointed — but then no cyclist ever does.

Routes

All of the routes in this book are loops except for the flat rides in Appendix A. In addition, all use the same starting and ending point for any of the five localities with the exception of the *Fort Harrison Frolic* which is included as a Bridgewater route but begins at the Daniel Harrison House in Dayton. We've tried to cover a range of routes in terms of mileage which in most cases translates into degree of difficulty. However, if the length of a particular ride seems too challenging, shorten it by riding to a reasonable half-way point given your ability level. Another option is to get a non-cycling friend to provide a sag wagon at a desirable end of the line.

The flat rides tend to be easy and usually accompany rivers making them especially scenic. We put them in for all those folks who either refuse to ride because of the hills around here or allowed one of us to coerce them into going for a ride on our say-so that, "It's not too bad." To all those disbelievers, there really are flat rides in the Shenandoah Valley.

After much deliberation, we opted not to include any riding on gravel roads which abound in these parts. If you do find yourself riding on gravel, check your map and directions again. You're definitely somewhere but not on one of the routes in this book.

Dogs

During the Fourth Annual Bike Virginia ride in June 1991 on which some 1,000 cyclists rode from Lexington to Berryville in five days, I was repeatedly asked the question, "How did you get all the people along the route to tie up their dogs?" I'd like to take credit for that amazing feat, but the fact is I can't. My guess is that the dogs and their owners got tired of chasing the procession after a while and took the path of least resistance which was to simply tie up their beasts. This is usually not the case, and so the age-old question arises: How to handle the dog or pack of dogs that takes a liking to those new clipless pedals and shoes?

Dogs are #1 Territorial and #2 Quite curious about the circular motion of cranks and wheels. In some 20 years of cycling, I've never had a dog problem that I couldn't handle through one of the following means:

a) Anticipate Fido's speed and trajectory and outrun him. Don't try this on an uphill unless you're really in fantastic shape. Usually a country dog won't run past his property line, and in many cases feels obligated to make only a token effort to defend his turf at that.

b) Yell at the dog. A display of dominance can go a long way toward establishing the pecking order. Keep it short and non-obscene. I like to yell "Git" in my most commanding tone, and that's always worked well.

c) If all else fails, dismount and walk, keeping your bike between you and the canine. This often defuses the attack and puts you in a better position of balance if more intrusive defenses are necessary.

Pepper sprays, kicking, cursing, and wildly flailing frame-mounted pumps are alternate methods which may be necessary as last ditch attempts to save life and limb. However, these are extremely undesirable and may do more to provoke the hapless cur and his owner than is actually called for. Like I said, I've been riding through rural Virginia for a long time and have yet to encounter a dog that I couldn't outrun, outshout, or outthink.

Food and Drinks Available

We've tried to list all the places on each route that might offer an oasis to weary, hungry, and thirsty cyclists. I would encourage you to patronize them, i.e. actually buy something, not just sit out front, solicit free water, or try to use their bathroom facilities. The flip side of this particular coin is that although these places are in business when we're scouting these routes, that might not be the case when you're reading this and out pedaling along through this beautiful countryside. Ergo, pack for a ride as if all of these facilities are non-existent, and then if they're closed or out of business, you won't be caught up the road without a Power Bar.®

Gearing

There are many books out there that will give all the nitty-gritty stuff about gearing. I had a cycling/tennis buddy way back when who would spontaneously wax poetic on the eternal conundrum regarding pitch height vs. thread width. I'm not a techie so I'll keep what I know simple and to the point. If you're not accustomed to riding decent hills, don't push big gears. Use all those 18-21 sprocket combinations, especially the nice little granny gears that you never get a chance to use in the flatlands. If that fails, don't feel too proud to dismount and walk uphill as opposed to overworking ill-prepared tendons and ligaments in the legs. In such situations, it seems that knees complain the loudest so listen closely to them. If you're prone to swollen patellae, pack plenty of Ibuprofen, a water bottle, and don't be a hero. It's better to cut one day's ride short, than to hobble around for the next two or three. When planning your particular ride from this book, it's best to err on the conservative side as far as mileage goes unless you're well accustomed to climbing hills. They are a great equalizer.

If we were to recommend the use of a bike with a triple chainwheel up front, there are many who would refuse to ride because of limited equipment or resources, and others would take this as a personal challenge just to prove us wrong. There was a fellow who used to ride on the local rides I led through the recreation department. He rode a bike with one gear and coaster brakes and never complained about having to walk up every hill, even the little ones. By his own admission, his riding would not have been hampered by the absence of a chain since he walked his bicycle up every hill and then coasted down the other side.

Neither option is desirable, but the fact remains that most of us will be better able to handle the varied terrain in the Shenandoah Valley with a range that includes 15-21 gears. Also, careening down from the Blue Ridge

Parkway is not a great time to remember to have your brakes overhauled. Make sure your bike is in good working order before you start riding.

Maps

As this book was being prepared, counties in the Shenandoah Valley were switching to the 911 emergency system which requires the use of road names and not merely road numbers. We've opted to stick with identification by numbers for several reasons. The road names are colorful and in many cases their derivation will be given by historical route information in *A Cyclist's Guide to the Shenandoah Valley*. In other cases, you can guess or do some research yourself. If at some point the maps and directions don't jive, go with the route directions. Although additional roads are shown on the maps, some of the ones that are not part of a specific bike loop may have been omitted in the interest of graphic clarity. If you opt to leave the prescribed path, you're on your own.

When to Come

My advice is to pick your favorite season, pack for the extremes of weather and head on out to the Shenandoah Valley. There's really no bad time to come — just better and worse depending on transient weather and crowds. The fall colors tend to attract a lot of visitors which means increased vehicular traffic with drivers who aren't necessarily looking out for cyclists who are likewise doing their share of rubber-necking.

Four season cycling is not unheard of in these parts. Last Christmas I took a ride with my neighbor on a 75-degree December day. However, the year before there were icicles in my gutter for the same entire month. Go figure. Both are extremes and both are flukes. The Harrisonburg Criterium in April was all but snowed out several years ago. It can be hot as you-know-where in July, or mild. We could offer a lot of statistics on mean and median temperature and barometric pressure, but find these to be ultimately meaningless.

The Blue Ridge and Allegheny Mountains have stood by for hundreds of millions of years. They've shaped everything about the Shenandoah Valley, watching life forms from the dinosaur to man come and go. For each of the locales covered in this book, a peak looms in the background as if it was a guardian sent to watch over the particular settlement in the Valley below. Staunton has its twin peaks, Betsy Bell and Mary Gray. Lexington is shadowed by Big and Little House Mountains. Afton Mountain looks down from the Blue Ridge onto Waynesboro. Round Hill and Mole Hill provide a backdrop for the towns of Bridgewater and Dayton. The southern tip of the 50-mile Massanutten looms large against the growing skyline of Harrisonburg.

Directly and indirectly, it is the mountains that define and give the Shenandoah Valley its unique character. As the hurried pace of everyday life produces all kinds of change, it's comforting to hop onto a bicycle and pedal past man's creations toward those enduring peaks waiting patiently as they've always done.

We hope that you'll enjoy riding through the Shenandoah Valley as much as we enjoyed putting this book together. May the wind be at your back, the uphills short, the downhills invigorating, and the rains just commencing as you pull into the driveway.

The goal of this publication is to provide the most accurate and useful information for cycling in the Shenandoah Valley. Shenandoah Odysseys and the authors assume no liability for bicyclists traveling on these routes or using the book in any way. As with cycling on any road or trail, the cyclist assumes the risk while riding. We advise the use of caution, follow all posted and unposted rules of the road, wear an approved helmet at all times, and assure that your bicycle is in good condition.

Harrisonburg
The Friendly City

ROUTES

Harrisonburg
The Friendly City

In 1716, Virginia Governor Alexander Spotswood stood atop the Blue Ridge Mountains and surveyed the scene stretched out before him. Gazing westward into what is now Rockingham County, he referred to the unsettled Shenandoah Valley as a "paradise" and named the river below the Euphrates. We know it now as the Shenandoah River.

Just a few years later, German, Scots-Irish, Swiss, and English settlers streamed into the same valley that Spotswood had previously seen from the mountaintop. The new arrivals began farming and soon established commercial centers for conducting business in the region. Rockingham was formed from Augusta County in 1778. Virginia Governor Patrick Henry promoted this name to honor an Englishman who had been sympathetic toward the colonists during the Revolutionary War.

Thomas Harrison, a prosperous local farmer, donated 2½ acres in 1779 near the geographic center of the Shenandoah Valley to be used as the site for Rockingham's courthouse. He laid out lots on an additional 50 acres and called this new town Rocktown because of the large number of limestone outcroppings in the area. In 1849 the growing community was incorporated and renamed Harrisonburg after its founder.

Harrisonburg was a thriving community of 2,000 residents by 1870, and court days filled the streets. Today there are more than 30,000 people living within the city limits. The surrounding Rockingham County has a population of 60,000 and is the third largest in Virginia by acreage. For many years, people entering the city passed a familiar landmark near the courthouse. The Big Spring was covered by a small domed building, but the springhouse was torn down in the early 1900s when town leaders feared that the structure in the middle of the street might impede traffic.

Although Harrisonburg's earliest school dates back to a 1794 program run by area Methodists, it's the impressive James Madison University campus with its bluestone buildings that stands out these days. JMU started as the State Normal and Industrial School for Women in 1908 under an act

Harrisonburg
City Map

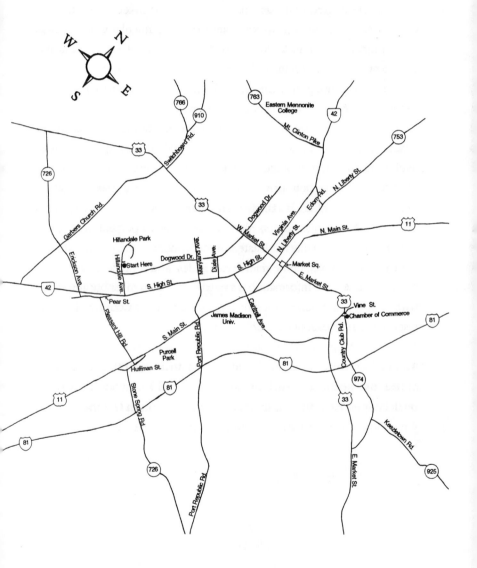

of Virginia's General Assembly. Today the school is a co-educational university with an enrollment of over 10,000 students. The city is also home to Eastern Mennonite College. Located at the north end of the city, EMC was founded in 1917 by the Mennonite Church and grew from a two-year junior college into a four-year school.

The city's industrial base has largely been linked with the rural traditions of neighboring Rockingham County, particularly flour milling and poultry production. A 220-foot feed mill located just a few blocks from downtown was constructed in 1985 by Rocco Industries to mill turkey and chicken feed. Since its formation in 1939, Rocco has grown to become the second largest turkey producer in the country.

As you cycle through the area, you'll see any number of facilities for raising these birds as well as other aspects of the county's agricultural livelihood. In fact, four of the seven largest employers in Rockingham are connected with the poultry industry. This county leads the state in agricultural production of grain, dairy products, and beef in addition to poultry. The area's Mennonite farmers alone account for 25 percent of Virginia's milk supply. The county fair in late summer continues to be a big attraction with animal exhibits, home-made crafts, rides, and food items.

Additional area information is available at the Harrisonburg-Rockingham County Chamber of Commerce at Vine Street and Country Club Road just off Route 33 east of the city.

All cycling routes begin and end at the entrance to Hillandale Park at the intersection of Hillandale Avenue and Dogwood Drive. The park is open 8AM-9PM daily from April 16 through October 31. The park closes at 5PM from November 1 until April 15.

Governor Spotswood and the Knights of the Golden Horseshoe saw a paradise stretched out before them from atop the Blue Ridge Mountains in 1716.

DAYTON DONUT
Harrisonburg • Route 1 • 12.5 miles

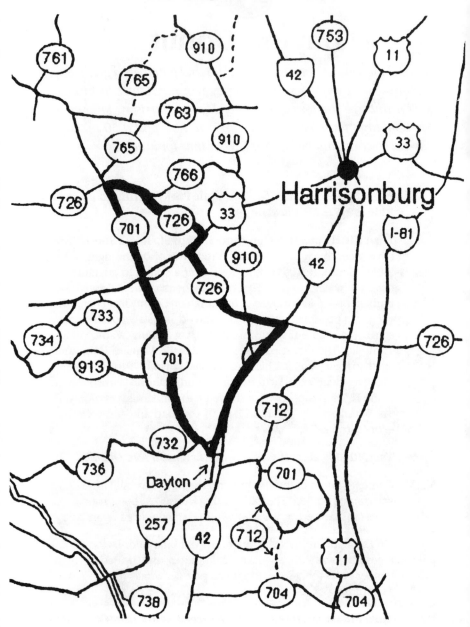

Dayton Donut

For some this ride will be just a warm-up and for others a great way to get out of the city and into the Mennonite countryside. Loop through Dayton and see the former home of Daniel Harrison, brother of Harrisonburg's founder Thomas Harrison. Ride past a 50-million-year-old volcano and be back at JMU in time for lunch.

0.0 **Begin at the entrance to Hillandale Park on Hillandale Ave. Ride EAST on Hillandale Ave.**

0.3 **Turn RIGHT at STOP sign onto S. High St./Rt. 42 South.** The olive-green brick house with the red tin roof on the right is the Bibler House. It was built in 1793 over a spring to guarantee a constant water supply. The original owners were Lewis and Barbara Bibler who moved to Rockingham County from Pennsylvania. It's possible that the house served as a stagecoach stop at some point. Route 42 was formerly the Harrisonburg-Warm Springs Turnpike. The oldest part of the road is the 11 miles from here south to Mossy Creek. This road was laid out in 1779 to give Mossy Creek residents access to the county court system in Harrisonburg. In the 1830s a company was chartered to connect this section and the Warm Springs-Staunton part of the road and complete the entire turnpike.

0.8 **Turn RIGHT at traffic light onto Erickson Ave./Rt. 726.**

1.3 Garbers Church of the Brethren on the right was built in 1822. It was formerly called "The Old Meeting House." Although once two miles outside the city, it is now within Harrisonburg's boundaries.

1.7 On the right are the remains of an old lime kiln. In the 1800s limestone was broken into small pieces and heated at high temperatures to reduce it to a white powder which was then used as fertilizer.

2.7 **Turn RIGHT at STOP sign and proceed with CAUTION on Rt.**

33 East. Route 33 was once known as the Rawley Springs Turnpike. The word *turnpike* means a tollroad. The name comes from the device used to stop traffic so that the toll would be paid. The turnpike itself was usually a tall wooden box with a pike, or pole, resting on it. The pole stretched across the road with the opposite end supported by a forked post. The pike was raised or turned after the toll had been paid.

3.0   Turn LEFT onto Rt. 726 opposite Weavers Mennonite Church on the right. This stone building is the third church to occupy this site. The first was a wooden structure known as Burkholder Church after Peter Burkholder. He was one of the ministers in 1827 when it was built. The name was changed sometime after 1840 to honor Samuel Weaver who moved into the area and became the church sexton.

3.1   The rocky limestone field on the right is indicative of a karst region and provided ample raw materials for area lime kilns.

4.3   The gray house with the tin roof on the left was built in 1902. The tan stone building sitting among the other barns is an early 1900s milking parlor. Look closely for a mound of dirt halfway between the house and road. This covers the family's arch cellar, a stone-lined cavity for keeping food cool. The German settlers brought the arch cellar style with them to the Shenandoah Valley. In front of the cellar is one of the springs marking the beginning of Cooks Creek. It was on this same creek in Dayton that Daniel Harrison built his house in 1749. It flows into the North River which in turn flows into the South Fork of the Shenandoah River.

4.8   Turn LEFT onto Rt. 701 across from Cooks Creek Presbyterian Church. This church began as the Old Erection Church in 1745 located near what is now Dayton. The church and its cemetery had been built near a spring which flooded the building after a dam was constructed. The original site is at the bottom of Dayton's Silver Lake. The congregation moved to the present site in 1780 with the construction of the New Erection Church. The church in front of you was built in 1912 and renamed after the home area of most of its members. The stairs and stones across the road are from an old schoolhouse.

5.2   The farms along this stretch of road offer a look at the variety of agricultural production in the Shenandoah Valley. There's an apple orchard on the hill to the right as well as long poultry houses for raising turkeys and chickens. The large barns and silos are part of a dairy operation where Luther Shank bottled his own milk in the early 1900s.

5.5 The woods to the right are called Burnt Woods. Legend has it that Civil War deserters hid out here, and gold was buried amid the trees to keep it out of Yankee hands.

5.8 Mole Hill is ahead and to the right. It is the remnant of a 50-million-year-old volcano, one of two in Virginia. Mole Hill rises 500 feet above the Valley floor with its top at 1,900 feet above sea level. Locals thought that it looked like it had been pushed up from underground by a giant mole, thus its name. Legend has it that area residents celebrated the end of the War of 1812 by leading an ox to the top and roasting it there. Be sure to pull off the road and enjoy the view.

6.3 **Proceed STRAIGHT on Rt. 701 at STOP sign after crossing Rt. 33.** The community at this intersection on the Rawley Springs Turnpike was known as Millersville after the family that operated a store here and owned a great deal of land in the 1800s. In the late 1800s a new store was built after a company was formed. The new enterprise was built near a valley, or dale, and the new community became **Dale Enterprise.**

6.4 **Bear RIGHT on Rt. 701. Rt. 702 goes left.** The building that once housed the Dale Enterprise store and post office is on the right.

8.1 The stately rock home on the left is Walnut Grove, aptly named for the 40 black walnut trees in the yard. Although the bitter nut can be eaten once the tough shell is cracked, many local artisans have also used the dark brown dye from the outer husk for staining cloth and wood. The house was built in 1931 from stones in the Dry River. It sits on the site of an old school called Paul's Summit.

8.5 Silver Lake was formed in the 1800s with the damming of Cooks Creek. Its name was apparently given by a local school teacher named Pearl Head who thought that such a pretty lake should have a name to match. It has also been called Mill Pond because of the mill at the south end of this 15-acre lake.

8.9 **Dayton** was settled in the mid-1700s and is one of the oldest towns in Rockingham County. Although it was known as Rifetown or

Rifeville after an early landowner named Daniel Rife, it was officially called Dayton when legally established in 1833. This name may come from Jonathon Dayton, youngest signer of the Constitution. He was from New Jersey but apparently had a relative living in this area.

9.0   Continue STRAIGHT on Rt. 732 through Dayton. Rt. 701 goes left and Cooks Creek Park is on the right. The Harrisonburg-Rockingham Historical Society and Museum is on the right across from Cooks Creek Park. ★ **Food and drinks are available at various restaurants in town.** ★

9.3   Turn LEFT at STOP sign onto Main St. For a taste of some wonderful homecooked Mennonite treats, bear right on Main St. and continue through town onto Rt. 42. Then ride **.5 mile** south on Rt. 42. The Dayton Farmers Market on the right is a mini-mall of 21 shops with everything from Shoo Fly Pie to hand-dipped ice cream. It's open Thursday through Saturday.

9.7   Continue STRAIGHT on Business Rt. 42 past STOP sign at Rt. 732. Daniel Harrison, brother of Harrisonburg's founder Thomas Harrison, built this stone house in 1749. In the 1750s, it served as protection against Indian attacks which were especially numerous during the French and Indian War. Supposedly the house once had a stockade around it and an underground passage to a nearby spring. The brick portion of the house was added by later owners who also enlarged the doors and windows. The house is open Saturday and Sunday afternoons from late May through the end of October, and at special times around Christmas.

10.0   Cross Rt. 42 South with CAUTION and turn LEFT onto Rt. 42 North.

11.5   Enter Harrisonburg.

12.2   Turn LEFT onto Hillandale Ave.

12.5   End ride at starting point.

Daniel Harrison. brother of Harrisonburg's founder Thomas Harrison, built this stone house in 1749 with fortification against Indian attacks.

EDOM EXPRESS
Harrisonburg • Route 2 • 20 miles

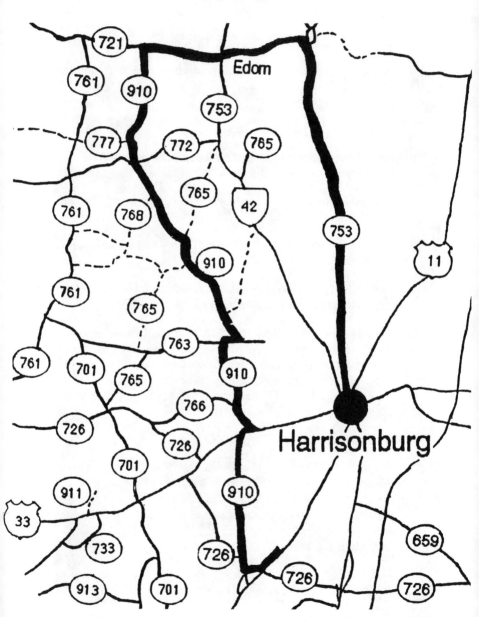

Edom Express

Cycle through countryside that was home to the area's first German and Swiss settlers. Be sure to take time to look around the old mill and mill town of Edom before returning to Harrisonburg.

0.0   **Start at the entrance to Hillandale Park at Dogwood Dr. and Hillandale Ave. Turn LEFT at STOP sign onto Dogwood Dr.**

1.5   **Turn RIGHT onto W. Water St. after passing Westover Park on the left.**

1.8   **Turn LEFT at STOP sign with CAUTION onto S. High St./Rt. 42 North.**

2.8   **Turn RIGHT onto Edom Rd.** Local farmers buy and sell their livestock here at the Shenandoah Valley Livestock Sales.

3.0   **Turn LEFT at STOP sign onto N. Liberty St.** Liberty Street was once called German Street, but this name was changed during WWI so as not to honor our enemy at the time. As early as the 1820s this was a thriving commercial district known as Back Street. There were carriage and cabinetmakers here, the latter being in the business of producing furniture and coffins.

3.1   **Cross RR tracks with CAUTION.**

3.3   Wetsel Seed Company on the left was started in 1897 by Daniel M. Wetsel. He was a farmer in Port Republic who specialized in quality corn seed. At first he sold his seed from a wagon, but after expanding his sales into other varieties of vegetables, he opened a downtown Harrisonburg store in 1911. Be sure to stop by the retail store downtown.

4.6   The field on the left was originally the Rockingham County Fairgrounds of which the small log structure on the hill was a part. The 140-acre fairground site operated here from 1952-1980. Book printer R.R. Donnelley and Sons Co. purchased the land over 10 years ago, and the fairgrounds are now located on Rt. 11 south of Harrisonburg.

4.9 The white weatherboard house on the right has a log portion that was built around 1800. Va Ag-Bags are sold by this farmer. You'll see these white bags all over the county used by area farmers to store animal feed with high moisture content, such as large round bales of hay and silage. These special bags allow the farmer to bag and seal 22 round bales in three minutes. This eliminates the need for an expensive storage facility for the oversized bundles.

5.0 Route 753, sometimes called Kratzer Road, was once an important transportation route from Harrisonburg to Linville, then called Kratzer Spring. Kratzer Road was also known as Middle Road because it ran parallel to the Valley Turnpike to the east, and Back Road, which skirted the mountains to the west. Middle Road ran from Harrisonburg to Forestville in Shenandoah County. To add to the confusion, it was also known by some as Ox Road because it was used to drive cattle to market.

7.4 The cemetery behind the Linville United Church of Christ on the right contains a number of interesting ornamental 1800s tombstones, especially among the large stand of cedars.

7.6 The village of **Linville** has an interesting and confusing history. In 1866 Jacob Funkhouser laid out the town of Kratzer Spring, named after the Kratzers who first settled here around 1750. The present name comes from the Linville family who came to the area in the 1740s from Pennsylvania and settled along what is now Linville Creek to the west. Present-day Linville does not lie on Linville Creek and was called Kratzer Spring until about 1870, when it was called Etna for a short time. The railroad once ran through town, and a limestone quarry operated just north of the village. A number of black families settled here after the Civil War. ★ **Food and drinks are available at Longs Service Center on the right.** ★

7.7 **Turn LEFT on Rt. 721.** Just ahead on Rt. 753 after the bend is the Old Sipe-Davis House, a 21-room limestone house built as a barn by the Kratzers around 1811. It was part of a 4,000-acre estate, and it is now an apartment complex. The datestone near the roof is inscribed "Anthoney Kratzer, May 29, 1811." It was converted into a dwelling just after the Civil War by Emanuel Sipe, who was related by marriage to the Kratzers. It has also been a general store, post office, and cheese factory over the years.

8.0 Cross RR tracks with CAUTION.

8.3 Farmingreen, the brick house on the right, was built by Henry Wenger in 1825. The Wengers came to this country from Switzerland, first arriving in Pennsylvania before moving south into the Shenandoah Valley in the 1780s. They purchased a 600-acre tract of land here for $1,700 in silver and then built a log house and barn, neither of which is still standing. Additions were built onto the present structure in 1906 and 1973.

8.4 The Linville-Edom School is the result of a competition between the two villages which in 1912 each wanted to have its own high school. The solution was to build a school equidistant between Linville and Edom and name it after both. The school grounds were used for the Rockingham County Fair in the 1940s.

8.8 The Joseph Wenger homestead on the left is unique because of the circular brick columns. He built this house in 1819 from bricks made on the property. The rounded ones are believed to be the only ones in Rockingham County. In 1835, the Wengers built a new house next to the older one with the idea of tearing down the first. Instead, they linked the two by enclosing the three-foot gap between them. They used this space to hide valuables during the Civil War.

9.0 Cross Linville Creek and turn LEFT at the Burruss House on the left. This large white house on the banks of Linville Creek was built in the late 1800s and was home for two generations of millers: first C.W. Burruss and then his son, I.L. Burruss. I.L. Burruss operated the mill until it burned. He also ran the Edom Post Office from the mill from the 1930s until the 1950s. The earliest settlers came to **Edom** in the late 1700s. John Chrisman, one of the first, operated the Edom Mill as early as 1826. The road once went behind the brick house on the south bank of the creek and crossed the old bridge which was built in 1914. Before the bridge was built, travelers forded the stream. By then the original mill was gone, a casualty of Northern conflagration in the Valley during the Civil War. The mill was rebuilt in 1867 and operated as the Edom Roller Mill until 1960 when once again a fire claimed most of it. Before then the mill was a four-story building, but the fire destroyed the upper structure and most of the machinery forcing its closing. The owners put a roof on the remaining stone walls and used it for storage. The mill in its heyday back in 1900 produced 50 barrels of flour or 3,500 gallons of cider daily.

9.1   The historical marker on the left tells of America's first caesarean operation being performed here on January 14, 1794. Fearing for the safety of his wife and unborn child, Dr. Jessee Bennett performed this procedure. The large brick structure on the right was once the general store operated by J.W. Myers. The building has two front entrances. One served the store, and the other with the porch, went into the Myers' residence. Before the 1930s, the Edom Post Office was in this store which offered grocery delivery service by wagon, and later by truck, into outlying areas.

9.3   Turn RIGHT with CAUTION at STOP sign onto Rt. 42 North.

9.4   Turn LEFT onto Rt. 721.

9.7   The stone house on the left dates back to around 1800, but only the two-foot thick walls remain of the early dwelling. The present house was built after fire destroyed the original structure. Linville Creek is on the left.

10.1   The stone portion of the house at Springfield Farm on the right was built in 1763 by George Chrisman, the same family which ran the Edom Mill. The farm was originally part of a large land grant called the Hite Grant. Portions of the house were supposedly burned during the Civil War, and the present owners have uncovered evidence of this. Additions were built in 1876 and 1898. An interesting footnote is that the driveway to the house was originally part of a road that went to West Virginia.

10.6   Bear LEFT onto Rt. 910 at grassy traffic islands with cattle pond on the right. CAUTION: Watch for loose gravel.

11.3   The stone house across the field to the right was built by Samuel Bowman around 1769. The Bowmans were early settlers in the area. Their driveway was once part of a public road that continued over the hill.

12.0   This hollow was once a thriving village called **Greenmount**. The reservoir for the former mill on the left still remains of this community which included a blacksmith shop, general store, church, post office, and shoemaker. All that stand now are empty log and stone structures and a few occupied residences. The bottom of this tiny valley is the headwaters for Linville Creek which flows out of a substantial spring from the hillside to the right.

12.4 **Continue STRAIGHT at STOP sign past Greenmount Church of the Brethren at the intersection with Rt. 772.** Behind the church, which was organized in 1859, is the brick and stone Christian Myers homeplace. Its original date is not known, but the newer brick section was added in 1849.

12.7 Don't be surprised if you see a few llamas wondering around in the fields to your left. The Five K Llamas Farm presently has about 25 of these relatives of the camel which they raise for sale. People buy them for their wool, as pets, and as pack animals.

13.1 Antioch United Methodist Church of Christ was organized by Rev. I.N. Walter around 1832. This building was erected in 1880. To the right is Little North Mountain which marks the western boundary of the Shenandoah Valley. Little North Mountain was formed as a thrust fault with the relatively older limestone and dolomite of the Shenandoah Valley being shoved onto the sandstone of the Alleghenies along the North Mountain Fault millions of years ago.

13.3 The large white, partially log house at the Martin Burkholder farm on the right was built in the late 1700s and still has the original siding on the front. The back part was added by Newton Burkholder, a local dentist. Fort Lynn, the name given the large limestone barn on the property, was built in 1803. Area stone buildings were often called *forts* because of the long vertical slits in the walls. It was believed, probably mistakenly, that slits in barn walls were for guns in case of attack. This is improbable for two reasons. Most of these barns were built around 1800, long after the threat of Indian attack was past, and long before the threat of Yankees was a reality. Also, the technique of building with such openings, narrow on the outside and wider on the inside, is found in Old World stone buildings. It was probably brought over by early immigrants and used as a means to provide light and ventilation while minimizing winds entering the barn.

13.8 **Bear RIGHT on Rt. 910. Rt. 765 goes straight and left.** The next **1.7 miles** is among the rockiest countryside in Rockingham

County. Residents often have to blast through limestone deposits to install a septic tank. Stone has been quarried from this area for foundations, chimneys, walls, and even the early buildings at JMU. This area and sometimes flowing-creek are called Willow Run because of the willow trees that used to grow along here.

15.5   Turn RIGHT at STOP sign onto Rt. 763.

15.6   Turn LEFT onto Rt. 910. The house on the right was built in the 1800s, with the oldest log portion reportedly salvaged from the nearby Weavers Mennonite Church after it was first torn down in the mid-1800s. Area residents hauled the building materials to this spot while the Mennonite congregation was erecting the second of three churches to be built at the intersection of Rt. 726 and Rt. 33.

16.6   Turn LEFT at STOP sign onto Rt. 910. Rt. 766 goes right.

16.9   The white house on the right once housed the West Central Switchboard, an early party line telephone system for this area, and is the reason for the name Switchboard Road. Instead of phone numbers, a combination of long or short rings distinguished one family's extension from another.

17.0   The white house on the left is part of the Liskey Farm. Although the house on the road was built in 1898, the older brick home back in the hollow has a longer history. Family members have passed down the story about hiding chickens and geese in the attic and turning their horses loose in the woods to keep them out of the hands of Yankee soldiers. Next to the brick house is a small white-sided log structure. It is believed that this building was the first post office in Rockingham County back in 1792. This farm was situated on the Williamsburg Trail and would have served as a drop-off for mail going east and west.

17.1   Turn RIGHT with CAUTION at STOP sign onto Rt. 33 West. The colonial-style brick house, atop the hill on the right, was the home of Dr. Ashby Turner, an eye, ear, nose and throat specialist. He built the house in 1910 for $6,500. For many years, he kept his office and even did surgery here. The waiting room and surgery were on the first floor, and the recovery room was upstairs.

17.2   Make a quick LEFT turn onto Garbers Church Road.

17.5   The large brick house on the right is about 160 years old.

17.6 The tan brick house on the right is known as the Jacob Shank House and was built between 1796 and 1805. The house was part of a 200-acre plantation, but slaves were never used to work the fields. It was always owned by Mennonite or Brethren families, both of which forbade slavery. Supposedly, the house was used by local Brethren as a meeting house before Garbers Church was built. According to another story, it was used as a hospital during the Civil War.

18.6 **Turn LEFT at STOP sign by Garbers Church of the Brethren onto Erickson Ave.** This church was built in 1822 and was the first area Dunker church, later called the Brethren. The Dunkers were German and got their name because of their practice of complete immersion in water, i.e. dunking, during adult baptism.

19.2 **Turn LEFT with CAUTION at traffic light onto S. High St./Rt. 42 North.**

19.7 **Turn LEFT onto Hillandale Ave.** The olive-green brick house with the red tin roof on the left is the Bibler House. It was built in 1793 over a spring to guarantee a constant water supply. The original owners were Lewis and Barbara Bibler who moved to Rockingham County from Pennsylvania. It's possible that the house served as a stagecoach stop at some point. Route 42 was formerly the Harrisonburg-Warm Springs Turnpike. The oldest part of the road is the 11 miles from here south to Mossy Creek. This road was laid out in 1779 to give Mossy Creek residents access to the county court system in Harrisonburg. In the 1830s a company was chartered to connect this section and the Warm Springs-Staunton part of the road and complete the entire turnpike.

20.0 **End ride at starting point.**

Mills

Easy access to fast-flowing streams coupled with an abundant supply of grain from area farms made milling the first industry to spring up on the Shenandoah Valley frontier. Staunton was the earliest commercial center for this part of the Valley, largely because of its suitable location on a potential millstream. By 1737, it was known as Beverley's Mill Place, and there were three more mills built in Augusta County by 1746.

A 1793 letter from Robert Gamble to Thomas Jefferson sums up the importance of milling in the Valley: "Our mills make flour that is not surpassed by any in America. In 4 years the 3 little counties of Augusta, Rockbridge, and Rockingham... from having but one manufacturing mill only had upwards of 100 merchant mills in great perfection."

By the mid-1800s, the production of grain in the Shenandoah Valley fed the entire nation. Rockingham and Augusta County boasted 41 mills apiece while Rockbridge had 16. These numbers increased until there were hundreds of mills within the three counties. In fact, more than 150 show up on old maps of Augusta County alone.

There were two kinds of local mills: grist mills and merchant mills, both of which ground grain. Grist mills did custom grinding and took a percentage of the flour as payment for the completed work. Merchant mills, on the other hand, purchased grain outright, ground it, and sold it under their own trade name. In addition to grinding grain, many of the millers took advantage of the water power to grind plaster, saw wood, turn woodworking machinery, and make textiles. Bridgewater was once home to several woolen mills on the North River. The Poage House, north of Staunton, has a marl mill across the road. This mill processed a clay and limestone mixture for fertilizer until well into the 1900s.

Most grain was milled with stone grindstones before the Civil War. The bottom stone remained stationary, and the upper stone was turned by a shaft connected to the water wheel. This was turned by the current of the creek or river. The space between the two stones was adjusted according to what was being ground. The stones were never allowed to touch, and the miller made minute adjustments to ensure that they remained balanced.

The flour would be ruined if the stones touched. Even worse, however, sparks created by contact could easily ignite the highly combustible dust. The reference to keeping one's nose to the grindstone was a daily necessity for millers who had to quickly detect the smell of the stones rubbing against each other.

Mills such as Edom Mill were frequent targets of Union burning during the Civil War. After the Civil War many mills converted to steel rollers instead of the stone grinding wheels, but the threat of fire remained. The Edom Mill on Linville Creek in Rockingham County is a prime example. The mill was rebuilt in 1867, but again burned down, this time accidentally in 1960. All that's left of this roller mill is the huge metal wheel and stone walls from what was once a four-story structure.

Few of the mills which once dotted the countryside are standing today. Some were casualties of the Civil War and others burned by accident. Many more disappeared during periodic flash floods which turned the millstream's power into an unharnessed source of destruction. Osceola Mill operated from 1849-1969 as one of seven mills on the McCormick Farm near Steeles Tavern. It is now a bed and breakfast inn. For most, only names like Franks Mill, Folly Mills, and Shutterlee Mill remain as a silent testimony to this former industrial mainstay. Cyclists who would like to learn more about the workings of a mill should stop off at the McCormick Farm near Steeles Tavern. A reconstructed mill is open to the public at this spot where Cyrus McCormick invented the reaper.

PLEASANT VALLEY ANYDAY

Harrisonburg • Route 3 • 23.4 miles

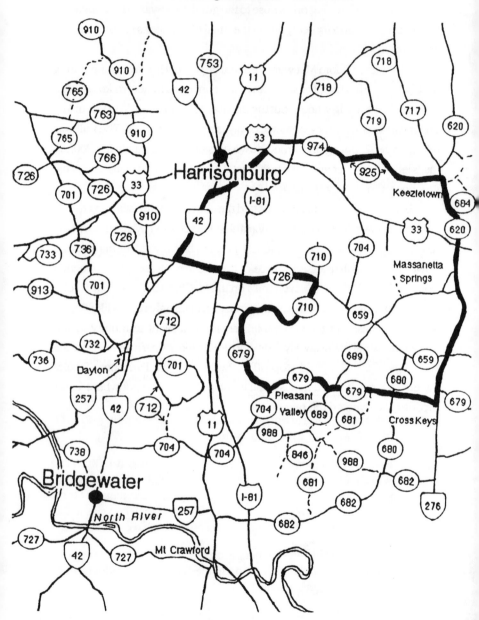

Pleasant Valley Anyday

Head out through the old railroad town of Pleasant Valley. Keep pedaling past Cross Keys where Gen. Stonewall Jackson scored one of his decisive Civil War victories. Return to Harrisonburg in the shadow of Massanutten Mountain.

0.0   **Begin at the entrance to Hillandale Park on Hillandale Ave. Ride EAST on Hillandale Ave.**

0.3   **Turn RIGHT at STOP sign onto Rt. 42 South/South High St.**

0.4   **Turn LEFT onto Pear St. and cross RR tracks with CAUTION.**

0.5   **Turn LEFT onto Pleasant Hill Rd.** Bethlehem Brethren Church on the left was dedicated in 1894 and built on land donated by Rev. J.H. Hall. This religious group was also known as the Progressive Dunkers and was first organized in this area in 1882 when members broke away from the local Dunker Brethren Church. The Progressive Dunkers' creed was: "The Bible, the whole Bible, and nothing but the Bible." The Pleasant Hill School, across the road, operated in the early 1900s.

1.3   **Cross Rt. 11 at traffic light with CAUTION. Then turn RIGHT just before the RR tracks onto Huffman St./Rt. 726.**

1.5   **Bear LEFT across RR tracks on Stonespring Rd./Rt. 726. Watch for heavy truck traffic.** At the end of Cline's gravel parking lot on the right before the RR tracks is the original Stone Spring. In the early 1900s, families would ride their bicycles to the square brick structure housing the spring and have picnics.

1.7   The Rocco Chicken Hatchery is on the left. Some 700,000 chicks per week are hatched here and supplied to area farmers for raising. That's 36 million annually!!

2.2   The white house with green trim on the left is actually a log house that was built in 1835. It served as a tollhouse on Port Road which came over the hill behind the house and then followed the existing road into Harrisonburg. Local farmers would drive their cattle along this road to pasture in the mountains. At one time there was a blacksmith shop next to the large oak tree beside the house as well as a pond across the road for watering livestock. The tollgate stopped collecting the five cent toll in 1929. **Watch out for heavy traffic through here.**

2.9 The red weatherboard house on the left, also a log house, was built in the late 1700s.

3.3 Turn RIGHT at STOP sign onto Port Republic Rd./Rt. 659.

3.6 Turn RIGHT onto Rt. 710.

5.0 Hopeful Hollow Farm is on the right. The house was built in the 1850s from 2x4s stacked horizontally like logs. The yellow pine weatherboards are original. The log cabin next to the house was moved from its former site on the Port Road. It was uncovered during the demolition of an eight-room house. Both the limestone and split rail fences are traditional Shenandoah Valley forms.

5.1 Re-enter Harrisonburg.

6.1 Bear RIGHT at sharp bend and cross two sets of RR tracks with CAUTION. The land directly ahead was once the Rockingham County Poor Farm. It encompassed 300 acres and at any time housed as many as 50 indigent people who helped on the farm.

6.2 Turn LEFT at STOP sign onto Pleasant Valley Rd./Rt. 679. Caution: Watch for heavy truck traffic from industrial area.

7.3 Cross RR tracks with CAUTION.

7.4 Turn LEFT at STOP sign onto Rt. 679/704 at Pleasant Valley. This community sprang up after the railroad came through in 1874. The depot was called Pleasant Valley, but the post office was called Rockingham due to the existence of a Pleasant Valley Post Office elsewhere in Virginia. With the closing of the second Pleasant Valley Post Office in 1964, this one assumed that name. The old mill and brick schoolhouse are off to the right.

8.1 Continue STRAIGHT on Rt. 679. Rt. 704 goes LEFT.

8.9 **Continue STRAIGHT on Rt. 679 at intersection with Rt. 689.** St. Jacobs Lutheran Church on the right was originally called Spaders Lutheran Church when formed in 1842. The Lutherans were German immigrants with religious beliefs similar to those of the English Episcopalians. They first settled in Rockingham County in the 1740s.

9.6 Apples and peaches are available in season at Osceola Orchard on the right.

10.8 The red brick house on the right dates back to the early 1800s. Notice that the chimneys are interior, i.e. built into the walls of the house, rather than being added on the outside of the walls. In general, interior chimneys are a feature of homes older than those with chimneys on the outside.

11.2 **Turn LEFT at STOP sign and ride with CAUTION on Rt. 276 North.** Standing in the middle of the wooded knoll on the left is a private residence which once served as a meeting hall for this community of **Cross Keys**. It's also been a farmers' cooperative and a church. It was built in the Mennonite church style with two front doors, one for men and one for women. The woodlot around the dwelling includes oak trees that are over 200 years old. The hub of the Cross Keys community is **.2 mile** south on Rt. 276 toward Weyers Cave. The former Cross Keys Tavern sits behind a furniture refinisher and the silos and building of the former Farm Bureau. The tavern structure was built around 1800 and is one of the oldest in the area. It was the hub of a village that included a Dunker church, stores, and a post office established by the 1830s. The community's name supposedly comes from a pair of crossed keys that hung above the doorway of the tavern. It served as a hospital during the Civil War Battle of Cross Keys that took place across the road. The brick house in the field across the road is said to have been used as a hospital as well.

11.4 Route 276 is one of the oldest roads in the Valley. The original Indian Trail and Great Wagon Road came through Keezletown and south into the present Waynesboro along this route. It's said that when George Washington visited the Shenandoah Valley in the 1750s, he surveyed the road and mapped out a straighter route along what is now Route 11, through Harrisonburg, Mt. Crawford, and Staunton. However, even after the move, Route 276 continued to be a major transportation route and was used by both armies in the Civil War.

11.5 The building that now serves as the Cross Keys/Mill Creek Ruritan Hall, to the right on Rt. 679, was a Union Church used for meetings by several different congregations in the 1800s. The Presbyterians acquired exclusive use and built the present building in 1872. The cemetery and churchyard were once part of a 450-acre farm owned by John Kiblinger. His son Jacob deeded the land to the trustees of Union Church. Civil War buffs may want to take a **3.6 mile** side trip to the Cross Keys Battlefield. To do so, turn right onto Rt. 679 and ride for **1.5 miles;** turn left onto Rt. 659 and go **.3 mile** to the top of the hill. The house to the left across from the battle marker was once the old Victory Hill School, named to commemorate Jackson's win here. Backtrack to Rt. 276 to rejoin route.

11.8 The detailed map of the Battle of Cross Keys on the right makes a good rest spot.

12.3 Cross Rt. 659 at traffic light with CAUTION.

12.7 Meadow View on the left was built in 1870 by Edward Kemper on the site of a former tavern that dated back to the 1790s. However, the name Meadow View predates this to a dwelling built here by John Stephenson around 1745. Supposedly the field across the road was the site of the first racetrack in western Virginia. According to one local story, a friend of Stephenson, and a Presbyterian minister at that, encouraged him to build the track. Rev. John Hindman, sometimes known as the "Racing Parson" because of his love of horseracing, founded Cooks Creek Presbyterian Church near Dayton in the 1740s. The pond just past the house on the left, as well as the holes on the right side of the road, were once rock quarries that supplied materials for the house and gravel for the road. There used to be a powder mill farther down Mill Creek that made gunpowder for the first settlers as well as for soldiers in the American Revolution.

14.0 Massanutten Mountain on the right is a 50-mile ridge of erosion-resistant sandstone that rises from the Valley floor to an elevation of 2,900 feet. This mountain splits the Shenandoah Valley in two. Many of the streams you'll encounter on other routes in the Valley, including the Middle, North, and South Rivers, flow into the South Fork of the Shenandoah which moves north along the eastern edge of Massanutten before joining the North Fork. The North Fork flows out of northern Rockingham County and then along the west side of the Massanutten Range. The sandstone composition is the remnant of a 430-million-year-old sand shoal deposit. The southernmost end of the range is Peaked Mountain. Behind the peak is a kettle, or canyon, at the bottom of which are a number of reliable springs.

14.5 **Cross Rt. 33 at traffic light with CAUTION and continue STRAIGHT on Rt. 620 North.** The large brick house on the right was built in 1844 by Jonathon Peale, thus the name Peales Crossroads for this intersection. Supposedly Stonewall Jackson used Peale's house for his headquarters during the Valley Campaign. Before Peale, Felix Gilbert had a store at this spot, simply known as Crossroads, which George Washington mentioned in his journal. Route 33, also known as the Rockingham Turnpike, runs from Harrisonburg east across the Blue Ridge Mountains at Swift Run Gap and on to Richmond. It was incorporated in 1850 with shares selling for $25.

15.6 The brick house on the right was built in 1869 by Archibald Taylor with bricks made on the property.

16.0 **Turn LEFT onto Rt. 925.** Henry Keezle, son of George Keisell, lived in the stone house on the right which dates back to the late 1700s. **Keezletown** once rivaled Harrisonburg as the hub of Rockingham County. Keisell's Town was established in 1791 on 100 acres of land owned by George Keisell. Both Keisell and Thomas Harrison, founder of Harrisonburg, wanted their respective towns to be the county seat. Supposedly a horse race to Richmond between the two men settled the issue. Despite losing the race, Keezletown thrived in the 1800s and had a population of over 200 residents.

16.6 The tan barn on the left is a good example of a forebay barn, so-called because of its overhang. The top floor was used to store hay while the overhang provided protection from the elements for livestock and wagons below.

17.5 **Bear LEFT on Rt. 925. Rt. 719 goes right.**

18.1 **Enter Harrisonburg.**

18.5 Although now called Keezletown Road, historically this was the name associated with Route 276. The large white house on the right is the Old Rutherford Place. It dates back to the 1800s and was one of the earliest houses on the road. The house next door was built in the 1940s and was the third along this stretch of road. In days gone by, the Van Pelt family owned a dairy farm and raised range turkeys on land that stretched from here past the nearby shopping centers. The former Fairview one-room school was built nearby in 1919 but is no longer standing.

18.8 Turn RIGHT at STOP sign onto Country Club Rd. and watch for increased traffic.

19.5 Cross RR tracks with CAUTION and pass under I-81.

20.0 Turn Left at the traffic light onto Vine St. Stop by the Harrisonburg-Rockingham Chamber of Commerce on the right for visitor information.

20.1 Turn LEFT at traffic light and proceed with CAUTION on East Market St./Rt. 33 East. ★ Food and drinks are available at a wide range of stores and restaurants in this vicinity. ★

20.4 Turn RIGHT onto Cantrell Ave. at traffic light before crossing I-81. Continue on Cantrell Ave. past JMU and Rockingham Memorial Hospital.

21.6 Cross S. Main St./Rt. 11 at traffic light and continue across overpass.

21.9 Turn LEFT onto S. High St./Rt. 42 South across from Harrisonburg High School.

23.1 Turn RIGHT onto Hillandale Ave.

23.4 End ride at starting point.

The Valley Road

The history of the road that roughly follows the present Route 11 goes back before the earliest European settlers entered the Valley. In the early 1700s, the only way through the Valley was a path controlled by the Iroquois nation. The Indian Road evolved into the Great Wagon Road in the 1740s as settlers began to funnel southwestward from Philadelphia. In 1745, the trail was authorized as a public road as far south as the New River, but travelers in southern Augusta County were still forced to use ropes to pull their wagons up muddy hills. Over the years, it's been known as the Valley Road, Valley Turnpike, and about 15 other names.

The road from Keezletown, in Rockingham County, to Waynesboro was part of the Valley Road in the early 1700s. According to one story, George Washington visited the Valley in the 1750s and mapped out a straighter course along what is now Rt. 11 through Harrisonburg, Mt. Crawford, Staunton, Greenville, Steeles Tavern, and Lexington. The Rockbridge section was authorized as a public road in 1745.

Road improvements continued with the establishment of the Valley Turnpike Company in the 1830s. Company stock was sold, and work crews went out with sledgehammers to create a roadway 40 feet wide with the middle 18 feet paved to a depth of one foot. This macadamized road, actually just packed gravel, ran from Winchester 95 miles south to Staunton with tollbooths every five miles. *Turnpike* was commonly used to connote a toll road. Stretched across the road was a pike, or pole, that was turned after the toll was paid.

By the mid-1800s the Valley Road was a major north-south thoroughfare. In 1844, stagecoach travelers could leave Staunton at 11 AM and arrive in Winchester at 8 AM the following day. The same stage would arrive in Baltimore by 2 PM costing the passenger $11.50 for the entire trip.

Most automobile travelers these days bypass the Valley Road for Interstate 81. For that reason, it's often a favorite for cyclists who want a straight shot up or down the Shenandoah Valley. Considerable history remains along Rt. 11 in former stagecoach stops like Greenville, Mt. Sidney, Mt. Crawford, and New Market.

SINGERS GLEN GALLOP

Harrisonburg • Route 4 • 26.7 miles

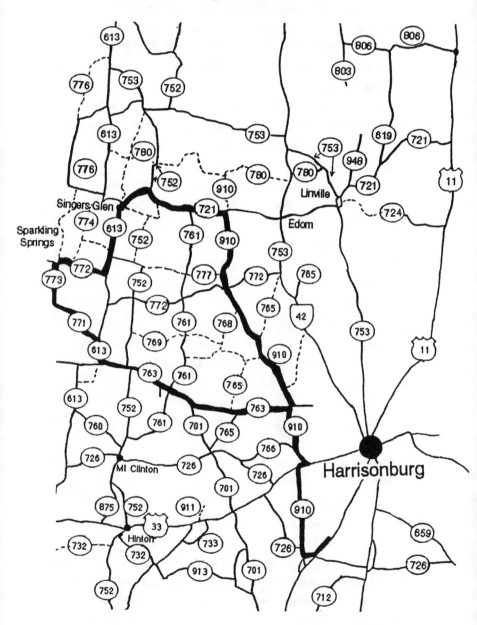

Singers Glen Gallop

The village of Singers Glen honors Joseph Funk and the tradition of music that he taught and wrote of in the 1800s. Despite a lack of formal training, Funk wrote song books that left his home-based print shop and acquired a national audience.

0.0   **Begin at the entrance to Hillandale Park on Hillandale Ave. Ride EAST on Hillandale Ave.**

0.3   **Turn RIGHT at STOP sign with CAUTION onto S. High St./Rt. 42 South.** The olive-green brick house with the red tin roof on the right is the Bibler House. It was built in 1793 over a spring to guarantee a constant water supply. The original owners were Lewis and Barbara Bibler who moved to Rockingham County from Pennsylvania. It's possible that the house served as a stagecoach stop at some point. Route 42 was formerly the Harrisonburg-Warm Springs Turnpike. The oldest part of the road is the 11 miles from here south to Mossy Creek. It was laid out in 1779 to give Mossy Creek residents access to the county court system in Harrisonburg. In the 1830s, a company was chartered to connect this section and the Warm Springs-Staunton part of the road and complete the entire turnpike.

0.8   **Turn RIGHT at traffic light onto Erickson Ave./Rt. 726.**

1.3   **Turn RIGHT onto Garbers Church Rd. at Garbers Church of the Brethren.** This church was built in 1822 and was the first area Dunker church, later called the Brethren. The Dunkers were German and got their name because of their practice of complete immersion in water, i.e. dunking, during adult baptism.

2.4   The tan brick house on the left is known as the Jacob Shank House and was built between 1796 and 1805. The house was part of a 200-acre plantation, but slaves were never used to work the fields. It was always owned by Mennonite or Brethren families, both of which forbade slavery. Supposedly the house was used by local

Brethren as a meeting house before Garbers Church was built. It's been said that it was used as a hospital during the Civil War.

2.5   The large brick house on the left is about 160 years old. The earthen ramp to the barn by the road allows the farmer easier access to the hay loft.

2.8   Turn RIGHT at STOP sign onto Rt. 33 East with CAUTION. Route 33 was once known as the Rawley Springs Turnpike. The word *turnpike* means a tollroad. The name comes from the device used to stop traffic so that the toll would be paid. The turnpike itself was usually a tall wooden box with a pike, or pole, resting on it. The pole stretched across the road with the opposite end supported by a forked post. The pike was raised or turned after the toll had been paid. The colonial-style brick house atop the hill on the left was the home of Dr. Ashby Turner, an eye, ear, nose and throat specialist. He built the house in 1910 for $6,500. For many years he kept his office and even did surgery here. The waiting room and surgery were on the first floor, and the recovery room was upstairs.

2.9   Make a quick LEFT turn onto Switchboard Rd./Rt. 910.

3.0   The white house on the right is part of the Liskey Farm. Although the house on the road was built in 1898, the older brick home back in the hollow has a richer history. Family members have passed down stories about hiding chickens and geese in the attic and turning their horses loose in the woods to keep them out of the hands of Yankee soldiers. Next to the brick house is a small white-sided log structure. It is believed that this building was the first post office in Rockingham County back in 1792. This farm was situated on the Williamsburg Trail and would have served as a drop-off for mail going east and west.

3.1   The white house on the left once housed the West Central Switchboard, an early party line telephone system for this area, and is the reason for the name Switchboard Road. Instead of phone numbers, a combination of long or short rings distinguished one family's extension from another.

3.3   Turn RIGHT onto Rt. 910. Rt. 766 goes left.

4.3   Turn LEFT at STOP sign onto Rt. 763. The house directly across the road was built in the 1800s, with the oldest log portion reportedly salvaged from the nearby Weavers Mennonite Church after it was first torn down in the mid-1800s. Area residents hauled the building materials to this spot while the Mennonite congregation was erecting the second of three churches to be built at the intersection of Rt. 726 and Rt. 33.

4.8   The brick Federal-style house on the left is called Brookdale and was built around 1822.

5.8   In the field off to the left is a pair of white houses. The first is the Emanuel Suter Homeplace made from native heart pine logs in 1764. The Suters are an old Mennonite family from Switzerland. The most famous Suter was probably Emanuel, a local potter in the mid to late 1800s. His workshop and kiln stood in this field between the house and the road. He made almost every type of utilitarian ceramic piece used in the home including crocks, pie plates, jugs, and flower pots. Suter even produced a brown money jug for children to save their pennies. During his peak production, anywhere from 2,000-4,000 finished pieces left his shop in a year. Many of these are worth thousands of dollars today, but in 1868 a gallon jug went for just 20¢.

5.9   Look off to the left at the next pair of houses. The one in a state of disrepair, the first of the two, was built in the early 1800s. Many of the original outbuildings are still standing, including a tobacco barn. Before the Civil War, tobacco was a fairly common crop in the Valley. After the war, it was grown less and by 1910, there were only about three acres grown in all of Rockingham County. The second house, which is still well kept up, was built as a retirement home for the farmer in the first house.

6.2   The white weatherboard house on the right was built in stages like many of the older farmhouses in the area. This one began as two rooms in the 1800s and was finally completed in 1904. The windmill still operates but no longer pumps water for the farm.

8.0   Cross Hopkins Ridge. Archibald and John Hopkins came to the area in 1749 from Ohio and owned a 1,700-acre plantation that stretched from this ridge west to the Alleghenies.

8.7   Maplewood on the left was built by either Archibald or John Hopkins around 1759. The bricks were made nearby. The plantation was split up after the Civil War. The Hopkins, along with another brother named Nathan, operated a mill here as well. The mill used the waters of Muddy Creek and was first called Hopkins Mill, and then Stultz's Mill in the 1900s. The Hopkins supposedly ground grain for American troops during the Revolution. It still stood in the 1970s, although it had been converted into a private residence. A fire later burned it to the ground.

8.9   Continue STRAIGHT on Rt. 613. Rt. 763 goes left.

9.4   Veer LEFT at sharp bend onto Rt. 771 and cross Muddy Creek. Rt. 613 goes straight. The community of **Chrisman** once stood here with a post office, mill, and general store to the right on the hill. The Chrismans were a branch of the same family that settled around Edom.

9.9   To the left is Little North Mountain marking the western boundary of the Shenandoah Valley. Little North Mountain was formed as a thrust fault with the relatively older limestone and dolomite of the Shenandoah Valley being shoved onto the sandstone of the Alleghenies along the North Mountain Fault millions of years ago.

10.2   The brick house on the right was built in the early 1800s.

10.9   Continue STRAIGHT on Rt. 773. Gravel Rt. 771 goes left.

11.7   A **.3 mile** sidetrip on Rt. 772 will take you to Sparkling Springs, a private resort. This was once called Baxter's Spring and was promoted by a group of Mennonites who were interested in developing a resort. The Sparkling Springs Co. bought the spring in 1898 and by 1910 had built 24 cabins. It actually consists of two springs: one produces bad-tasting sulfur water, and the other a liquid with a more desirable mineral content.

11.9   Bear RIGHT onto Rt. 772. Rt. 773 goes left.

12.9   The white house with the white board fence on the right is part of May Meadows Farm. It was built in the 1850s and has been added onto four times since then.

13.0   Turn LEFT at STOP sign onto Rt. 613.

13.6   The house on the left marks the headwaters of Muddy Creek which flows through Mount Clinton and then into Dry River near Bridgewater. Look at the east side of the house, and you'll see the spring flowing out from beneath the house and under the small footbridge. However, when you pass the other side, you'll notice that there is no creek.

14.0   The community of **Singers Glen** was called Mountain Valley prior to the Civil War. The land was first owned by the Harrison family-more than likely Daniel Harrison, builder of Fort Harrison in Dayton. Henry Rhodes was the first known settler here. However, his son-in-law Joseph Funk is most associated with Singers Glen. Funk was born in 1778 in Pennsylvania, but his family moved here in the 1780s. He married Rhodes' daughter and bought 100 acres of land in 1809. Although he had very little formal education, Funk taught school, farmed, and wrote religious and music books. He was best known for his musical ability, and his books were distributed across the country. The first books were published in Harrisonburg, but in 1847 he purchased a printing press and hauled it home by horse and wagon. This printing shop in his loom house marked the first Mennonite printing house in America. The success of his publishing necessitated having a post office here, and in 1860 Joseph's son, Solomon, became the first postmaster. He renamed the village Singers Glen in honor of his father's musical talent.

14.1   On the right is the last of four schools that served this community. This one operated from 1923-1973.

14.3   The Joseph Funk House is on the left. This small white house with dormer windows is actually log under the siding. It is listed on the National Register of Historic Places.

14.4   The next two houses on the left were built by Joseph Funk for two of his sons. His first wife left him with five children when she died. He remarried and together they had nine more offspring. The brick store on the right housed one of the town's two mercantile businesses around 1900. This was called T. Funk & Sons and was built in 1895. The Singers Glen Baptist Church on the left was formed in 1876, and the present building was dedicated in 1888.

14.5   The Donovan Memorial United Methodist Church on the right was built in 1905. It was named for Rev. John D. Donovan, a former member and pastor of the church. The parking lot was the site of the first Singers Glen school.

14.6   ★ **Food and drinks are available at O&R Country Store.** ★

14.7   **Continue STRAIGHT on Rt. 721. Rt. 613 goes left.**

15.4   **Turn RIGHT onto Rt. 721/752 and cross bridge over Joes Creek.** William Linville, one of the early settlers on Linville Creek, named Joes Creek for his son. There is a legend of the Soothing Fountain associated here with **Green Hill.** It seems that there was once a Native American village here, an idea substantiated by a considerable number of artifacts found. Near the foot of the hill was a spring from which water flowed very gently with a musical sound. The Indians would go the spring to gain information about their lovers.

15.6   Bear LEFT on Rt. 721. Gravel Rt. 752 goes right.

16.4   The Massanutten Mountain range is straight ahead. It extends north for 50 miles through the middle of the Shenandoah Valley.

17.3   Bear RIGHT onto Rt. 910 at grassy traffic island with the cattle pond on the left. Watch for gravel in the road.

18.0   The stone house to the right in the hollow across the pasture was built by Samuel Bowman around 1769. The Bowmans were early settlers in the area. Their driveway was once part of a public road that continued over the hill.

18.5   The oldest part of the white board and batten house on the left is the low wing on the far end made of log. Notice the old mill reservoir behind the house.

18.7   This hollow was once a thriving village called **Greenmount.** The reservoir for the former mill still remains of this community which also included a blacksmith shop, general store, church, post office, and shoemaker. What remains now are empty log and stone structures and a few occupied residences. The bottom of this tiny valley is the headwaters for Linville Creek which flows out of a substantial spring from the hillside to the right.

19.1   Continue STRAIGHT at STOP sign at intersection with Rt. 772 past Greenmount Church of the Brethren. Behind the church, which was organized in 1859, is the brick and stone Christian Myers homeplace. Its original date is not known, but the newer brick section was added in 1849.

19.3   Don't be surprised if you see a few llamas wondering around in the fields to your left. The Five K Llamas Farms presently has about 25 of these relatives of the camel which they raise for sale. People buy them for their wool, as pets, and as pack animals.

19.8   Antioch United Methodist Church of Christ was organized by Rev. I.N. Walter around 1832. This building was erected in 1880.

20.0 The large white, partially log, house at the Martin Burkholder farm on the right was built in the late 1700s and still has the original siding on the front. The back part was added by Newton Burkholder, a local dentist. Fort Lynn, the name given the large limestone barn on the property, was built in 1803. Area stone buildings were often called *forts* because of the long vertical slits in the walls. It was believed, probably mistakenly, that slits in barn walls were for guns in case of attack. This is improbable for two reasons. Most of these barns were built around 1800, long after the threat of Indian attack was past, and long before the threat of Yankees was a reality. Also, the technique of building with such openings, narrow on the outside and wider on the inside, is found in Old World stone buildings. It was probably brought over by early immigrants and used as a means to provide light and ventilation while minimizing winds entering the barn.

20.5 **Bear RIGHT on Rt. 910 at sharp bend. Rt. 765 goes left and straight.** The countryside for the next 1.7 miles is among the rockiest in Rockingham County. Residents often have to blast through limestone deposits even to install a septic tank. Stone has been quarried from along here for foundations, chimneys, walls, and even the early buildings at JMU. This locale and sometimes-flowing creek are called Willow Run because of the willow trees that used to grow along here.

22.2 **Turn RIGHT at STOP sign onto Rt. 763.**

22.3 **Turn LEFT onto Rt. 910.**

23.3 **Turn LEFT onto Rt. 910/Switchboard Rd. Rt. 766 goes right.**

23.5 **Enter Harrisonburg.**

23.8 **Turn RIGHT at STOP sign onto Rt. 33 West.**

23.9 **Make a quick LEFT turn onto Garbers Church Rd.**

25.3 **Turn LEFT at STOP sign onto Erickson Ave. by Garbers Church of the Brethren.**

25.9 **Turn LEFT at traffic light with CAUTION onto South High St./Rt. 42.**

26.4 **Turn LEFT onto Hillandale Ave.**

26.7 **End ride at starting point.**

The Shenandoah Valley has a considerable number of limestone outcroppings such as these. Along with sinkholes and caverns, all are indicative of a karst typography.

Geology

The Shenandoah Valley is called a karst region because its landscape is dominated by carbonate rocks like limestone and dolomite which are easily dissolved by groundwater. Caverns, limestone outcroppings, and sink-holes are the most common indicants of a karst topography. Most of this limestone was created from the sediment of a tropical sea which covered the area during the Paleozoic Era some 600 million years ago.

You'll notice that the relatively flat Valley floor is often interrupted by small conical hills. The majority of these, like Staunton's twin peaks, Betsy Bell and Mary Gray, are made of a hard mineral called chert or flint. Scattered pockets of chert resisted the erosion which eventually leveled the surrounding limestone landscape. An exception is Mole Hill, near Dayton, which is actually the remnant of a 50-million-year-old volcano. Trimble Knob, in Highland County, is the only other known volcanic plug in Virginia.

Massanutten Mountain splits the Shenandoah Valley for 50 miles north of Harrisonburg. Its erosion-resistant sandstone was relatively unaffected by the forces of wind and water which smoothed the carbonate rock of the Valley floor. Little House and Big House Mountains, which dominate the landscape of western Rockbridge County, are made of the same mineral.

The Blue Ridge Mountains underwent massive transformation until about 200 million years ago with more recent changes being due to erosion and road building. The most recent major change in the Valley topography occurred about 15,000 years ago during the last ice age. Bare, rocky places along the crest of the Blue Ridge Mountains and near Sherando Lake in eastern Augusta County are the result of the constant freezing and thawing that took place then.

The abundance of limestone figured heavily into the Valley's early economy as a building material as well as for the production of caustic lime for use in agriculture, leather tanning, and making mortar. The area has also been a major source of high grade iron ore and manganese. The Crimora mines near Waynesboro, although now closed, still hold records for production of manganese oxide.

NORTH TO ZENDA
Harrisonburg • Route 5 • 27.8 miles

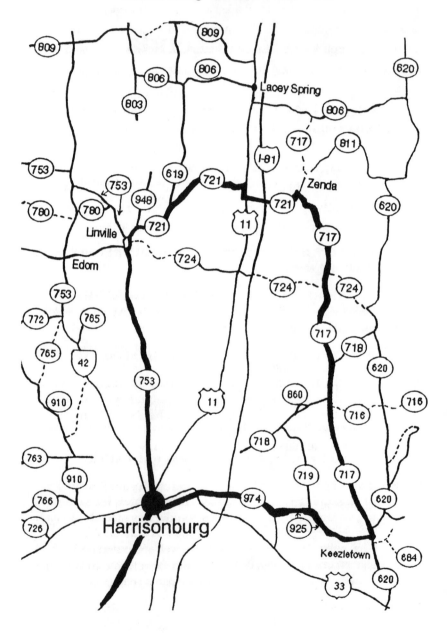

North to Zenda

Not much remains of Zenda, or Little Africa, a community said to have been started by freed slaves at the end of the Civil War. However, one still gets a strong sense of time and place on this loop that skirts Massanutten Mountain.

0.0   **Begin at the entrance to Hillandale Park on Hillandale Ave. Turn LEFT at STOP sign onto S. Dogwood Drive.**

1.1   **Turn RIGHT onto Dixie Ave.**

1.4   **Turn LEFT at STOP sign and ride with CAUTION on S. High St./Rt. 42 North.**

1.5   **Turn RIGHT at traffic light onto Cantrell Ave. with Harrisonburg High School on the left. Ride with CAUTION across overpass.**

3.0   **Turn LEFT at traffic light onto E. Market St./Rt. 33 East.**

3.3   **Turn RIGHT at traffic light onto Vine St. Turn RIGHT at second intersection onto Country Club Rd./Rt. 974.** Stop by the Harrisonburg-Rockingham County Chamber of Commerce at this intersection for visitor information.

3.9   **Ride under I-81 and cross RR tracks with CAUTION.**

4.6   **Turn LEFT onto Keezletown Rd. and catch your first glimpse of Massanutten Mountain. CAUTION: Watch for fast-moving vehicular traffic on this shoulderless stretch of road.** Former Virginia Senator Robert Leedy was born on a farm along here in the 1800s. There used to be a well and pump on the road that attracted travelers on the turnpike from Elkton to Harrisonburg (now Rt. 33) giving this area the name Leedy's Pump.

4.9   Although now called Keezletown Road, historically this was the name associated with Route 276. The large white house on the left is the Old Rutherford Place. It dates back to the 1800s and was one of the first houses on the road. The house next door was built in the 1940s and was the third house on this stretch of road. In days gone by, the Van Pelt family owned a dairy farm and raised range turkeys on land that stretched past the nearby shopping centers. The former Fairview one-room school was built nearby in 1919 but is no longer standing.

6.8   The tan barn on the right is a good example of a forebay barn, so-called because of its overhang. The top floor was used to store hay, while the overhang provided protection from the elements for livestock and wagons below.

7.3   Turn LEFT onto Rt. 620 at Keezletown. This village once rivaled Harrisonburg as the hub of Rockingham County. Keisell's Town was established in 1791 on 100 acres of land owned by George Keisell. Both Keisell and Thomas Harrison, founder of Harrisonburg, wanted their respective towns to be the county seat. Supposedly a horse race to Richmond between the two men settled the issue. Despite losing the race, Keezletown thrived in the 1800s and had a population of over 200 residents. The stone house, across the road on your right, dates back to the late 1700s. It was the home of George's son, Henry Keezle.

7.5   Cross RR tracks with CAUTION.

7.6   Continue STRAIGHT on Rt. 717 by the old Keezletown School. Rt. 620 goes right.

8.0   The 14-room house, behind the towering shrubs on the left, was built in 1892 by George Bernard Keezell, grandson of founder George Keisell. George Keezell was elected justice of the peace in 1879 at the age of 24. He was elected to the Virginia State Senate four years later.

8.3   Dutch Lord Farm on the left has many outbuildings dating back to the 1800s. The name refers to a legend about a wealthy Dutch lord who came to this area and settled near Massanutten Mountain. It's said that he was not enamored with frontier life, and he moved away leaving his gold buried at Peaked Mountain, the southern-most tip of the Massanutten range. Rocky ledges are supposedly the result of people excavating the mountainsides in search of the lost fortune.

9.8   The white house on the knoll on the right was built by pouring a mortar mixture into a wooden form that's been filled with rubble rock. This house was built in 1869. Supposedly, the walls were partially poured when a heavy rain washed them away, and the builders had to begin anew.

10.0   Seven Oaks on the left was built by Brock White in 1903. After building a similar home across the road, he and his wife decided to build a second one with more adequate closet space — the first had none. The timber was cut from nearby woods. There were originally seven oaks, but lightning has claimed three.

10.4   Continue STRAIGHT on Rt. 717. Rt. 718 goes left.

11.0   Bear LEFT on Rt. 717. Rt. 718 turns right.

12.6   The square white house on the right with the two-story portico is the former Blue Ball Tavern. It was built around 1800 and served as a refresher stop on the Wagon Road. Supposedly, the Flook family who operated the tavern kept a blue cast iron ball mounted on a pole out front. Trinity Lutheran Church with its red doors and open belfry stands on the left at the top of the hill. It was first organized in 1857. The view of Massanutten from the church is well worth the short climb. Massanutten Mountain is a 50-mile ridge of erosion resistant sandstone that rises from the Valley floor to an elevation of 2,900 feet. This mountain splits the Shenandoah Valley in two. Many of the streams you'll encounter on other routes in the Valley, including the Middle, North, and South Rivers, flow into the South Fork of the Shenandoah which moves north along the eastern edge of Massanutten before joining the North Fork. The North Fork flows out of northern Rockingham County and then along the west side of the range. The sandstone composition is the remnant of a 430-million-year-old sand shoal deposit. The southern tip of the range is Peaked Mountain. Behind the peak is a kettle, or canyon, at the bottom of which are a number of reliable springs.

12.7   Notice the sycamore trees growing along Smith Creek on the right. The creek is named for Daniel Smith, an early settler in 1764 and one of Rockingham County's first justices. The creek flows north along Massanutten before entering the North Fork of the Shenandoah River.

13.6   The house on the right was built in 1812 by the Christian Flook family and was known as Yellow Tavern. Legend has it that the house had a trap door through which one of the sons, a Northern sympathizer, fled during the Civil War.

14.6   Chestnut Ridge to the left is riddled with limestone caverns. Chestnuts were once a common tree in the Valley. The wood was used for fencing and building, and the nuts themselves were used to fatten pigs. Very few of these trees survived the blight that spread across the country in the early 1900s.

15.0   Turn LEFT onto Rt. 721. There is little here to indicate the former community of **Zenda** which supposedly means Little Africa. It is thought that this community was settled by slaves who had been freed from a nearby plantation after the Civil War. The last black descendants moved away around 1950. The site of the old general store and post office is **.3 mile** to the right on Rt. 717. Turn right on Rt. 811 and go **.2 mile,** and you'll see the ruins of what was once Zenda's school and church with an interesting cemetery obscured by the underbrush.

15.3   The limestone wall on your left encloses the Lawson-Long Cemetery. There are still vacant plots, but the last burial was in 1948. High corn in the adjacent field may hide this private cemetery.

15.4   The Fellowship United Methodist Church on the left was first organized in 1854 by Andrew Sellers. There have probably been two earlier meeting houses here, but their history is unclear. This church was built in 1912.

15.8   Cross over I-81.

16.2   Turn RIGHT at STOP sign onto Rt. 11 North and proceed with CAUTION. The community of **Melrose** scattered along Route 11 probably got its name from the Harrison family's nearby Melrose Manor farm. This area was once a drover's stop in the 1700s and 1800s when cattle and pigs were driven north on this road to market. The person moving the cattle, the *drover,* could only cover a few miles before having to stop to water and feed the animals. The plantation house, across the road to the left, is the Harrison-Moore House, and was built in 1859. The Melrose Service Station across the road is made of gray limestone.

16.5   **Turn LEFT onto Rt. 721 toward Linville and Edom.** Notice the old limestone quarry on the right.

16.6   The limestone buildings with green roofs on the left are part of Melrose Caverns. These are privately owned although they were once open to the public. They've been referred to over the years as Harrison's Cave, Virginia Caverns, and Caverns of Melrose. Some say that the first settlers in the 1700s hid from Native Americans in these caves, but the earliest record of them is from 1818 when David Harrison presumably discovered them. Both Confederate and Union soldiers camped in the caverns during the Civil War.

18.6   **Continue STRAIGHT on Rt. 721. Rt. 619 goes right.**

19.5   On the right against the cliff are the remains of a limestone quarry and lime kiln. The railroad carried the stone away from here.

19.8   The Old Sipe-Davis House on the right before the bend is a 21-room limestone house built as a barn by the Kratzers around 1811. It was part of a 4,000-acre estate, and it is now an apartment complex. The datestone near the roof is inscribed "Anthoney Kratzer, May 29, 1811." It was converted into a dwelling just after the Civil War by Emanuel Sipe, who was related by marriage to the Kratzers. The building has also been a general store, post office, and cheese factory over the years.

19.9   **Continue STRAIGHT on Rt. 753 at Linville after road bends sharply to the left. Rt. 721 goes right to Edom.** This small village has an interesting and confusing history. In 1866 Jacob Funkhouser laid out the town of Kratzer Spring, named after the Kratzers who first settled here around 1750. The present name comes from the Linville family who came to the area in the 1740s from Pennsylvania and settled along, what is now, Linville Creek to the west. Present-day Linville does not lie on Linville Creek and was called Kratzer Spring until about 1870, when it was called Etna for a short time. The railroad once ran through town, and a limestone quarry operated just north of the village. After the Civil War, a number of black families settled here.

20.1   ★ **Food and drinks are available at Longs Service Center on the left.** ★

23.5   **Harrisonburg City Limits.**

24.6 Cross RR tracks with CAUTION and continue STRAIGHT on N. Liberty St.

25.1 Continue STRAIGHT at traffic light across Rt. 33.

25.2 Cross RR tracks with CAUTION at STOP sign.

25.9 Bear RIGHT onto S. Main St.

26.0 Turn RIGHT at traffic light onto W. Cantrell St. and cross RR overpass.

26.2 Turn LEFT at traffic light onto S. High St. across from Harrisonburg High School.

27.5 **Turn RIGHT onto Hillandale Ave.** The olive-green brick house with the red tin roof on the left is the Bibler House. It was built in 1793 over a spring to guarantee a constant water supply. The original owners were Lewis and Barbara Bibler who moved to Rockingham County from Pennsylvania. It's possible that the house served as a stagecoach stop at some point. Rt. 42 was formerly the Harrisonburg-Warm Springs Turnpike. The oldest part of the road is the 11-mile stretch from here south to Mossy Creek. This road was laid out in 1779 to give Mossy Creek residents access to the county court system in Harrisonburg. In the 1830s, a company was chartered to connect this and the Warm Springs-Staunton part of the road to complete the entire turnpike.

27.8 **End ride at starting point.**

African-Americans

African-Americans arrived in the southern Valley of Virginia in 1727, the same year that the Germans and Swiss established one of the earliest permanent settlements near Massanutten Mountain. These first blacks were 15 escaped slaves who had fled from eastern Virginia into the mountains near present-day Lexington. Although they were eventually caught, their presence began the existence of separate European and African cultures within the region.

Most of the early African-Americans were brought to the Shenandoah Valley as slaves, destined for agricultural and domestic labor. When the Civil War broke out in 1861, 20-25 percent of the population of Augusta, Rockbridge, and Rockingham Counties was black. The majority worked on small family farms, in local businesses, and in regional industries like iron foundries and canal building. In comparison to life on large plantations, local slaves worked side by side with whites.

A small number of free blacks struggled to survive in the shadow of slavery. Most of them toiled at menial jobs, but some did indeed prosper. Robert Campbell, a Staunton barber, became one of Virginia's wealthiest free blacks. Joseph T. Williams, a Harrisonburg barber, served four years in the Confederate army as a personal servant and then became a Harrisonburg policeman in 1874. Rev. John Chavis was said to have attended Washington College, now Washington and Lee University, around 1802 and then had a rich career as a Presbyterian minister in North Carolina. Another free black man, named Patrick Henry, was hired by Thomas Jefferson to live and work as caretaker at Natural Bridge, which Jefferson owned. Henry purchased a black woman named Louisa, whom he freed and married, before he died in 1829.

The harsh legal system that defined slave society in the Valley, as well as the rest of the South, made it difficult for blacks to establish institutions or perpetuate their culture. Although several black-owned businesses did prosper, no fraternal organizations, churches, or schools existed in this part of the Valley until after the Civil War.

After the war, black schools, businesses, and communities, albeit segregated, were established. But the Valley's black population steadily declined from 1865 through the 1960s as social, educational, and employment opportunities beckoned from elsewhere. As you ride through the Shenandoah Valley, you'll pass through communities like Cedar Green, west of Staunton; Madrid, near Waynesboro; Kiddsville, near Fishersville; and Smokey Row, near Arbor Hill. Churches such as Reid's Chapel in Stuarts Draft and Hatton Pond, near Greenville, have continued the traditions begun by their black founders just after the Civil War.

The former community of Zenda, in northern Rockingham County in the shadow of Massanutten Mountain, holds a particular interest for historians. Supposedly a group of freed blacks moved a short distance from the plantation on which they'd labored and started this small village, whose name means *Little Africa*. All that remains of the old Zenda is an empty building, once used as a school and church, and a grown-over cemetery.

Massanutten Mountain is a 50-mile range looming large to the east of Harrisonburg.

WHERE'S THE CAVE?

Harrisonburg • Route 6 • 47.1 miles

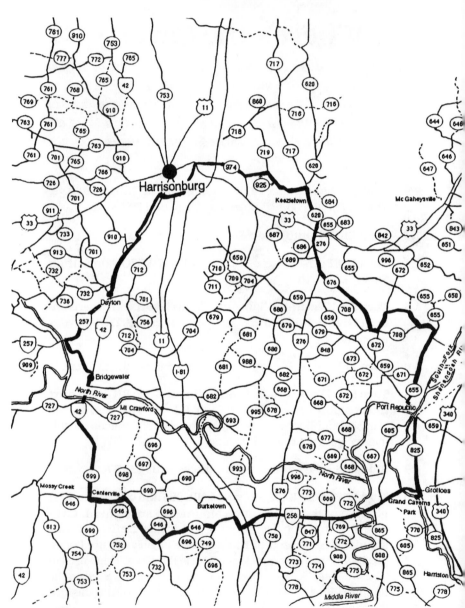

Where's the Cave?

Bernard Weyer had no idea what he'd uncover when he started digging up one of his raccoon traps back in 1804. Explore Weyer's Cave, now known as Grand Caverns, as well as the historic towns of Keezletown, Port Republic, Dayton, and Bridgewater on this extended tour of southern Rockingham and northern Augusta County.

0.0 **Begin at the entrance to Hillandale Park on Hillandale Ave. Turn LEFT at STOP sign onto S. Dogwood Dr.**

1.1 **Turn RIGHT onto Dixie Ave.**

1.4 **Turn LEFT at STOP sign and ride with CAUTION on S. High St./Rt. 42 North.**

1.5 **Turn RIGHT at traffic light onto Cantrell Ave. with Harrisonburg High School on the left. Ride with CAUTION across overpass.**

3.0 **Turn LEFT at traffic light onto E. Market St./Rt. 33 West.**

3.3 **Turn RIGHT at traffic light onto Vine St. Turn RIGHT at next intersection onto Country Club Rd./Rt. 974.** Stop by the Harrisonburg-Rockingham County Chamber of Commerce at this intersection for visitor information.

3.9 **Ride under I-81 and cross RR tracks with CAUTION.**

4.6 **Turn LEFT onto Keezletown Rd./Rt. 925 and catch your first glimpse of the Massanutten Mountain Range ahead. CAUTION: Watch for fast-moving vehicular traffic on this shoulderless stretch of road.** Former Virginia Senator Robert Leedy was born on a farm along here in the 1800s. There used to be a well and pump on the road that attracted travelers on the turnpike from Elkton to Harrisonburg (now Rt. 33) giving this area the name Leedy's Pump.

4.9 Although now called Keezletown Road, historically this was the name associated with Route 276. The large white house on the left is the Old Rutherford Place. It dates back to the 1800s and was one of the first houses on the road. The next house on the road was built in the 1940s and was the third house on this stretch. In days gone by, the Van Pelt family owned a dairy farm and raised range turkeys on land that stretched past the nearby shopping centers. The former Fairview one-room school was built nearby in 1919 but is no longer standing.

6.8 The tan barn on the right is a good example of a forebay barn, so-called because of its overhang. The top floor was used to store hay, while the overhang provided protection from the elements for livestock and wagons below.

7.3 Turn RIGHT onto Rt. 620 at Keezletown. This village once rivaled Harrisonburg as the hub of Rockingham County. Keisell's Town was established in 1791 on 100 acres of land owned by George Keisell. Both Keisell and Thomas Harrison, founder of Harrisonburg, wanted their respective towns to be the county seat. Supposedly a horse race to Richmond between the two men settled the issue. Despite losing the race, Keezletown thrived in the 1800s and had a population of over 200 residents. The stone house across the road on your left after the turn dates back to the late 1700s. It was the home of George's son, Henry Keezle.

7.8 The brick house on the left was built in 1869 by Archibald Taylor with bricks made on the property.

8.8 Cross Rt. 33 at traffic light with CAUTION and proceed on Rt. 276 South. Route 33 stretches east to Richmond. It was incorporated in 1850 as the Rockingham Turnpike with shares of stock selling for $25. The large brick house on the left was built in 1844 by Jonathon Peale, thus the name Peales Crossroads for this intersection. Supposedly, Stonewall Jackson used Peale's house for his headquarters during the Valley Campaign. Before Peale, Felix Gilbert had a store here simply known as Crossroads, a place which George Washington mentioned in his journal. Route 276 is one of the oldest roads in the Valley. The original Indian Trail and Great Wagon Road came through Keezletown and south into the present Waynesboro along this route. It's said that when George Washington visited the Shenandoah Valley in the 1750s, he applied his surveying skills and mapped out a straighter route, along what is now Route 11, through Harrisonburg, Mt. Crawford, and Staunton. However even after the move, Route 276 continued to be a major transportation route and was used by both armies in the Civil War.

10.2   Turn LEFT onto Rt. 676 at Liskey Truck Sales.

10.4   On your rides through the countryside, you may notice houses with two front doors, side by side, like the white house on the left. Although the exact reason for this design is unknown, it's believed to be a German tradition and was used by immigrants from Pennsylvania and on into the Valley of Virginia.

10.6   Massanutten Mountain on the left is a 50-mile ridge of erosion resistant sandstone that rises from the Valley floor to an elevation of 2,900 feet. This mountain splits the Shenandoah Valley in two. Many of the streams you'll encounter on other routes in the Valley, including the Middle, North, and South Rivers, flow into the South Fork of the Shenandoah which moves north along the eastern edge of Massanutten before joining the North Fork. The North Fork flows out of northern Rockingham County and then along the west side of the Massanutten Range. The sandstone composition is the remnant of a 430-million-year-old sand shoal deposit. The southernmost end of the range is Peaked Mountain. Behind the peak is a kettle, or canyon, at the bottom of which are a number of reliable springs.

10.9   The ruins of the limestone chimney on the left were once part of a farm owned by the Harshbergers, a family of early German settlers in the area.

13.0   Turn LEFT at STOP sign onto Rt. 708.

13.2   Turn LEFT at STOP sign onto Rt. 672.

14.0   Turn RIGHT onto Rt. 658 just after the Mt. Olive Church of the Brethren at Pineville. The village at this intersection was once a beehive of activity and was named for a stand of pines that grew here. The Lam and Coakley general stores operated on the left and right respectively. Directly across the road was the brick home of Dr. Frank Miller. His office was in the gray building in the side yard.

14.8   **Turn RIGHT onto Rt. 657.**

15.3   **Turn LEFT at STOP sign onto Rt. 708.**

16.0   **Turn RIGHT at STOP sign onto Rt. 655/Rt. 708.**

16.2   **Proceed STRAIGHT on Rt. 655. Rt. 708 goes left.** A mile sidetrip of flat riding on Rt. 708 will take you down to the South Fork of the Shenandoah River and the remains of a former milling complex. Also down Rt. 708, in the stand of trees on the left, is one of the area's most stately mansions, Bogota, built in 1847 by Jacob Strayer. There is a fireplace and mantel in each of the 12 rooms. Family legend has it that the Strayers sat on their front porch as the Civil War Battle of Port Republic raged nearby in June, 1862. Their land was originally part of Jacob Stover's Massanutten Settlement land grant of 5,000 acres in 1733. Of this, 244 acres were purchased by Gabriel Jones in 1733. Jones was a very influential man in the area and built his home a few hundred yards from where Bogota now sits. He was born in Williamsburg, went to England to get his law degree, and was the first English lawyer to live in what was then Augusta County. Jones practiced in Harrisonburg and traveled every day on the same road that today is still called Lawyer's Road. In addition to his legal practice, Gabriel Jones was a member of the House of Burgesses and Virginia's Constitutional Convention. It's said that George Washington dined with him at his home in 1784.

17.3   The traditional German hex signs on the bank barn on the left are an expression of good luck. These are commonly found on the barn doors in the Shenandoah Valley, whereas those on Pennsylvania barns are more often located on the side of the building under the eaves.

18.4   **Turn LEFT at STOP sign and proceed with CAUTION on Rt. 659.** This road, also called Wayland Highway, is named for Dr. John Wayland, a local teacher and historian who published over 20 books and treatises on the history of the Shenandoah Valley. He attended Bridgewater College and then got his Ph.D. from the University of Virginia. Dr. Wayland died in 1962.

18.8   **Cross first bridge over North River into Port Republic.** This is one of the oldest towns in Rockingham County and was possibly part of Jacob Stover's 5,000-acre land grant in 1733. It is located where the North and South Rivers merge to form the South Fork of the Shenandoah River. In the early 1800s, this was a port from which "gundalows" laden with freight, particularly iron, went down the river to the Potomac River at Harper's Ferry, and sometimes farther onto the C&O Canal into Washington, D.C. Gundalows were flat bottomed boats that could be as large as nine feet wide and 90 feet long. Polemen would pilot the boats in flotillas of up to 20 of the craft to Harper's Ferry. There the boats were sold for lumber, and it's said that the town of Harper's Ferry was built from the wood of these Shenandoah River gundalows. Port Republic became a town with an 1802 act of the Virginia Assembly. Twenty-eight half-acre lots were sold on which the buyer had to build a "dwelling house 16 feet by 16 feet at the least, with a brick or stone chimney" which was fit for habitation within 10 years. ★ **Food, drinks, and canoe rentals are available at the Village Country Store.** ★ At the edge of the parking lot is a map and description of the Battle of Port Republic, one of Gen. Stonewall Jackson's victories during his famous Valley Campaign.

19.2 **Cross second bridge over South River. Turn RIGHT onto Rt. 825.** The tan house with blue trim on the left is the Turner Ashby House. This Confederate general was killed on June 6, 1862 during a nearby skirmish at Chestnut Ridge, part of Jackson's otherwise successful Valley Campaign. Supposedly this dashing calvary hero's last words were, "Charge men! For God's sake, charge!" He was taken to this home, that of Frank Kemper, where his body lay in state. Area women placed a red rose through the bullet hole in his uniform. Stonewall Jackson came to the house to pay homage to his fallen comrade before burial.

20.4 **Grottoes** was called Liola in 1882 and renamed Grottoes in 1888. Its name was then changed to Shendun (after the first syllable of *Shenandoah* and the Gaelic word *dun*, which means fort or town). It was finally changed back to Grottoes in 1893. Samuel Miller, owner of the Mossy Creek Ironworks, operated an iron forge near Grottoes in the early 1800s. His son, William, established the Mount Vernon Forge here in 1848. Take a detour through the side streets of this town for a look at some interesting architecture. There are a number of houses along the railroad tracks that were built by the locally famous Eustler Brothers in the late 1800s and early 1900s. ★ **Food and drinks are available at several stores along this road.** ★

21.6   **Proceed STRAIGHT after STOP sign at intersection with Rt. 256.**

21.9   **Turn RIGHT onto Rt. 844 to enter Grand Caverns Regional Park.** Picnic facilities make this an excellent lunch and rest stop. Bernard Weyer discovered the caverns in 1804 while looking for a raccoon trap. They were opened to the public in 1806 as Weyer's Cave and are among the oldest publicly toured caves in the country. The name Grand Caverns was adopted in 1906, but the former railroad stop, Weyer's Cave, has retained the original name. It's said that Thomas Jefferson rode his horse over the Blue Ridge to see the underground formations, and Gen. Stonewall Jackson and his troops camped here during the Valley campaign. There are still signatures of Confederate soldiers on the inner walls. **After a break at the park, turn LEFT onto Rt. 825 to continue on the route.**

22.2   **Turn LEFT at STOP sign onto Rt. 256 West.**

22.9   After crossing the South River, the birthplace of painter George Caleb Bingham is on the right. Bingham was born in 1811 in a house that was located behind the present brick home. He and his family moved to Missouri in 1819. He left behind a legacy of paintings of the American West when he died in 1879. The Old Chaney House that you see now was built in 1856 and marks the Augusta-Rockingham County line.

24.1   Look off to the left and you'll see the white Octagonal Barn built by Robert Harnsberger around 1867. It's listed as a Virginia Landmark.

24.2   Stop by Mountain River Gardens on the right for fresh produce and strawberry picking in season.

24.4   **Cross the North River.**

26.9   The present site of the Wildlife Center of Virginia is on the right. This facility offers veterinary and rehabilitation services to injured wildlife. It is not open to the public.

27.4   **Weyers Cave** developed as a stop, halfway between Harrison-burg and Staunton, along the Baltimore and Ohio Railroad in 1874. It was named for the closest landmark, the cave discovered by Bernard Weyer in what is now Grottoes. However, even though there was a railroad station, post office, and much construction, there were no roads into the town at first. With the subsequent addition of roads, Weyers Cave became an important shipping point. The Future Farmers of America was formed here in 1927.

27.4 ★ **Food and drinks are available at Super Save Market on the left.** ★

27.6 **Cross RR tracks with CAUTION.**

28.4 **Watch for traffic entering and exiting I-81.**

28.7 **Turn RIGHT at STOP sign onto Rt. 11 North.** ★ **Food and drinks are available at the convenience store at this intersection.** ★ Rocky's Antique Mall, .2 mile on the left, is an antiquers paradise and is open Thursday through Sunday.

29.1 **Turn LEFT onto Rt. 646.** The brick home on the left named Maple Lane Farm was built by Samuel Byers II after he returned from service in the Civil War. His father, Samuel Byers Sr., acquired and combined a number of parcels of land starting in 1824. It is now the residence and office of veterinarians Drs. Ann and David Gardner.

30.7 The Georgian brick house on the right was built in 1827 by a man named Green for John Seawright II and his wife Jane. It was called King Meadow Manor in honor of Seawright's mother, Jane King Seawright. Various Seawrights lived here through the 1940s.

31.2 The community of **Stonewall** once stretched along the banks of Naked Creek through here and south. There were several water powered mills in operation.

32.1 **Bear RIGHT on Rt. 646. Rt. 732 goes left.** The red forebay barn on the left is a popular style in the Valley. The overhang, or forebay, was used to shelter animals and wagons from inclement weather.

34.1 **Bear LEFT on Rt. 646 at bend. Rt. 690 goes right.**

35.1 **Turn RIGHT onto Rt. 699 at Centerville.** This was known as Milnesville Post Office in the 1885 area atlas. The gray weatherboard building on the right was once Centerville's general store. The Centerville United Methodist Church on the left was organized in 1880.

36.8 A .2 mile sidetrip to the right goes back to St. Michaels United

Church of Christ. It was organized in 1764 as the Lutheran or Lutheran Reformed Church. The original building was made of logs and had a dirt floor. Legend has it that in 1794 one of the early ministers, Rev. Benjamin Henkel, was buried under the chancel, the part of the floor under the altar. That church was remodeled in 1830 and then torn down in 1876. A brick structure was built in 1876, and the present one erected in 1916.

37.3 Look across the curve toward Bridgewater with Round Hill and Mole Hill in the distance.

38.2 The house on the right at the bend is called Long Glade. It was built by the Irvine family around 1790 and expanded in four sections over the next 200 years. Only Irvines and Millers have ever lived in this house. Frances Irvine lived on the farm in 1774. According to family history, she was home alone when a Native American woman friend came to the house to warn her of an impending Shawnee attack on local settlers. Mrs. Irvine got on her horse and rode through the night, Paul Revere-style, to warn settlers in Mossy Creek and Mount Solon of the raid. Her warning apparently caused the tribe to cancel its plans.

38.3 Turn RIGHT at STOP sign onto Rt. 42 North. This road was once the Harrisonburg-Warm Springs Turnpike, and there was a tollgate opposite Bridgewater by the North River bridge.

39.0 Cross North River and enter Bridgewater. ★ Food and drinks are widely available. ★

39.8 Turn LEFT onto North River Rd.

40.0 The Dry River District Ranger Station on the left has a wealth of free information regarding recreational opportunities in the nearby George Washington National Forest.

40.0 Turn RIGHT onto Dry River Rd./Rt. 738. Dry River on the left is named because its waters dry to a trickle during the summer. However, it is the largest tributary of the North River which merges into the South Fork of the Shenandoah River.

41.2 The Hollen homeplace, the yellow brick house on the right at the curve in the road, was built in 1834. The adjacent barn was built around 1840 and was one of the few area barns not burned by Yankee troops as they marched through the Valley in 1864. The mill on the left was built around 1883. Powered by the waters of Dry River, the mill ground flour, animal feed, and corn as well as milling wood until closing in the 1930s. There was a dam across the road where the Mill Cabinet Shop now stands. The cabinet shop used to be located in the mill itself where craftsmen made antique reproduction furniture. They now specialize in wooden cabinets and wardrobes. Ray Simmons, one of the shop's founders, is retired but continues the woodworking tradition in a shop behind the mill.

41.6   Turn RIGHT at STOP sign and proceed with CAUTION on Rt. 257 East.

42.2   The community of **Stemphleytown** was named for David Stemphley who lived here in the 1840s. The small gray building on the left was once a store. A school formerly stood down the road near the Dry River.

43.0   The Chesapeake and Western Railroad, sometimes nicknamed the Crooked and Weedy, ran through Dayton beginning in 1895. The train ran from Elkton and went west to Stokesville at the foot of the Allegheny Mountains. The line ceased operations in the 1930s as the supply of mountain timber was exhausted. Those with sharp eyes may be able to spot the raised ridge from the old railbed on the right.

43.7   Turn LEFT onto Rt. 42 Business and ride through Dayton.
Dayton was settled in the mid 1700s and is one of the oldest towns in Rockingham County. Although first known as Rifetown or Rifeville after an early landowner named Daniel Rife, it was legally established as Dayton in 1833. This name may come from Jonathon Dayton, youngest signer of the Constitution. He was from New Jersey but apparently had a relative living in this area. **★ Food and drinks are available.** ★ For a taste of some wonderful homecooked Mennonite treats, turn right and ride **.5 mile** on Rt. 42 South. The Dayton Farmers Market, on the right, is a mini-mall of 21 shops with everything from Shoo Fly Pie to hand-dipped ice cream. They're open Thursday through Saturday year-round.

44.1   Cross Cooks Creek.

44.2   Daniel Harrison, brother of Harrisonburg's founder Thomas Harrison, built this stone house which was used in the 1750s as protection against Indian attacks. These were especially numerous during the French and Indian War. The house apparently once had a stockade around it and an underground passage to a nearby spring. The brick portion of the house was added by later owners who also enlarged the doors and windows. It is open Saturday and Sunday afternoons from late May through the end of October.

44.6   **Cross Rt. 42 South at STOP sign and turn LEFT onto Rt. 42 North with CAUTION.**

46.8   **Turn LEFT onto Hillandale Ave.**

47.1   **End ride at starting point.**

Jackson's Valley Campaign

Thomas Jonathan "Stonewall" Jackson was a paradox — a Confederate hero in what was ultimately a losing endeavor. His rural beginnings hardly prepared him for study at West Point, but he consistently made up for any shortcomings with hard work and amazing powers of concentration. For 10 years while teaching at the Virginia Military Institute in Lexington, he was gaining knowledge for the part in the Confederate defense of the Shenandoah Valley which would ultimately define his genius in military strategy.

The Shenandoah Valley, with its role as the "Breadbasket of the Confederacy" in addition to being a producer of iron for munitions, played a key role in the South's success or failure in the Civil War. Its relative proximity to the Union capital at Washington, D.C. and the Confederate capital in Richmond also made it strategically important for the Northern army. So it was that in the spring of 1862, Gen. Stonewall Jackson used a relatively small army to defeat Union armies that were 10 times larger. In doing so, he not only held onto the Valley's considerable resources, at least for the time being, but also drew the enemy away from its primary target, the Confederate capital.

While teaching military strategy at VMI, Jackson immersed himself in studying Napoleon and the other great generals of military history. It was this information that he put to use as he kept his "foot calvary" constantly on the move during what's become famous as the Valley Campaign. Between March 22 and June 25, 1862, his army covered 676 miles during 48 actual days of marching, fought six battles, and confounded 175,000 federal troops, in the process diverting the Union forces from attacking Richmond. Despite a shortage of supplies, reinforcements, and consistently accurate information, he was able to accomplish these military feats with never more than 17,000 soldiers, and sometimes as few as 3,500.

Some of the credit for Jackson's victories should go to Jedediah Hotchkiss. This former New Yorker had moved to the area in the 1840s. A self-taught map-maker and engineer, he volunteered his services to the Confederacy when the war broke out. After assignment to Jackson's army, Hotchkiss became "the best topographical engineer in the Confederate

General Stonewall Jackson's tactical genius brought him much acclaim with victories in his Valley Campaign during the Civil War in the spring of 1862.

Army. He was the man more responsible than any other for Jackson's ability always to proceed in a sure knowledge of the terrain... ," according to one source. His former Staunton home is on E. Beverley Street across from the Virginia School for the Deaf and the Blind.

Two concluding victories in the Valley Campaign were fought near Cross Keys and Port Republic in Rockingham County. Inspired by a battle fought by Napoleon in his Italian Campaign, Jackson used Massanutten Mountain and the forks of the Shenandoah River to his advantage to separate and attack the flanks of larger Union armies. He followed these strikes with quick movements and forced marches so as to minimize his own losses.

On June 9, 1862, the day after the Battle of Cross Keys, Jackson moved his troops across the North River at Port Republic and burned the bridge behind him so as to halt the pursuit of Union troops on his heels. The Southern contingent engaged the rest of the enemy troops on the east side of the river, and after a hard-fought encounter, drove them back. The North lost about 1,000 men, half of whom were captured, to the South's 800. With victories at Port Republic and Cross Keys and the retreat of Northern soldiers, Jackson rushed his troops east to help defend Richmond.

Stonewall Jackson never returned to his Lexington home. Less than a year after the Valley Campaign, he was accidentally wounded by his own men at the Battle of Chancellorsville and died May 10, 1863. Jackson's arm was successfully amputated, but he died of pneumonia. In the days that Jackson lay near death, Confederate Gen. Robert E. Lee wrote, "He has lost his left arm; but I have lost my right arm."

JOURNEY TO MOUNT JACKSON
Harrisonburg • Route 7 • 72.4 miles

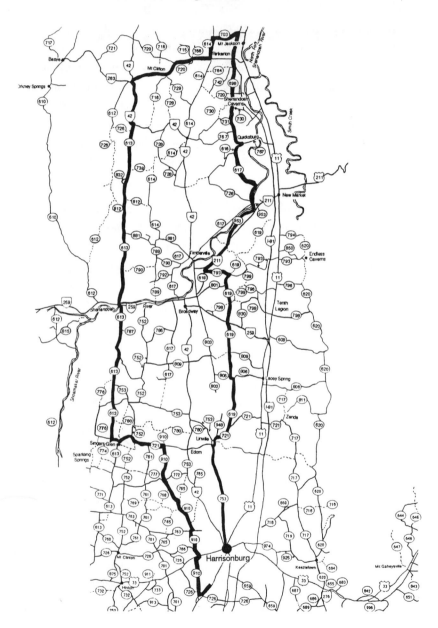

Journey to Mount Jackson

This long ride is a good one for those who measure their enjoyment in miles as well as sights along the way. It features a possible sidetrip to Endless Caverns and another stop at Shenandoah Caverns, Virginia's only cavern with its own elevator. For those who shudder at the thought of a 70+ miler in one day, take some plastic and spend the night at Widow Kip's B&B in Mount Jackson.

0.0   **Start at the entrance to Hillandale Park at S. Dogwood Dr. and Hillandale Ave. Turn LEFT at STOP sign onto S. Dogwood Dr.**

1.5   **Turn RIGHT onto W. Water St. after passing Westover Park on the left.**

1.8   **Turn LEFT at STOP sign with CAUTION onto S. High St./Rt. 42 North.**

2.8   **Turn RIGHT onto Edom Rd.** Local farmers buy and sell their livestock at the Shenandoah Valley Livestock Sales on the left.

3.0   **Turn LEFT at STOP sign onto N. Liberty St.** Liberty Street was once called German Street, but this name was changed during WWI so as not to honor our enemy at the time. As early as the 1820s, this was a thriving commercial district known as Back Street. There were carriage and cabinetmakers here, the latter being in the business of producing furniture and coffins.

3.1   **Cross RR tracks with CAUTION.**

3.3   Wetsel Seed Company on the left was started in 1897 by Daniel M. Wetsel. He was a farmer in Port Republic who specialized in quality corn seed. At first he sold his seed from a wagon, but after expanding his sales into other varieties of vegetables, he opened a downtown Harrisonburg store in 1911. Be sure to stop by the downtown store.

4.6   The field on the left was originally the Rockingham County Fairgrounds, of which the small log structure on the hill was a part. The 140-acre fairground site operated here from 1952-1980. Book printer R.R. Donnelley and Sons Co. purchased the land 10 years ago, and the fairgrounds are now on Rt. 11 south of Harrisonburg.

4.9   The house on the right has a log portion that was built around 1800. Va Ag-Bags are sold by this farmer. You'll see these white bags all over the county used by area farmers to store their animal feed with high moisture content, such as large round bales of hay and silage, in the fields. These special bags allow the farmer to bag and seal 22 round bales in three minutes. This eliminates the need for an expensive storage facility for these oversized bundles of feed.

5.0   Route 753, sometimes called Kratzer Road, was once an important transportation route from Harrisonburg to Linville, which was then called Kratzer Spring. Kratzer Road was also known as Middle Road because it ran parallel to the Valley Turnpike to the east and Back Road skirting the mountains to the west. Middle Road ran from Harrisonburg to Forestville in Shenandoah County. To add to the confusion, it was also known by some as Ox Road because it was used to drive cattle to market.

7.4   The cemetery behind the Linville United Church of Christ on the right contains a number of interesting ornamental 1800s tombstones, especially among the large stand of cedars.

7.6   ★ **Food and drinks are available at Longs Service Center on the right.** ★

7.7   **Continue STRAIGHT on Rt. 721 after sharp bend to the right. Rt. 753 goes left and Rt. 725 goes right. Linville** has an interesting and confusing history. Jacob Funkhouser laid it out in 1866 as Kratzer Spring, named after the Kratzers who first settled here around 1750. The present name comes from the Linville family who came to the area in the 1740s from Pennsylvania and settled along what is now Linville Creek to the west. Present-day Linville does not lie on Linville Creek and was called Kratzer Spring until about 1870, when it was called Etna for a short time. The railroad once ran through town, and a limestone quarry operated just north of the village. After the Civil War, a number of black families settled here.

7.8   After the bend to the right is the Old Sipe-Davis House, a 21-room limestone house built as a barn by the Kratzers around 1811. It was part of a 4,000-acre estate, and it is now an apartment complex. The datestone near the roof is inscribed "Anthoney Kratzer, May 29, 1811." It was converted into a dwelling just after the Civil War by Emanuel Sipe, who was related by marriage to the Kratzers. It has also been a general store, post office, and cheese factory.

9.0   Turn LEFT onto Rt. 619.

10.6   The white frame Pine Grove Church of the Brethren on the right was established around 1850.

11.6   Turn LEFT on Rt. 619/806 at bend. Rt. 806 also goes straight.

11.7   Turn RIGHT onto Rt. 619. Rt. 806 goes straight.

13.9   The log building on the left, although in a sad state of decay, shows the chinking and daubing that filled the spaces between logs. Chinking often consisted of wooden pieces stuffed between the logs. Daubing was a mixture of clay and animal hair placed over the chinking to seal the space.

14.4   Bethel Church of the Brethren on the right was probably established in the late 1800s. It was the first church in this community.

14.5   Continue STRAIGHT after STOP sign at intersection with Rt. 259. Mayland was first known as The Pines. As more settlers arrived in the 1700s, it was later renamed Newtown. It was ultimately named Mayland after John May who lived here. The building on the left side of the road across the intersection used to be Spitzer's General Store, one of two stores in town. ★ **Food and drinks are available at Keppie's Store.** ★

14.6   Mayland Christian Church on the left was established in 1899.

14.9   Massanutten Mountain, off to the right, is a 50-mile ridge of erosion-resistant sandstone that rises from the Valley floor to an elevation of 2,900 feet. It splits the Shenandoah Valley in two. Many of the streams you'll encounter on other routes in the Valley, including the Middle, North, and South Rivers, flow into the South Fork of the Shenandoah which moves north along the eastern edge of Massanutten before joining the North Fork. The North Fork flows out of northern Rockingham County and then along the west side of the Massanutten Range. The sandstone composition is the remnant of a 430-million-year-old sand shoal deposit. Those with good eyes may see the letters spelling out Endless Caverns on the side of the mountain.

16.0 This area is referred to as **Long Meadows.** This is one of the earliest placenames in this section of the Valley and occurs in land transactions as early as the 1730s. However, there have never been any definite boundaries connected to this name. It's also been known as **The Plains** and today lies in the Plains Magisterial District of Rockingham County. Few trees grew here in the mid-1700s when this area was surveyed, giving rise to the early names.

16.9 The Wampler family cemetery on the left is the resting place for many of the area's early German settlers.

17.0 **Turn LEFT at STOP sign onto Rt. 793.** Turn right onto Rt. 793 and ride **4.5 miles** to see **Endless Caverns.**

17.6 Rt. 793 crosses Long Meadows Run along here. The stream feeds into the North Fork of the Shenandoah River. The white house, in the grove of trees to the right, was built by the Cline family in the late 1800s. John and Katie Cline were the first of this early family in the area. John was born in Mount Crawford in 1796, and later earned the nickname Apple John Cline because of the major apple orchard he established here. He and his wife are buried in the Wampler cemetery.

18.5 **Turn RIGHT at STOP sign onto Rt. 618.**

18.6 **Turn RIGHT at STOP sign onto Rt. 211 East.** Nearby **Timberville** has gone by a number of names over the years. It was first named Williamsport after Abraham Williamson who opened a store here in 1814. When William G. Thompson took over the store in 1872, the town became known as Thompson's Store. When the post office was established in 1827, it was named Timberville because of the large wooded tract to the north of town. The village was incorporated as Timberville in 1844. It has been home to a marble works, tannery, hemp mill, and blacksmith shop.

19.5 The white weatherboard house with gray trim, next to the Timberville Church of the Nazarene on the left, is actually a covered log structure. It was built in the late 1700s by the Hoovers, one of this area's earliest families.

20.0   **Veer LEFT onto Rt. 953.** This road looks like someone's driveway so be careful not to miss it. The single story green veterinary office on the left is a good landmark for this turn. Route 953 is called Old River Road because it is the original route along the North Fork of the Shenandoah River. The North and South Forks of the Shenandoah River join above the northern end of the Massanutten Range and then flow into the Potomac River at Harpers Ferry.

20.5   The house on the left with the four-columned porch and twin bay windows as well as the red barn were once the Old Coffman Farm. The house was supposedly built by a Brethren minister in the Hoover family before the Civil War.

20.7   Although its age is unknown, the brick house on the right was here in 1846 when it passed into the Jordan family which has owned it ever since. It contains original windows with six panes over six panes, typical of the mid-1800s. The present generation of Jordans has extended an invitation for cyclists to get water from the outside faucet and picnic down by the river. Be sure to ask first and leave the area clean so that this courtesy will continue to be extended to others.

21.3   This community was once called **Plains Mill.** The flour mill to the left along the North Fork of the Shenandoah River was built in 1848 by Siram P. Henkel. It ceased operation about 1950. The Henkels built the house on the right in 1882. There was also an iron forge here at one time.

22.2   **Shenandoah County** was formed in 1772 from Frederick County to the north. It was first named **Dunmore** in honor of Virginia's last colonial governor. With the outbreak of the American Revolution and the ousting of Governor Dunmore, the name was changed to Shenandoah in 1777.

22.8   **Turn LEFT at STOP sign onto Rt. 617 and cross the North Fork of the Shenandoah River.** Turn right onto Rt. 953 and then left onto Rt. 211 to take a 1.7 mile sidetrip into **New Market.** The first Europeans came to this area around 1727 and formed the Massanutten Settlement. Legend has it that the Senedo tribe once resided near here, but was wiped out around 1700 by the warring Catawbas from the south. Senedo is one possible source of the word *Shenandoah*. Peter Palsel founded this town after buying land from John Sevier and laying out 32 lots in 1775. The town is still remembered for the Civil War battle in May 1864 in which 247 VMI cadets marched from Lexington to help turn back Union troops. ★ **Food and drinks are widely available here.** ★

22.9 **Cross bridge over the North Fork of the Shenandoah and turn RIGHT onto Rt. 617/728. Rt. 617 goes straight.**

23.0 **Proceed STRAIGHT on Rt. 617. Rt. 728 goes left.** The tan brick farmhouse to the left is called Riverlawn and was built by Jacob Price in 1847. Slaves built the home over a five-year period and made the bricks on the property for which Price paid an overseer $10,000. It was once part of a 600-acre plantation and reportedly served as a hospital after the Battle of New Market.

23.3 The cemetery on the left is the resting place for members of the Zirkle family, early German settlers.

23.4 The large white Georgian house on the left is one of the oldest homes along the river. George Adams Zirkle owned the house and 1,000 acres. According to family stories, this house was built in the late 1700s using the remnants of an older structure that stood here and burned down.

23.9 The ruins of Manors Mill are visible on the left after the bend in the road. It opened in 1847 and could turn out 200 barrels of flour a day. At one point the entire area was dammed, and an early power plant operated off the mill's energy until it burned in 1926.

24.4 **Cross RR tracks with CAUTION.**

24.5 The white frame church with bell and two wooden crosses on the left is St. Martin Evangelical Lutheran Church. It was built in 1890.

26.0 The white house in the field to the left is typical of the early 1800s with its two brick end chimneys and symmetrical door and window placement.

26.1 **Proceed STRAIGHT on Rt. 617. Rt. 616 goes left.**

26.8 **Turn LEFT onto Rt. 616 at Quicksburg.** This village was previously called Forest Station, but the name was changed at the insistence of William A. Quick whose family provided the land on which the town was built.

27.4 **Turn LEFT at STOP sign onto Rt. 767.** ★ **Food and drinks**

are available at the Quicksburg Grocery Store to the right on Rt. 767. ★

27.7 **Turn RIGHT onto Rt. 698 and cross Holman Creek.**

29.0 **Proceed STRAIGHT on Rt. 698 at intersection with Rt. 730.** Or turn right onto Rt. 730 to take a **.2 mile** sidetrip to Shenandoah Caverns. This is the only cavern in Virginia with its own elevator.

31.2 Frederickson Orchard was once called Turkey Knob. The orchard was planted in 1945, and now contains about 400 acres in trees. Apple orchards such as this one are a major agricultural crop in the northern Shenandoah Valley.

31.6 **Ride under I-81 overpass and enter Mount Jackson. Cross Mill Creek.** Survey maps from 1746 show this as Benjamin Allen's Mill Creek. This stretch where the road crosses the creek was an area of early settlement and supposedly the site of Allen's 1730s mill. The house on the right with the stone foundation and two-story porch was built in the 1830s and was associated with a milling complex across the road. The house and mill were advertised for sale in 1863 for Confederate money. There were no buyers, and Gen. Sheridan's Union troops burned the mill in October 1864. It was rebuilt, but accidentally burned again in 1918. Local entrepreneur, J.I. Triplett, used the site for one of the area's first power plants with electricity guaranteed every Tuesday when housewives did their ironing.

31.7 The restored 1800s gray house and outbuildings on the hill on the right are Widow Kip's Bed and Breakfast.

31.8 **Cross Mill Creek.**

31.9 **Turn RIGHT at STOP sign onto Rt. 263 East/Bryce Blvd. and ride under RR overpass.**

32.1 **Turn LEFT at STOP sign onto Rt. 11 North/Main St.** Mount Jackson was planned and developed in 1812 as Mount Pleasant. However, President Andrew Jackson's frequent stops here on his way from Washington to his home in Nashville, Tenn., prompted a name change in 1826. This town offers some interesting architecture, a number of antique shops, and the only cemetery in Virginia whose clientele were all Confederate soldiers.

32.5 ★ Food and drinks are available at IGA Market on the right. ★

33.0 ★ Food and drinks are available at **Red Apple Deli** on the right. ★

33.5 Turn LEFT onto Rt. 292 West/Rt. 703 at 7-Eleven store. Watch for increased traffic entering and exiting I-81 and truck stop.
★ Burger King is ahead on the right. ★

35.3 Turn LEFT at STOP sign onto Rt. 614.

35.9 Otterbein United Methodist Chapel was founded in 1835. The beautiful stained glass window in front is worth a good look.

36.5 Turn RIGHT at STOP sign onto Rt. 263 at Rinkerton. CAU-TION: Watch for high speed traffic on this road.

38.7 ★ Food and drinks are available at Powers Grocery on the right. ★

39.0 **Mount Clifton** used to have a telephone exchange and a mill down below on Mill Creek. Mount Clifton United Methodist Church was founded in the 1880s.

41.2 Turn LEFT onto Rt. 42 South with CAUTION and cross Mill Creek.

43.5 Turn RIGHT onto Rt. 613 at Getz Corner after 90-degree bend to the left. Stay on Rt. 613 for the next 16.7 miles. Although just a spot along the road now, Evan Jones and a number of other settlers resided here by the mid-1700s. Sometime in the 1800s, William Getz obtained land from the Jones family and built a store from which he also ran the post office. There was a school and butcher shop here as well. Getz's store closed after WWI.

43.7 The former Kerline School, named for Thomas Kerline who gave the land, served this community from the late 1800s until it closed in 1929. The building on the right was converted into a house.

44.1 Samuel Jones, a descendant of Evan Jones, built the white weatherboard house on the right in 1918.

45.3 The log house, across the road on the left, was supposedly built by Evan Jones himself. Some of the weatherboard remains. Tin shingles like these were applied in the 1850s before whole tin roofs were used.

46.4 St. Luke's United Methodist Church to the right was founded in 1848.

48.2 Get some freshly picked produce in-season at Ryan's Fruit Market.

49.2 The 1880s area atlas shows Mt. Olivet Church of the Brethren as a "Dunker" church. Dunker is an older term for the Brethren who practiced adult baptism by total immersion or dunking. The road through here was once called The Back Road and ran along the foothills of the Allegheny Mountains, the western edge of the Shenandoah Valley. It was used a lot by drovers moving their cattle to market.

52.2 Brocks Gap crosses Little North Mountain to the right. The Brock family settled here in the 1780s.

52.7 The tan board and batten house on the right was built in the early 1800s and served as a stopover for travelers along the Back Road. Many took advantage of cold water from the stone springhouse along the road.

52.8 Turn LEFT at STOP sign onto Rt. 259 East at Cootes Store. The North Fork of the Shenandoah River breaks through the mountain at Brocks Gap. The effects of this river over time lowered the elevation of the pass so that it is equal to that of the Valley. This was once the site planned for a hydroelectric dam, but it was never built. Samuel Cootes lived in the area from 1792 until he died in 1882. He was a sheriff and member of the Virginia House of Delegates.

52.9 Cross the North Fork of the Shenandoah River and turn RIGHT onto Rt. 613.

55.0 **Watch for heavy equipment and debris in road.** Just past the lumber mill on the left are the remains of a large mill with the huge wheel still intact. The mill was powered by Brocks Creek. This community of **Turleytown** was named for Giles Turley who stopped on his way to Kentucky and remained here. There was once an inn on this road that led to the cattle markets in Baltimore.

55.1 **Cross Joes Creek named for Joe Linville.**

59.9   Stay on Rt. 613 as it bends sharply to the left. Rt. 774 goes right.

60.3   **Turn LEFT at STOP sign onto Rt. 721.** The community of **Singers Glen** to the right was called Mountain Valley prior to the Civil War. The land was first owned by the Harrison family-more than likely Daniel Harrison, builder of Fort Harrison in Dayton. Henry Rhodes was the first known settler here. However, his son-in-law Joseph Funk is most associated with Singers Glen. Funk was born in 1778 in Pennsylvania, but his family moved here in the 1780s. He married Rhodes' daughter and bought 100 acres of land in 1809. Although he had very little formal education, Funk taught school and wrote religious and music books, as well as farmed. He was best known for his musical ability, and his books were distributed across the country. The first books were published in Harrisonburg, but in 1847 he purchased a printing press and hauled it home by horse and wagon. This printing shop in his loom house marked the first Mennonite printing house in America. The success of his publishing necessitated having a post office here, and in 1860 Joseph's son, Solomon, became the first postmaster. He renamed the village Singers Glen to honor his father's musical talent. ★ **Food and drinks are available at O&R Grocery to the right on Rt. 613.** ★

61.1   **Turn RIGHT onto Rt. 721/752 and cross bridge over Joes Creek.** There is a legend of the Soothing Fountain associated here with **Green Hill.** It seems that there was once a Native American village here, an idea substantiated by a considerable number of artifacts found. Near the foot of the hill was a spring from which water flowed very gently with a musical sound. The Indians would go to the spring to gain information about their lovers.

61.3   **Bear LEFT on Rt. 721. Gravel Rt. 752 goes right.**

62.1   The Massanutten Mountain range is straight ahead.

63.0   **Bear RIGHT onto Rt. 910 at grassy traffic island. Watch for loose gravel in the road at this intersection.**

63.7   The stone house to the right in the hollow across the pasture was built by Samuel Bowman around 1769. The Bowmans were early settlers in the area. Their driveway was once part of a public road that continued over the hill.

64.2   The oldest part of the house on the left is the low wing on the far end made of log. Notice the old mill reservoir behind the house.

64.3   This hollow was once a thriving village called **Greenmount**. The reservoir for the former mill still remains of this community which also included a blacksmith shop, general store, church, post office, and shoemaker. Most of what remains now are empty log and stone structures and a few occupied residences. The bottom of this small valley is the headwaters for Linville Creek which flows out of a substantial spring from the hillside to the right.

64.8   **Continue STRAIGHT at STOP sign at intersection with Rt. 772 past Greenmount Church of the Brethren.** Behind the church, which was organized in 1859, is the brick and stone Christian Myers homeplace. Its original date is not known, but the newer brick section was added in 1849.

65.1   Don't be surprised if you see a few llamas wondering around in the fields to your left. The Five K Llamas Farm presently has about 25 of these relatives of the camel which they raise for sale. People buy them for their wool, as pets, and as pack animals.

65.5   Antioch United Methodist Church of Christ was organized by Rev. I.N. Walter around 1832. This building was erected in 1880.

65.7   On the right is the large white, partially log, house at the Martin Burkholder farm. It was built in the late 1700s and still has the original siding on the front. The back part was added by Newton Burkholder, a local dentist. Fort Lynn, the name given the large limestone barn on the property, was built in 1803. Area stone buildings were often called *forts* because of the long vertical slits in the walls. It was believed, probably mistakenly, that slits in barn walls were for guns in case of attack. This is improbable for two reasons. Most of these barns were built around 1800, long after the threat of Indian attack was past, and long before the threat of Yankees was a reality. Also, the technique of building with such openings, narrow on the outside and wider on the inside, is found in Old World stone buildings. It was probably brought over by early immigrants and used as a means to provide light and ventilation while minimizing winds entering the barn.

66.2   **Bear RIGHT on Rt. 910. Rt. 765 goes left and straight.** The countryside for the next 1.7 miles is among the rockiest in Rockingham County. Residents often have to blast through limestone deposits even to install a septic tank. Stone has been quarried from this area for foundations, chimneys, walls, and even the early buildings at JMU. This area and sometimes-flowing creek are called Willow Run because of the willow trees that used to grow along here.

67.9 **Turn RIGHT at STOP sign onto Rt. 763.**

68.0 **Turn LEFT onto Rt. 910.** The white house on the right was built in the 1800s, with the oldest log portion reportedly salvaged from the nearby Weavers Mennonite Church after it was first torn down in the mid-1800s. Locals hauled the building materials to this spot while the Mennonite congregation was erecting the second of three churches to be built at the intersection of Rt. 726 and Rt. 33.

69.0 **Turn LEFT at STOP sign onto Rt. 910/Switchboard Rd. Rt. 766 goes right.**

69.3 The white house on the right once housed the West Central Switchboard, an early party line telephone system for this area, and is the reason for the name Switchboard Road. Instead of phone numbers, a combination of long or short rings distinguished one family's extension from another.

69.4 **Enter Harrisonburg.** The white house on the left is part of the Liskey Farm. Although the house on the road was built in 1898, the older brick home, back in the hollow, has a longer history. Family members have passed down the story about hiding chickens and geese in the attic and turning their horses loose in the woods to keep them out of the hands of Yankee soldiers. Next to the brick house is a small white-sided log structure. It is believed that this building was the first post office in Rockingham County back in 1792. This farm was situated on the Williamsburg Trail and would have served as a drop-off for mail going east and west.

69.5 **Turn RIGHT at STOP sign onto Rt. 33 West.** The colonial-style brick house, atop the hill on the right, was the home of Dr. Ashby Turner, an eye, ear, nose and throat specialist. He built the house in 1910 for $6,500. For many years, he kept his office and even did surgery here. The waiting room and surgery were on the first floor, and the recovery room was upstairs.

69.6 **Make a quick LEFT turn onto Garbers Church Rd.**

69.9   The large brick house on the right is about 160 years old.

70.0   The tan brick house on the right is known as the Jacob Shank House and was built between 1796 and 1805. The house was part of a 200-acre plantation, but slaves were never used to work the fields. It was always owned by Mennonite or Brethren families, both of which forbade slavery. Supposedly the house was used by local Brethren as a meeting house before Garbers Church was built. Another story has it that it was used as a hospital during the Civil War.

71.0   Turn LEFT at STOP sign onto Erickson Ave. by Garbers Church of the Brethren. This church was built in 1822 and was the first area Dunker church.

71.6   Turn LEFT at traffic light with CAUTION onto S. High St./Rt. 42 North.

72.1   Turn LEFT onto Hillandale Ave. The olive-green brick house with the red tin roof on the left is the Bibler House. It was built in 1793 over a spring to guarantee a constant water supply. The original owners were Lewis and Barbara Bibler who moved to Rockingham County from Pennsylvania. It's possible that the house served as a stagecoach stop at some point. Route 42 was formerly the Harrisonburg-Warm Springs Turnpike. The oldest part of the road is the 11 miles from here south to Mossy Creek. This road was laid out in 1779 to give Mossy Creek residents access to the county court system in Harrisonburg. In the 1830s a company was chartered to connect this section and the Warm Springs-Staunton part of the road and complete the entire turnpike.

72.4   End ride at starting point.

Caverns

The majority of the more than 2,800 caves in Virginia are found west of the Blue Ridge Mountains. Endless, Grand, Luray, Skyline, Shenandoah, and Natural Bridge Caverns are all in the Shenandoah Valley and open to the public. They formed over millions of years from easily dissolved rocks, like limestone, which occurred near the earth's surface.

Distinctive dripstone formations formed as surface water seeped through the earth and limestone and picked up minerals. The mixture was then redeposited, drop by drop, onto the floor and ceiling of the cave below. Stalactites, stalagmites, columns, and draperies are the most typical formations you'll find. Stalactites hang from the ceiling, while stalagmites rise from the floor. Columns are the result of the above two formations meeting to create a solid pole from floor to ceiling. Draperies occur when the dissolved minerals move across the cave surfaces at odd angles and then harden into unusually wide formations.

No two caverns are alike-each has its own unique limestone sculpture as well as a fascinating history. Among the oldest open to the public is Grand Caverns near the town of Grottoes. Bernard Weyer happened onto this discovery while trying to recover a raccoon trap in 1804. After Weyers Cave opened to the public in 1806, Thomas Jefferson rode over the Blue Ridge from Monticello to admire it. In those early days, the 5,000-square-foot subterranean Grand Ballroom was the scene of many dances. During the Civil War, it served as a stop-over for General Stonewall Jackson's Confederate troops. The cave's name was later changed to Grand Caverns, although the former railroad stop to the west retained the name Weyers Cave.

Endless Caverns, near New Market in southern Shenandoah County, is true to its name. Since the discovery in 1879 by two boys chasing a rabbit down a hole, no one has yet found an end to this limestone labyrinth. These caverns were officially opened to the public on August 14, 1920.

Shenandoah Caverns, also near New Market, has the distinction of being the only Virginia cavern with an elevator. This spot was uncovered in 1884 during the construction of the Southern Railway. A mile-long tour

The natural limestone formations of Endless Caverns near New Market are an awe-inspiring sight.

will take you through a series of chambers, most famous of which are the Bacon Formations in "Bacon Hall."

Your cycling journeys may also take you to Natural Chimneys, northwest of Staunton, and Natural Bridge, south of Lexington. These limestone formations give few clues that each was once in fact a cavern whose roof has long since collapsed. The grotto that once contained Natural Chimneys, formerly called the Cyclopean Towers, was large enough to hold a 40-story building. These pinnacles now stand as high as 120 feet.

Natural Bridge, one of the Seven Natural Wonders of the World, stands 23 stories high and is 90 feet long. George Washington surveyed this monument, and Thomas Jefferson purchased it in 1774 from King George III for 20 shillings—about $2.40. Don't miss the nearby caverns while you're touring Natural Bridge.

It's hard not to be awed by these magnificent underground structures which stand as monuments to the fragile beauty that nature can create. These and all other caves are sensitive environments which should be treated with care — geologic formations, if destroyed, will never regenerate. Any life forms in this subterranean world have had to develop adaptations that are unique to that environment and may not exist anywhere else.

Bridgewater
Spanning the North River

ROUTES

Bridgewater
Spanning the North River

The small-town, rural atmosphere remains in Bridgewater, making it a perfect setting for cyclists visiting this area of southern Rockingham County. Antique stores, bed and breakfast inns, and plain old friendliness are part of this town of 3,900 people. The history of the community goes back to the 1750s, but it was not until the early 1800s that John Dinkle saw the potential in harnessing the power of the North River. Dinkletown, as it was then called, grew with the establishment of a water-powered carding machine, sawmill, and gristmill. At one time in the 1800s, the town was also called Bridgeport because of its proximity to the bridge at a flatboat port on the North River.

In 1835 the town was chartered as Bridgewater, and lots were surveyed and laid out on 20 acres owned by John and Jacob Dinkle. The name was fitting since bridges have spanned the waters of the North River as far back as 1820. Over the years at least eight structures have stood at the same spot on the south end of town. The most impressive was a 240-foot covered wooden bridge that was completed in 1878. The present 339-foot span was erected in 1955.

Like much of the Shenandoah Valley, Bridgewater saw a real boom in the late 1800s with the construction of the railroad. At its peak, the town had numerous flour mills, woolen mills, and saw mills in close proximity. However, the town has also seen its share of tragedy over the years. A fire in 1880 caused widespread destruction; and severe floods in 1870, 1877, 1896, and 1949 did their share of damage as well. The 1949 flood prompted the construction of a flood control dam along the North River at what is now Wildwood Park.

No history of the town would be complete without mentioning Bridgewater College. It was Virginia's first co-educational college and the first affiliated with the Church of the Brethren to offer degrees. Daniel Flory founded the school in 1880 as Spring Creek Normal and Collegiate Institute in the nearby community of Spring Creek. He moved the campus to

Bridgewater
City Map

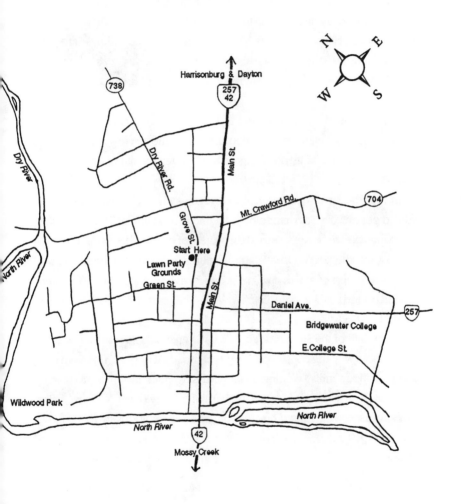

Harrisonburg & Dayton

738

257
42

N
E
W
S

Dry River Rd.

Main St.

Dry River

Mt. Crawford Rd.

704

Grove St.

North River

Start Here

Lawn Party
Grounds

Green St.

Main St.

Daniel Ave.

257

Bridgewater College

E. College St.

Wildwood Park

North River

North River

42

Mossy Creek

Dairy farmers are an important part of the local agricultural economy. Area Mennonite farmers alone account for 25% of Virginia's milk supply.

Bridgewater in 1887 and renamed it Virginia Normal School. It officially became Bridgewater College in 1889 and offers a liberal arts program today for approximately 1,000 students.

Several miles north of Bridgewater on Route 42 is the town of Dayton. Daniel Rife and his family owned large quantities of land in the area, a probable reason why it was first called Rifetown or Rifeville. Daniel Harrison, the brother of Harrisonburg's founder, Thomas Harrison, settled in the area and built a stone house on Cooks Creek around 1749. The house was also called Fort Harrison because of its fortification against Indian attacks. It is open to the public on weekends from May through October, and hosts a special Christmas celebration on the weekend just after Thanksgiving.

The Mennonite culture is very much in evidence as you pedal out of Bridgewater and Dayton. Before taking pictures of these folks, it is best to ask permission. Some members of the Old Order sects may be offended by this, although others may not mind. Those who cycle on Sunday will be delighted by the numbers of horse-drawn buggies on the roads going to and from worship services. Give them plenty of room and watch out for droppings in the road. Be sure to stop by the Dayton Farmers Market on Route 42 just south of Dayton. Many of the local Mennonite homemade foods, snacks, and craft items are available at this 21 shop mini-mall, open Thursday through Saturday.

Most routes start and stop at the parking area of the Bridgewater Lawn Party Grounds on North Grove St. The exception to this is the *Fort Harrison Frolic* which loops from the Daniel Harrison House in Dayton.

GETTING CENTERED

Bridgewater • Route 8 • 13.0 miles

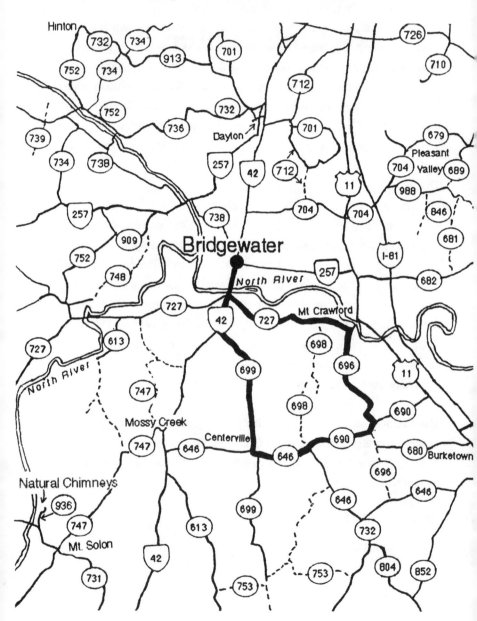

Getting Centered

This short 13-miler is a nice warm-up or perhaps a way to get your ying and yang on speaking terms again as you ride through Centerville. The views are outstanding, and for some this may be the ideal outing.

0.0 Start at Bridgewater Lawn Party Grounds parking lot on North Grove St. Ride SOUTH on N. Grove St.

0.1 Turn LEFT onto Green St. at STOP sign.

0.2 Turn RIGHT at traffic light onto Rt. 42 South.

0.8 Turn LEFT onto Rt. 727 after crossing North River and leaving Bridgewater.

2.6 Bridgewater Airport is privately owned. The large planes on the field are DC-3s. The .5 mile landing strip serves about 15 planes, most of which are used to eradicate gypsy moths locally.

3.1 The brick house on the right was built in two sections by the Wise family. The rear of the building was built in 1820, and as the physician-owner prospered, a second one was added directly in front in the 1860s. It was not until recently that the present owners connected the two with a passageway.

3.7 Turn RIGHT onto Rt. 696 and cross Silver Creek named for the silver maples that once graced its banks.

3.8 The house on the left is one of the area's oldest buildings. Andrew Lago built the most historic part around 1800. Lago was born on board the ship bringing his parents across the Atlantic to the New World. The part of the house facing the road was originally the back since the main road used to run along Silver Creek. The course of the roadway was changed in the late 1800s, and the orientation of the house was altered accordingly. The concrete stile along the driveway was installed to help horseback riders dismount. During the spring, cyclists will see the yard come alive with peonies, jonquils, and narcissus which the occupants in the late 1800s sold at the city market in Harrisonburg.

5.1 The bamboo on the left side of the road is not native to this area, but it has thrived since being planted 20 years ago. The next **.3 mile** on both sides of the road to the Augusta County line were once part of a huge farm called the Old Keyser Place. Andrew Lago's house was part of this same tract.

6.0 Bear RIGHT onto Rt. 690/696. Rt. 690 also goes left.

6.1 Continue STRAIGHT on Rt. 690. Rt. 696 goes left.

6.8 Summit Church of the Brethren was originally a Dunker or Tunker church. The Dunkers were a religious sect which settled in the Shenandoah Valley shortly after the American Revolution. They dressed plainly, espoused pacifism, and practiced adult baptism through total body immersion. *Dunker* comes from the German word, *tunken,* which means to immerse. A rift developed among the group in 1885, and one faction split off to form the Brethren Church. The others called themselves the German Baptist Brethren before changing after WWI to become the Church of the Brethren. The church sits at the top of Grattan Hill named for John Grattan, an early settler who owned some 1,000 acres of land in the area.

7.6 Bear LEFT on Rt. 690. Then turn RIGHT at STOP sign onto Rt. 646.

8.6 Turn RIGHT onto Rt. 699 at Centerville.

10.1 A **.2 mile** sidetrip to the right goes back to St. Michaels United Church of Christ. It was organized in 1764 as the Lutheran Reformed Church. The original building was made of logs and had a dirt floor. Legend has it that in 1794 one of the early ministers, Rev. Benjamin Henkel, was buried under the chancel, the part of the floor under the altar. That church was remodeled in 1830 and then torn down in 1876. A brick sanctuary was built in 1876, and the present one erected in 1916.

10.7 Look across the curve toward Bridgewater for a great view of Round Hill and Mole Hill in the distance.

11.4   The house on the right at the bend is called Long Glade after the nearby creek of the same name. It was built by the Irvine family around 1790 and has been expanded in four sections since then. Only Irvines and Millers have lived here. Frances Irvine lived there in 1774. According to family history, she was home alone when a Native American woman came to warn her of an impending Shawnee attack on the local settlers. Mrs. Irvine supposedly got on her horse and rode through the night, Paul Revere-style, to warn the residents of Mossy Creek and Mt. Solon of the raid. Her warning is said to have caused the tribe to cancel its plans.

11.5   Turn RIGHT at STOP sign onto Rt. 42.

12.3   Cross North River and enter Bridgewater

12.7   Turn LEFT onto Green St.

12.8   Turn RIGHT onto N. Grove St.

13.0   End ride at starting point.

DRY RIVER RUN
Bridgewater • Route 9 • 15.3 miles

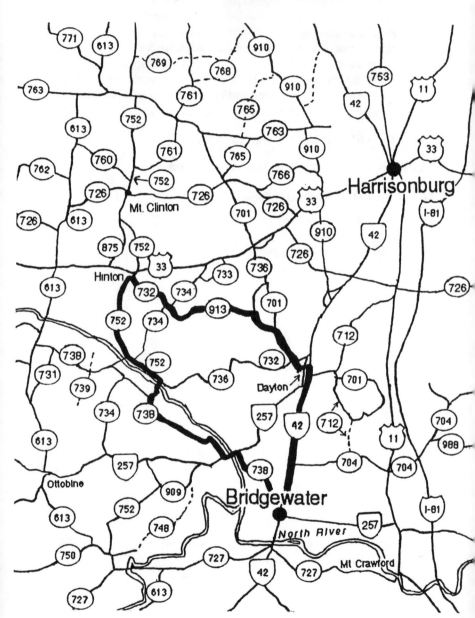

Dry River Run

Share the road with Mennonite horse-drawn buggies in the Dry River Valley. Then step back a little farther in time while climbing Mole Hill, the remnants of a 50-million-year-old volcano. Stop off and sample home-cooked Mennonite dishes at the Dayton Farmers Market on your way back to Bridgewater.

0.0   **Start at Bridgewater Lawn Party Grounds parking lot on North Grove St. Ride NORTH on N. Grove St.**

0.2   **Turn LEFT at STOP sign onto North River Rd.**

0.3   **Turn RIGHT onto Dry River Rd./Rt. 738.**

1.4   The Hollen homeplace, a yellow brick house on the right at the curve in the road, was built in 1834. The adjacent barn was built around 1840, and was one of the few area barns not burned by Yankee troops when they marched through the Shenandoah Valley in 1864 and 1865.

1.5   The mill on the left was built around 1883. Powered by the waters of Dry River, it ground flour, animal feed, and corn as well as milling wood until closing in the 1930s. There used to be a dam across the road where the Mill Cabinet Shop now stands. The cabinet shop was once located in the mill where craftsmen made antique reproduction furniture. The craftsmen now specialize in wooden cabinets and wardrobes. Ray Simmons, one of the shop's founders, is retired but continues the woodworking tradition in a shop behind the mill.

1.9   **Turn LEFT at STOP sign and proceed with CAUTION on Rt. 257. Cross bridge over Dry River.** Dry River is named because its waters dry to a trickle during the summer. However, it is the largest tributary of the North River which forms the South Fork of the Shenandoah River at Port Republic.

2.1 **Turn RIGHT onto Rt. 738.** The next seven miles are rich with Old Order Mennonite farms. The roads have a special surface applied so that the hooves of horses pulling buggies don't slip. Sunday cyclists on this route should be especially observant for horse droppings from the large number of buggies going back and forth from worship.

3.4 The Martin Speck house on the right was part of an 1,100-acre land grant from the 1700s. The Specks were the original owners, but two previous houses on the property burned down before the present one was built in 1838. The bricks for this home were made on the farm. It was the only one of three houses on the land that escaped Yankee conflagration.

4.0 **Turn RIGHT onto Rt. 752.**

4.2 **Continue STRAIGHT on Rt. 752. Rt. 738 goes left.**

4.6 **Cross Dry River and turn LEFT at STOP sign onto Rt. 752.**

5.4 The Bank Mennonite Church on the right was built in 1964. Although German and Swiss Mennonites were among the area's first settlers in the 1720s, there were no Mennonite churches for 100 years due to the strict Old Order belief that "the Lord of Heaven and Earth dwelleth not in temples made with hands." Acts: 17:24. Instead they held their Sunday worship in the homes of their congregation members. Despite its relative youth, this church has an interesting story attached to it. Some years ago, a local man with a reputation for exaggeration was walking past the graveyard one evening. What should he see but a ghost rising from a newly dug plot. He rushed to tell his neighbors, who were rather skeptical. They followed him back to disprove his sighting, and were amazed to, in fact, see an apparent apparition emerging from the grave. On closer inspection, however, it turned out that a white sheep had fallen into the hole, and was jumping up and down trying to extricate itself.

7.1 Mount Horeb United Methodist Church on the left was built by the United Brethren who used it from 1875 to 1945. Also known as German Methodists, all of the services of this sect were conducted in German until 1820. The United Brethren merged with the Methodists to form the United Methodists. They have used this building for services since 1950.

7.4   **Cross Muddy Creek.**

7.5   **Turn RIGHT onto Rt. 732 just before Rt. 33. Hinton** used to be known as Karicofe after a local family. Supposedly the Karicofes were Northern sympathizers during the Civil War, and the town was renamed in honor of a Confederate colonel who lived nearby. ★ **Food and drinks are available at the Hinton Market on the left.** ★

8.5   **Bear LEFT on Rt. 732 at grassy island. Rt. 734 goes right.**

8.6   **Continue STRAIGHT on Rt. 732. Rt. 734 goes left.**

9.0   **Turn LEFT at STOP sign onto Rt. 732. Rt. 914 goes right.**

9.1   **Bear LEFT on Rt. 913 and begin to climb Mole Hill. Gravel Rt. 732 goes right.** Mole Hill rises 500 feet above the Valley floor with its top at 1,900 feet above sea level. It is the remnant of a 50-million-year-old volcano, one of two in Virginia. Locals thought that it looked like it had been pushed up from underground by a giant mole, thus its name. Legend has it that area residents celebrated the end of the War of 1812 by leading an ox to the top and roasting it there. Be sure to pull off the road and enjoy the view.

10.7   **Turn RIGHT at STOP sign onto Rt. 736.**

10.8   **Turn LEFT onto Rt. 913. Gravel Rt. 736 goes straight.**

11.3   **Turn RIGHT at STOP sign onto Rt. 701.** The stately stone house across the road is Walnut Grove named for the 40 black walnut trees in the yard. The house was built of Dry River rock in 1931 on the site of an old schoolhouse called Paul's Summit.

11.6   Fifteen-acre Silver Lake was formed in the 1800s by the damming of Cooks Creek. Its name was apparently given by a local school-teacher, Pearl Head, who said that such a pretty lake should have a name to match. It's also been called Mill Pond because of the mill at the south end of the lake.

12.0   **Continue STRAIGHT on Rt. 290 East./College St. Rt. 701/732 goes left to Fort Harrison. Dayton** is one of the oldest towns in Rockingham County with its first settlers arriving in the mid-1700s. It was first known as Rifetown and Rifeville after Daniel Rife, an early landowner. However, the town was legally established as

Dayton in 1833, possibly to honor Jonathon Dayton, the youngest signer of the Constitution. He had a relative living in this area at the time. ★ **Food and drinks are widely available.** ★

12.1 The Harrisonburg-Rockingham Historical Society and Museum is on the right across from Cooks Creek Park.

12.5 Bear RIGHT at STOP sign onto Main St./Rt. 290 East.

12.7 Continue STRAIGHT at STOP sign across Rt. 257/Mason St.

12.8 Bear LEFT and then turn RIGHT onto Rt. 42 South with CAUTION. Route 42 was incorporated during the 1829-30 session of the Virginia General Assembly as the Warm Springs and Harrisonburg Turnpike.

13.0 For a taste of some wonderful homecooked Mennonite treats, stop by The Dayton Farmers Market, on the right. This 21 shop mini-mall has everything from Shoo Fly Pie to hand-dipped ice cream. It's open Thursday through Saturday so plan your ride accordingly.

14.1 Enter Bridgewater.

15.0 Turn RIGHT onto North River Road.

15.1 Turn LEFT onto N. Grove St. The Dry River District Ranger Station on the left has a wealth of free information regarding recreational facilities in the nearby George Washington National Forest.

15.3 End ride at starting point.

Mennonites

Today there are roughly 4,500 Mennonites living in the Shenandoah Valley, primarily in the Dayton and Bridgewater areas south of Harrisonburg and the Stuarts Draft area east of Staunton. They represent a wide range of sects, sharing many of the same beliefs but practicing them in different ways. Most noticeable to the outsider are the Old Order Mennonite families who travel by horse and buggy or bicycle. You'll see a number of businesses around Dayton, such as the Dayton Farmers Market, that still provide hitching posts to accommodate the horse and buggy.

The Shenandoah Valley Old Orders split off in 1901 from the other area Mennonites. However, a second splinter group has emerged since the 1901 schism. "The Black Bumper Mennonites" drive automobiles which must be dark in color with the chrome painted over. Conservative dress with men wearing plain coats without lapels and women wearing head coverings and an apron over modest dresses may identify some Mennonites, while the clothing of others may be no different than their non-Mennonite neighbors.

The history of the Mennonite religion goes back almost 500 years to Switzerland where a group of Protestants with beliefs in adult baptism, simplicity, and pacifism organized themselves as the Swiss Brethren. Also known as Anabaptists because of their practice of adult baptism, they were persecuted in Switzerland and other areas of Europe. In the 1500s, a Dutch ex-Catholic priest named Menno Simmons influenced some of these people. They became known as Menoists (now Mennonites) or followers of Menno. The Amish are Mennonites who broke away in 1693 to follow Jacob Ammon and his belief in shunning those who had left the faith.

Seeking relief from persecution, large numbers of German-speaking Swiss Mennonites came to America. Many made their homes in the Lancaster area of Pennsylvania, which even today represents the largest concentration of Mennonites in the United States. As the farmlands there filled, these German-speaking pioneers moved southward along the Valley Road into the Shenandoah Valley. Adam Miller and other Mennonites began settling near Massanutten Mountain around 1727.

FORT HARRISON FROLIC

Bridgewater • Route 10 • 18.3 miles

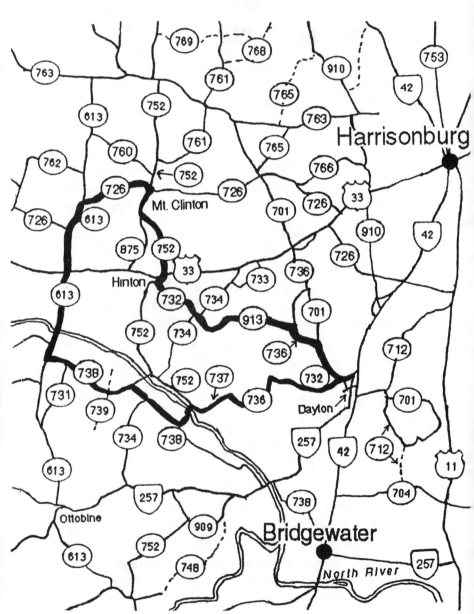

Fort Harrison Frolic

Begin and end your journey at the Daniel Harrison House, home of one of Dayton's early settlers. Along the way, you'll ride on primarily flat roads through Mennonite farm lands before climbing a 50-million-year-old volcano.

0.0 **Begin at Daniel Harrison House on Rt. 42 Business in Dayton. Ride NORTH (away from Dayton) on Rt. 42 Business.** Daniel was the brother of Thomas Harrison, Harrisonburg's founder. Daniel Harrison settled in this area in the late 1740s, and built the stone portion of this existing structure soon thereafter. It was fortified against Indian attacks with a stockade fence and an underground passage to a nearby spring.

0.1 **Turn LEFT at STOP sign onto Rt. 732.**

0.2 **Turn LEFT at STOP sign onto Rt. 732.** The mortarless limestone wall is typical of many that once lined roads in the Shenandoah Valley. As settlers cleared the roads and fields of these rocks, they piled them along their property lines to mark boundaries.

0.3 **Turn RIGHT onto Rt. 732/Bowman Rd. at Cooks Creek Park.** The Harrisonburg-Rockingham Historical Society and Museum is on the left after making this turn.

0.4 The house on the left with fancy trim was built in the late 1800s. Its riverboat design trim around the porch and eaves on the front of the house, the part facing the road, is unique and occurs on only a few homes in Rockingham County.

0.5 The oldest grave in Dayton's cemetery on the left is that of Mary Harrison, a relative of Daniel Harrison. She died in 1792. Dr. J.H. Jackson was buried here, supposedly in a standing position. The cemetery is the site of the former Anglican Chapel of Ease, Rockingham County's first church built in 1745. It was taken over by Methodists after the American Revolution, then sold and used as a barn until it was torn down about 1900.

1.8   **Turn LEFT onto Rt. 736/732. Watch for loose gravel.**

1.9   **Continue STRAIGHT on Rt. 736. Rt. 732 goes right.** This area has a large number of Old Order Mennonite residents. You'll see these folks on the road riding bicycles, tractors, or in horse-drawn buggies. The roads have a special surface applied so that the hooves of horses pulling buggies don't slip. Sunday cyclists on this route should be especially observant for horse droppings from the large number of buggies going back and forth from worship.

2.6   **Turn RIGHT onto Rt. 237. Gravel Rt. 736 goes straight.**

3.0   **Turn LEFT onto Rt. 737. Gravel Rt. 810 goes straight.** Notice Mole Hill off to the right.

3.8   **Turn LEFT onto Rt. 752 and cross Dry River.** Dry River is named because its waters dry to a trickle during the summer. However, it is the largest tributary of the North River which forms the South Fork of the Shenandoah River. During the infamous flood of November 1985, it jumped its banks and inundated this entire area.

4.2   **Turn RIGHT at YIELD sign onto Rt. 738. Rt. 752 goes straight.**

5.3   **Bear LEFT onto Rt. 738. Gravel Rt. 734 goes right.**

7.1   **Turn RIGHT onto Rt. 613.**

7.4   This crossroads of **Lilly** is named after William Lilly who started the post office here. He had 19 children, one of whom became an army major in the 1880s and later a Wild West showman named Pawnee Bill Lilly. ★ **Food and drinks are available at Dry River Grocery Store.** ★

7.5   The long hill to the left is called Giants Grave. Previously known as Cooper's Mountain, a storyteller spread a tale among the local children in the 1890s that was instrumental in renaming the mound. According to this legend, a lonely giant had lived in these mountains for most of his life and longed for the companionship of other giants. When he was very old, a second giant came and befriended him allowing him to die happy. His new companion buried him under this rise which still retains his shape despite the growth of trees and flowers on top.

8.6 On the left behind the white pines is the Abram Andes House. It is thought to have been built by Thomas Beery before 1822. The bricks, laid in Flemish bond style, were made on the farm. The land was originally part of a large grant that described the property not in acres, but "as far as the eye could see." There was once a large springhouse where the small brick springhouse now stands along the driveway. Local farmers once brought their cans of milk to the old structure for cool storage. After emptying them, they would wash the containers in the nearby creek until it ran milky white. From this the stream came to be known as Buttermilk Run.

8.7 **Cross Rt. 33 at STOP sign with CAUTION and stay on Rt. 613.** Route 33 was originally known as the Rawley Springs Turnpike, and this particular crossroads was called Whitmore's Shop. In addition to Joe Whitmore's blacksmith shop, the Oakdale School educated children here from 1885 through the early 1900s.

9.4 The house on the right is known as the Old Kline Place and dates back about 200 years. The creek that runs behind the house and through the property is War Branch. There's a story that a great battle between Native Americans and early settlers occurred here. The true story about the battle has been transferred into legend, but over the years residents in the house have uncovered a large number of Native American artifacts in the fields after plowing.

9.5 **Cross War Branch.**

10.1 **Turn RIGHT onto Rt. 726.**

10.3 The Hillside Dairy Farm on the right was built about 125 years ago with a fireplace in every room of the house.

10.7 Mt. Clinton Mennonite Church was first built in 1874. Although German and Swiss Mennonites were among the area's first settlers in the 1720s, there were no Mennonite churches for 100 years due to the strict Old Order belief that "the Lord of Heaven and Earth dwelleth not in temples made with hands." Acts: 17:24. Instead, they held their Sunday worship in the homes of their congregational members.

11.4 **Turn RIGHT onto Rt. 752 at Mt. Clinton.** Known previously as Muddy Creek for the stream that runs through town, the derivation of the present name is a bit cloudy as well. One possibility is the notion that the town received its name by a popular vote in 1833 with free applejack given to those in favor of the present name. Another stems from a story that a Confederate officer struck a chord with some of the local ladies while stopping to water his horse in town. When it was time to leave one of the other officers was heard to say, "Mount up, Clinton." His female admirers thought this would make a good name. The white brick house with green trim on the left upon entering Mt. Clinton belonged to Samuel Firebaugh. He lost the use of his arm during the Civil War and ran a general store that used to stand at the end of the driveway. The house itself was built in 1804. A father and son medical practice and residence was located in the house next door that was built just before the Civil War. The doctors worked out of this location through the late 1800s.

11.5   Mt. Clinton United Methodist Church was formerly a United Brethren Church. This sect was often referred to as German Methodist because services were conducted in German. In the 1920s the United Brethren and Methodists merged to become the United Methodist Church.

11.9   **Bear LEFT on Rt. 752. Rt. 875 goes right.**

13.1   **Turn RIGHT at STOP sign with CAUTION onto Rt. 33.** Hinton used to be known as Karicofe after a local family. Supposedly, the Karicofes were Northern sympathizers during the Civil War, and the town was renamed in honor of a Confederate colonel who lived nearby. ★ **Food and drinks are available at the Hinton Market on the left.** ★

13.2   **Make a quick LEFT turn with CAUTION onto Rt. 752.**

13.3   **Turn LEFT onto Rt. 732. Rt. 752 goes straight.**

14.4   **Bear LEFT on Rt. 732. Rt. 732 also goes straight and right.**

14.5   **Continue STRAIGHT on Rt. 732. Rt. 734 goes left.**

14.9   **Turn LEFT at STOP sign onto Rt. 732. Rt. 914 goes right. Watch for loose gravel in the road.**

15.0   **Bear LEFT on Rt. 913 and begin to climb Mole Hill. Gravel Rt. 732 goes right.** Mole Hill rises 500 feet above the Valley floor with its top at 1,900 feet above sea level. It is the remnant of a 50-million-year-old volcano, one of two in Virginia. Locals thought that it looked like it had been pushed up from underground by a giant mole, thus its name. Legend has it that area residents celebrated the end of the War of 1812 by leading an ox to the top and roasting it there. Be sure to pull off the road and enjoy the view.

16.6   **Turn RIGHT at STOP sign onto Rt. 736.**

16.7   **Turn LEFT onto Rt. 913. Gravel Rt. 736 goes straight.**

17.2   **Turn RIGHT at STOP sign onto Rt. 701.** The stately stone house across the road is Walnut Grove named for the 40 black walnut trees in the yard. The house was built of Dry River rock in 1931 on the site of an old schoolhouse called Paul's Summit.

17.4   Fifteen-acre Silver Lake was formed in the 1800s by the damming of Cooks Creek. Its name was apparently given by a local schoolteacher, Pearl Head, who said that such a pretty lake should have a name to match. It's also been called Mill Pond because of the mill at the south end of the lake.

18.0   **Turn LEFT onto Rt. 732. Dayton** is one of the oldest towns in Rockingham County with its first settlers arriving in the mid-1700s. It was first known as Rifetown and Rifeville after Daniel Rife, an early landowner. However, the town was legally established as Dayton in 1833, possibly to honor Jonathon Dayton, the youngest signer of the Constitution. He had a relative living in this area at the time.

18.2   **Turn RIGHT onto Rt. 42 Business.**

18.3   **End ride at starting point.**

The French & Indian War

For the first pioneers in the Shenandoah Valley, frontier life meant not only settling new land; it also meant armed conflict. The French and Indian War, 1754-1763, was comparable to more modern wars that pit armies from separate continents against each other on the field of battle. The American settlers along with the British Redcoats fought the French and their Native American allies, primarily Shawnees. Despite the name of this tumultuous period, some tribes, such as the Cherokees, allied themselves with the Colonial army.

George Washington, Adam Stephens, and Augusta County's Andrew Lewis retrained the Valley soldiers to use their military skills as frontier fighters battling on a wilderness battlefield. The Native Americans called the local militia "Long Knives" because they carried tomahawks as they fought to defend their western lands. Much of the war was fought in Augusta County; but keep in mind that, at that time, Augusta County stretched all the way to the Mississippi River.

Life on the Augusta County frontier was unsettled and perilous during these years. Many settlers who had started farms in the relative peace of the 1730s, fled in fear in the 1750s. The county's population plummeted from 9,000 to 5,500 during the 1754-1758 period as residents headed for safer country in Virginia's Tidewater and Piedmont as well as into the Carolinas. About 100 people were killed and another 200 wounded or captured in Indian raids, which accompanied the unrest.

However, even after a peace treaty was signed in 1763, sporadic raids and atrocities continued on both sides. Perhaps the area's worst attack occurred near Kerr's Creek in what is now Rockbridge County. According to accounts of the raid, which may have been exaggerated, on October 10, 1765, a band of Shawnees swept down on the settlement at Big Spring and killed between 50 to 60 settlers. Some of these same warriors, who had allied with the French, headed to within a few miles of Staunton. John Trimble became Augusta's last victim of the Indians as he encountered them near the present village of Churchville. A hastily organized militia force drove the Shawnees back into the mountains.

On the other hand, a band of Cherokees, allies with the Colonial cause, passed through the county in 1765. Ten of them spent the night in a barn near Verona, and five were murdered during the night. Two of the murderers were subsequently arrested, but they were never tried for their acts.

Rockingham County settlers were affected by the same unrest during this period of strife. Daniel Harrison built his stone house in 1749 in the present town of Dayton and fortified it to provide a defense against Indian attacks. Fort Harrison, as it is still called, became a refuge for residents of that area with its stockade fence and underground passage to a nearby spring. The Augusta Stone Church, on the Valley Road near Verona, was also said to have offered protection from Indian attacks, as did Timber Ridge Presbyterian Church in Rockbridge County.

SPRINGHILL SOJOURN
Bridgewater • Route 11 • 41.3 or 50.1 miles

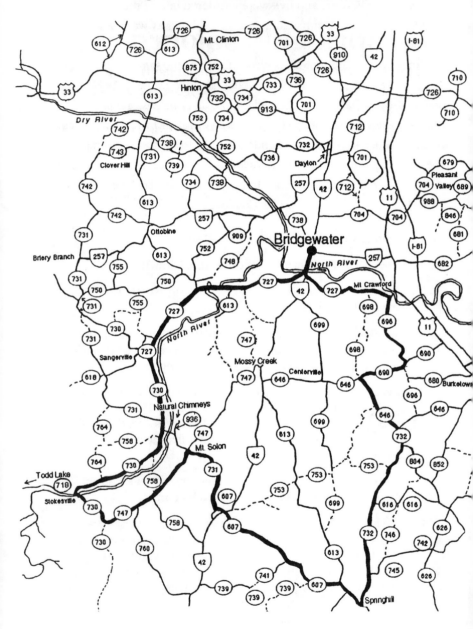

Springhill Sojourn

Head south toward Springhill and explore former railroad towns whose architecture recalls memories of bygone days. The early 1900s passenger depot and caboose are still accessible at the Stokesville Park. Picnic at Natural Chimneys or plan to cool off in the swimming pool there.

0.0 **Start at Bridgewater Lawn Party Grounds parking lot on North Grove St. Ride SOUTH on N. Grove St.**

0.1 **Turn LEFT onto Green St. at STOP sign.**

0.2 **Turn RIGHT at traffic light onto Rt. 42 South.**

0.8 **Turn LEFT onto Rt. 727 after crossing North River and leaving Bridgewater.**

2.6 Bridgewater Airport is privately owned. The large planes on the field are DC-3s. The .5 mile landing strip serves about 15 planes, most of which are used to eradicate gypsy moths locally.

3.1 The brick house on the right was built in two sections by the Wise family. The rear of the building was built in 1820, and as the physician-owner prospered, a second one was added directly in front in the 1860s. It was not until recently that the present owners connected the two with a passageway.

3.7 **Turn RIGHT onto Rt. 696 and cross Silver Creek named for the silver maples that once graced its banks.**

3.8 The house on the left is one of the area's oldest buildings. Andrew Lago built the most historic part around 1800. Lago was born on board the ship bringing his parents across the Atlantic to the New World. The part of the house facing the road was originally the back since the main road used to run along Silver Creek. The course of the roadway was changed in the late 1800s, and the orientation of the house was altered accordingly. The concrete stile along the driveway was installed to help horseback riders dismount. During the spring, cyclists will see the yard come alive with peonies, jonquils, and narcissus which the occupants sold at the city market in Harrisonburg in the late 1800s.

5.1   The bamboo on the left side of the road is not native to this area, but it has thrived since being planted 20 years ago. The next **.3 mile** on both sides of the road to the Augusta County line were once part of a huge farm called the Old Keyser Place. Andrew Lago's house was part of this same tract.

6.0   Bear RIGHT onto Rt. 690/696. Rt. 690 also goes left.

6.1   Continue STRAIGHT on Rt. 690. Rt. 696 goes left.

6.8   Summit Church of the Brethren was originally a Dunker or Tunker church. The Dunkers were a religious sect which settled in the Shenandoah Valley shortly after the American Revolution. They dressed plainly, espoused pacifism, and practiced adult baptism through total body immersion. *Dunker* comes from the German word, *tunken,* which means to immerse. A rift developed among the group in 1885, and one faction split off to form the Brethren Church. The others called themselves the German Baptist Brethren before changing after WWI to become the Church of the Brethren. The church sits at the top of Grattan Hill named for John Grattan, a settler who owned some 1,000 acres of land nearby.

7.6   Bear LEFT on Rt. 690 and turn LEFT at STOP sign onto Rt. 646.

9.7   Continue STRAIGHT on Rt. 732. Rt. 646 bends to the left. The barn on the left side of the road is called a forebay barn because of the overhang, or forebay. This was designed to protect animals and wagons from inclement weather. The ramp on the roadside leads to the second floor. There is also a wagon shed on the side.

10.2   Continue STRAIGHT on Rt. 732 at Y-intersection. Rt. 804 goes left.

10.8   The white house on the right was constructed using a technique called rubble construction that was developed in the late 1800s. Wooden forms were built, into which native rock was placed, followed by a cement-like slurry to form the walls. This is the home of renowned cornhusk artist, Pat Broyles. Her work is available at the Woodrow Wilson Birthplace Gift Shop in Staunton.

12.0   **Roman** was a thriving community from 1885 to 1920. The village had a post office, school, church, stores, and a blacksmith shop. It even had its own town band that performed at special events.

13.9   The brick home on the right was built in the 1780s.

15.1   The Middle River on the left snakes its way north through Augusta County, ultimately flowing into the North River near Grottoes, which then merges with the South River to form the South Fork of the Shenandoah River at Port Republic.

15.3   **Turn RIGHT at STOP sign onto Rt. 613 and begin climb to Springhill.** The Federal brick I-house, across the road at this intersection, is called the Gamble House after the name of early owners. It was built sometime between 1820 and 1840 and was associated with several mills nearby on the Middle River. For the time the house was quite lavish and indicative of the wealth of the owner.

15.7   The post office in **Springhill** was established before the Civil War, and was known as Long Glade after the nearby creek of the same name that flows north into Mossy Creek. The road through town was also known as Long Glade. Jacob Miller Crist and Jacob Crist Spitler mapped out this "planned town" in 1838, and water was piped from a spring uphill to the town, a likely rationale for the present name. An 1834 deed from the Crist family mentions this same spring. Area development eventually moved eastward toward the Valley Road, and so the architecture of Springhill is well preserved from its early days.

16.3   **Bear LEFT onto Rt. 607 at Y-intersection.**

18.2   The house on the left was built by William Howell in the 1840s. The current owners call it Short Glade Farm. This was the manor house for a large plantation known as the East property. Howell, who is buried across the road, had a daughter who married into the East family. The plantation included considerable acreage along both sides of the present road. The bank barn is not as old as the house.

20.9   **Cross Rt. 42 at STOP sign with CAUTION and stay on Rt. 607.** Route 42 was incorporated during the 1829-30 session of the Virginia General Assembly as the Warm Springs and Harrisonburg Turnpike. The word *turnpike* means a tollroad. The name comes from the device used to stop traffic so that the toll would be paid. The turnpike itself was usually a tall wooden box with a pike, or pole, resting on it. The pole stretched across the road with the opposite end supported by a forked post. The pike was raised or turned after the toll had been paid. **Moscow** was supposedly named by a Russian immigrant who settled in the area.

21.1   Bear RIGHT on Rt. 731.

21.7   The house on top of the hill to the right was built just before the outbreak of the Civil War in 1860. It has a log structure at its center.

23.2   The McCue House on the left was built in the early 1800s by stacking two-inch thick boards like logs.

23.4   The brick building on the right was built in 1908 during **Mt. Solon's** heyday. It housed Planters Bank until 1944. In 1947 the Mt. Solon Post Office operated here and continued to do so until the new one was built in 1964. Across the road, O.A. Flippo opened his general store in 1906. The Chesapeake and Western Railroad ran through here from the late 1800s until 1930. There are still some traces of the old railbeds. The depot was located at the site of the present post office. The Mount Solon United Methodist Church, around the bend on the right, was established in 1843. It's the only church that has ever been in Mt. Solon. It's said that Samuel Curry named this town after Solon, a Greek statesman from 600 B.C. Although the railroad caused increased prosperity here, this was an established settlement by the late 1700s with a store, distillery, several mills, and a tanyard.

23.5   Turn LEFT at four-way STOP onto Rt. 747 after passing overflow area from the old mill ponds. As soon as you turn, look to the right. The small multi-sided building at the edge of the gravel parking lot served as a community bandstand in the 1800s. It was later boarded over and used as a music classroom until the early 1900s.

23.7   The building in the middle of several others, on the right on top of the hill, is over 200 years old. The former C&W rail line crossed the road here at the bend in the road. It's said that the locals referred to the line as the "Crooked and Weedy."

24.4   Crest the top of Castle Hill. Local legend has it that Gen. Stonewall Jackson met some of his officers and camped here after their victory at the Battle of McDowell fought west of here in 1862.

25.2   Cross Freemason Run.

25.7   Mt. Olivet United Brethren Church on the left was founded in 1893.

26.0   **Continue STRAIGHT at three-way STOP on Rt. 747 by Mt. Zion United Methodist Church.**

27.0   Stribling Springs, one of the Shenandoah Valley's famous therapeutic resorts, was located down Rt. 730 on the left. Dr. Erasmus Stribling, then mayor of Staunton, opened the resort in 1817. Nothing remains of this spot which was reportedly used as a hospital during the Civil War as well as temporary headquarters for Gen. Stonewall Jackson.

28.1   **Bear LEFT on Rt. 730. Stokesville** was another railroad boom town in the early 1900s. The office for the Stokesville Park Campground on the left used to be the passenger depot at the end of the line for the C&W. The train carried timber, locally cut from what is now the George Washington National Forest, to Harrisonburg. Stokes City, as it was then called, was named after W.E.D. Stokes. His financing helped establish the rail line through here. The town dried up after the trains stopped running in 1930. Stop by the campground office for more information about this beautiful spot. ★ **Food and drinks are available at the campground office.** ★

28.3   **Cross bridge over the North River. Turn RIGHT onto Rt. 730 to continue route or continue STRAIGHT for 8.8 mile loop to Todd Lake.** This bridge was built around 1900 for the train. There was once a roundhouse across the bridge which turned the engine around for its return trip to Harrisonburg.

28.5   Stokesville Church was built in 1903.

28.6   ★ **Food and drinks are available at Stokesville Market on the left.** ★

32.1   **Turn right onto Rt. 731 and ride .4 mile to visit Natural Chimneys Regional Park. Otherwise, continue STRAIGHT on Rt. 730 to return to Bridgewater.** The naturally formed limestone "chimneys" have been referred to as the "Cyclopean Towers," "Towers of Solon," and "Pillars of Hercules." The seven peaks range in height from 65 to 120 feet. They are the remnants of what was once a cavern whose roof collapsed and filled in the grotto long ago. At one time, this cavern would have been large enough to contain a 40-story building. In addition to facilities for swimming, picnicking, and camping, this park is host to the Oldest

Continuous Sporting Event in America. The Natural Chimneys Jousting Tournament started in 1821 over competition for a local girl. On the third Saturday in August every year, 20th century knights gallop on horseback and attempt to spear small rings from a crossbar. ★ **Food and drinks are available at Werners Store on the left.** ★

33.6　The brick house on the left was built in the early 1800s. The original windows are those with 12 panes on the bottom and top halves. As a general rule, older houses tend to have a larger number of small panes in the original windows since larger panes were harder to make and ship.

34.5　Turn RIGHT onto Rt. 727 at Sangerville. The Old Earhart Place on the left was built around 1815. Although a Capt. Smith settled here around 1740, it wasn't until Jacob Sanger established a paper mill in the 1840s that the town started to prosper. In the late 1800s, Sangerville included a post office, general store, blacksmith shop, two churches, and close to 100 residents.

37.1　Turn RIGHT onto Rt. 613/727.

37.2　The Devier House on the right was built around 1830. There's a story associated with this house relating to a wedding in 1860. In the 1800s, it was the custom to bother newlyweds on their wedding night through a practice called belling. The group, which often got rowdy, would arrive at the couple's residence, serenade them, and demand an appearance. On this particular occasion, the bride's older brother came outside to ask the bellers to leave. Tempers flared, and one of the crowd shot and killed the brother.

37.4　Cross the North River.

37.9　The stately brick home on the right with columns on the top two floors was built right after the Civil War in 1865 by Dennis Miller. Miller was a carpenter and built the house for himself, his wife, and nine children. To keep the five boys and four girls apart, he built a wall in the middle of the third floor between their respective sides. The only way to cross from side to side was to go down to the second floor, cross over, and then go back upstairs. The barn is pre-Civil War and was probably spared burning by Yankee troops because Miller was a Dunkard, a pacifist group that remained neutral during the war. George Jordan lived here during the 1930s and started one of the area's first electric poultry hatcheries. Jordan's family still lives in the house which is heated geothermally using water from the spring in front of the house.

38.5 **Cross Mossy Creek.**

39.3 Round Hill is on the left. Named for its shape, it is composed of a flint-like rock called chert. The hill has been a local landmark since the early settlers mentioned it in a deed dating back to 1750.

40.6 **Turn LEFT at STOP sign onto Rt. 42 North. Cross North River and enter Bridgewater.**

41.1 **Turn LEFT onto Green St.**

41.2 **Turn RIGHT onto N. Grove St.**

42.3 **End ride at starting point.**

8.8 MILE TODD LAKE SIDETRIP

0.0 **Start from 28.3 mile point at the intersection of Rt. 730 and Rt. 718. Continue STRAIGHT at STOP sign on Rt. 718.**

1.0 **Turn LEFT on Forest Development Road 95 after passing Camp May Flather on the left. FDR 101 goes straight.** As the result of the extensive logging in these mountains around the turn of the century, by 1915 there was little standing timber left. In April 1912, the federal government began buying cut-over tracts for management by the U.S. Forest Service. Today there are over one million acres in the George Washington National Forest that are managed for recreation, timber harvest, and biological diversity.

4.2 **Turn RIGHT onto FDR 523.**

4.4 Entrance to Todd Lake. Swimming, camping, and picnic facilities are available during the summer. **To return, backtrack down FDR 523.**

4.6 **Turn LEFT at STOP sign onto FDR 95.**

7.8 **Turn RIGHT onto FDR 95 and pass Camp May Flather on the right.**

8.8 **Turn LEFT onto Rt. 730 before North River bridge to resume route.**

Two-wheel travelers in the Shenandoah Valley come in all sizes, shapes, and... even species.

Poultry

The history of poultry farming in the Shenandoah Valley goes back to the days before the automobile. At that time, range turkeys were raised in big fields at the base of the hills and mountains to the west. Although much has been said about cattle drives, it's interesting that turkeys were similarly driven by foot to markets in Staunton and Harrisonburg. The advent of the railroads in the 1850s allowed farmers to load their birds onto the cars for shipment to large eastern cities. Chickens were raised in area barnyards, and their eggs were either sold or used for barter at the general store.

The ingenuity of several Rockingham County farmers helped increase poultry production and allowed the county to proclaim itself, "The Turkey Capital of the World." Essential to this was perfecting a means of artificial incubation. Samuel H. Blosser of Dayton devised Virginia's first incubator in 1884 using a box filled with sawdust kept warm by adding hot water from his teakettle.

Other area farmers improved on his idea by using electricity in this process. The Jordan farm on Rt. 727 south of Bridgewater was one of the first to use electric hatcheries in the 1930s. Rural electrification was rare in those days, and so George Jordan had his line run directly from the main power plant rather than along the road. You can still see those early hatcheries and the power lines running back over the hill. Rockingham County had 34 facilities hatching more than 1.4 million chicks per week by the 1930s. Today's state-of-the-art technology produces a staggering amount of poultry. Rocco, one of the largest local companies, has two hatcheries out of which come 13 million turkeys and 68 million chickens annually to be raised by area farmers.

Turkey production took another step forward in 1926 when Charles W. Wampler Sr. helped his daughter raise a flock of artificially brooded turkeys for her 4-H project. He continued to raise the birds, and they were the beginning of a business, now known as Wampler-Longacre, that has become one of the Valley's leading poultry producers. The importance of feed should not be forgotten amidst all the high-tech equipment. D.W. Detwiler's special blend of grains for feed in 1899 helped speed up the fattening process. The 13-story Rocco Mill in downtown Harrisonburg continues to dominate the skyline of this growing city as a testimony to its feathered heritage.

Rockingham County ranks among the 10 highest poultry producers in the nation. As you ride through this area, as well as in Augusta and Rockbridge Counties, you'll see the long brood houses on local farms. These buildings can reach 900 feet in length and use computers to maintain a controlled temperature. Farmers start baby chicks or turkeys (poults) at one end of the brood house and move them along as they mature. When the birds reach marketable size, they are shipped to one of several local processing plants. The Rocco plant in Dayton employs 1,100 people who process 17 million turkeys annually, about 5,000 birds every hour.

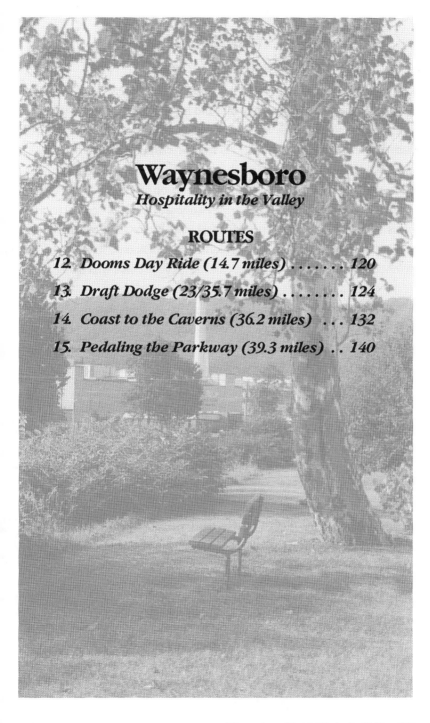

Waynesboro

Hospitality in the Valley

ROUTES

Waynesboro
Hospitality in the Valley

This city at the foot of Afton Mountain and Rockfish Gap has been offering hospitality in a variety of ways since the 1730s when Joseph Tease opened a tavern on land that he'd purchased from William Beverley. In the 1700s and 1800s, roads through town took people and produce east to Richmond and west to the new frontier. With the construction of railroads in the 1800s, Waynesboro was a natural spot for the east-west and north-south tracks to cross. Even now the town remains a focal point for travelers, whether on a straight shot on Interstate 64, the less hurried pace of Route 250, or the scenic splendor of the Blue Ridge Parkway and the Skyline Drive which meet east of the city at Rockfish Gap.

The village of Teasville had grown up around Tease's Tavern by the late 1700s. The name was changed to Waynesborough in 1797 to honor the valor of General "Mad Anthony" Wayne during the American Revolution and French and Indian War. The new name became official in 1801, and the city was incorporated in 1834.

The town's location along major transportation corridors as well the South River helped attract early industries. Mills and iron foundries sprang up on both sides of the river until there were essentially two cities in the late 1800s. Waynesboro sat on the western, and Basic City was on the eastern bank of the river. Basic City got its name from Jacob Reese's basic process for making steel. The Basic City Car Works earned its reputation by manufacturing railroad cars. It also tried, in vain, to produce the two cylinder Dawson Steam Auto-Mobile. Waynesboro and Basic City merged in 1926, and today has a population of approximately 20,000 residents.

Corporate giants like Genicom, Du Pont, Hoechst Celanese, and Corning continue Waynesboro's industrial tradition. Virginia Metalcrafters began as a stove manufacturer over 100 years ago, but today produces brass and iron decorative items, many of which are marketed through Colonial Williamsburg.

The town's architecture has been altered by several natural disasters

Waynesboro
City Map

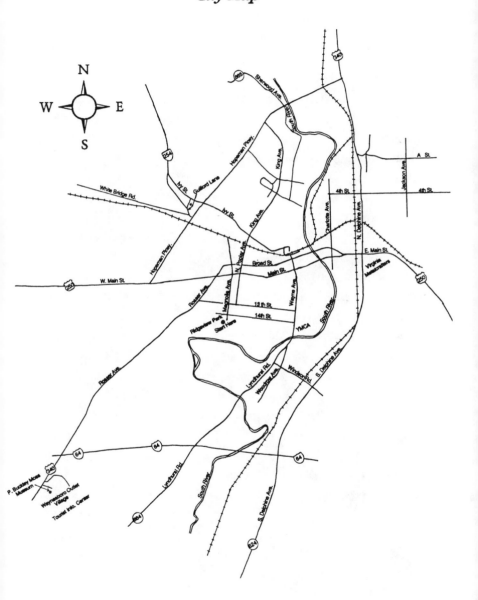

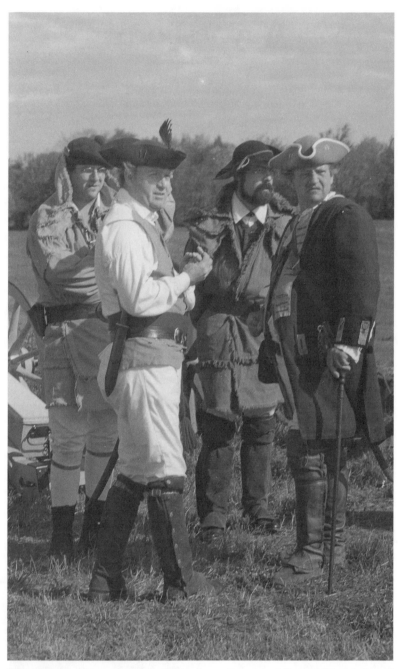

"Waynesborough" was named in 1797 to honor the valor of General "Mad Anthony" Wayne during the Revolutionary War.

over the centuries. Periodic flooding of the South River has taken its toll, but fire has been even more devastating. Widespread flames in 1861 destroyed most of the downtown area leaving little of Waynesboro's early architecture.

Opportunities for shopping can be found downtown as well as at the Waynesboro Outlet Village at the intersection of Interstate 64 and Route 340. Just a stone's throw from the Outlet Village and visible across the meadow is the P. Buckley Moss Museum. Ms. Moss is best known for her watercolors depicting Shenandoah Valley Mennonites and other rural scenes. The museum was built for visitors to learn more about the woman behind the paintings which have earned her international acclaim.

Waynesboro's Fall Foliage Festival is very popular among visitors. Aside from the splendor of the leaf colors on the Blue Ridge Mountains, this is a time when the city closes off downtown streets to showcase the works of hundreds of artists and their exhibits of sculpture, photography, pottery, paintings, and other media. Additional tourist information is available from the Chamber of Commerce at the corner of Main and Arch Streets in the downtown area as well as at the Travel Information Centers at the Outlet Village on Rt. 340 and Rockfish Gap on Afton Mountain.

All cycling routes begin and end at the entrance to Ridgeview Park near the intersection of Magnolia Avenue and 14th Street. The park offers swimming, picnicking, fishing, and an elaborate playground on the banks of the South River. It is open daily from sunrise to sunset.

DOOMS DAY RIDE

Waynesboro • Route 12 • 14.7 miles

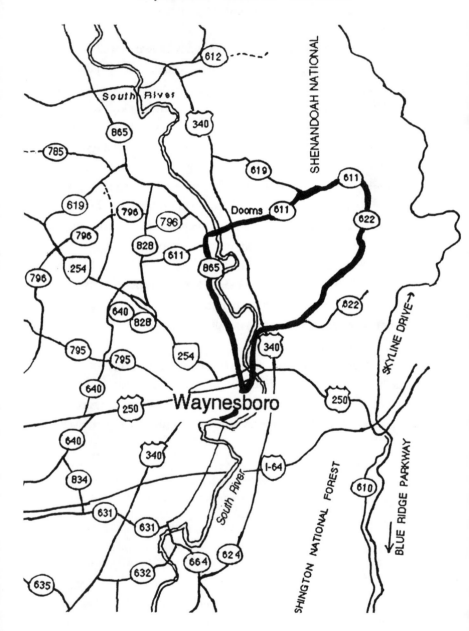

Dooms Day Ride

This short ride loops out of Waynesboro through the former Dooms Crossing railroad stop. Pedal along the base of Sawmill Ridge and try to pick out the bovine-shaped clearing that gave Calf Mountain its name.

0.0 Begin at the entrance to Ridgeview Park on Magnolia Ave. Proceed NORTH on Magnolia Ave. away from the park.

0.3 Turn RIGHT at four-way STOP onto 12th St.

0.4 Turn LEFT onto Poplar Ave.

0.6 Proceed with CAUTION on Poplar Ave. past traffic lights at Main St. and Broad St.

0.8 Cross RR tracks with CAUTION.

0.9 Poplar Ave. becomes King Ave. after crossing Ivy St.

1.4 Bear LEFT on King Ave. at the intersection with Hemlock Ave. and Dogwood St.

2.1 Turn RIGHT at STOP sign with CAUTION onto Hopeman Pkwy.

2.4 **Turn LEFT onto Sherwood Ave./Rt. 865.** The South River on the right joins the North River at Port Republic and forms the South Fork of the Shenandoah River. Farther ahead on Rt. 865 was the old Rockfish Gap Road. It was used throughout much of the 1800s to haul produce over the Blue Ridge Mts. to the port of Scottsville on the James River. Valley residents could exchange for goods arriving from Virginia's towns to the east. Salt was one of the commodities highly sought by Valley residents.

2.6 Windmills like the one at the house on the left were once a familiar sight in the Shenandoah Valley. This particular one was used to pump water into the house for more than 50 years. It's no longer being used, although still in working condition.

3.7 Southwick Farm on the right was built in the 1800s and was a major breeding farm for Percheron draft horses around 1900.

4.1 **Turn RIGHT onto Rt. 611 just before passing the high voltage towers on the right.**

4.3 **Cross bridge over the South River.**

4.4 **Cross RR tracks with CAUTION.**

4.5 **Cross Rt. 340 at STOP sign. Dooms** was originally called Dooms Crossing for John Dooms, owner of the land where the Norfolk and Western railroad crossed in the 1880s. The oldest houses in this area are down along the South River. More recently this community was the home of ex-Shenandoah Park ranger, Roy Sullivan, who passed away in September 1983. He is listed in the *Guinness Book of Records* as the only man in the world to be struck by lightning on seven occasions. These occurred between 1942 and 1977.

5.3 The old cemetery on the left side of the road, behind the mobile home, marks the original site of Smyrna Church. Now located back on Rt. 340, this was organized in 1889 as an outpost for the Presbyterian Church in Waynesboro.

6.2 **Proceed on Rt. 611. Rt. 619 intersects from the left. Rt. 611 becomes Rt. 622.** This is also called Calf Mountain Road. Although it's questionable whether it occurred naturally or by someone's design, in the late 1800s there was a calf-shaped clearing on the side of the mountain. One theory is that the body emerged naturally, and the tail was intentionally cut later to complete the figure.

11.1 **Turn RIGHT onto A St. (unmarked).**

11.4 **Turn LEFT at STOP sign onto Jackson St.**

11.7 **Turn RIGHT onto 4th St. at the top of the hill.**

12.2 **Proceed STRAIGHT at STOP sign across N. Delphine Ave./ Rt. 340. ★ Food and drinks are available at Dave's Meat and Grocery at this intersection. ★**

12.2 **Cross wooden bridge over RR tracks.** Notice the Basic City Lodge building on the right.

12.5 **Turn LEFT at STOP sign onto N. Charlotte Ave. across from the former Stanley Furniture Co.**

13.1 **Proceed with CAUTION across Broad St. at traffic light.**

13.2 **Turn RIGHT at YIELD sign onto E. Main St. Proceed through downtown Waynesboro.**

14.1 **Turn LEFT at traffic light by Waynesboro High School onto Poplar Ave.**

14.4 **Turn RIGHT at YIELD sign onto 13th St.**

14.5 **Turn LEFT at four-way STOP onto Magnolia Ave.**

14.7 **End ride at starting point.**

DRAFT DODGE
Waynesboro • Route 13 • 23 or 35.7 miles

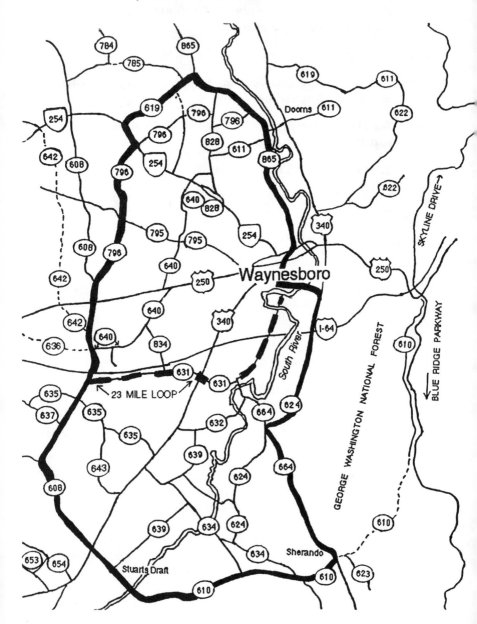

Draft Dodge

The toughest stretch on this route is past the Hershey plant in Stuarts Draft with the irresistible aroma of chocolate in the air. Stop at the Candy Shop for some Reeses Pieces, or Kinsingers Bakery and The Cheese Shop for Mennonite goodies. The shorter route will take you past the P. Buckley Moss Museum.

0.0   **Begin at the entrance to Ridgeview Park on Magnolia Ave. Proceed NORTH on Magnolia Ave. away from the park.**

0.3   **Turn RIGHT at four-way STOP onto 12th St.**

0.4   **Turn LEFT onto Poplar Ave.**

0.6   **Proceed with CAUTION on Poplar Ave. past traffic lights at Main St. and Broad St.**

0.8   **Cross RR tracks with CAUTION.**

0.9   **Poplar Ave. becomes King Ave. after crossing Ivy St.**

1.4   **Bear LEFT on King Ave. at the intersection with Hemlock Ave. and Dogwood St.**

2.1   **Turn RIGHT at STOP sign with CAUTION onto Hopeman Pkwy.**

2.4   **Turn LEFT onto Sherwood Ave./Rt. 865.** The South River, on the right, joins the North River at Port Republic and forms the South Fork of the Shenandoah River. Farther ahead was the old Rockfish Gap Road. It was used throughout much of the 1800s to haul produce over the Blue Ridge Mts. to the port of Scottsville on the James River. Valley residents could exchange for goods arriving from Virginia's towns to the east.

4.9   Turk Mountain is the large peak to the right. It is part of the Blue Ridge Mts. and lies within Shenandoah National Park.

6.3 Col. Robert Porterfield settled along here after the Revolutionary War. He served with the Continental army at Valley Forge. He later became a general in the Virginia militia.

6.5 Turn LEFT onto Rt. 619.

7.4 Hildebrand Mennonite Church was established in 1825, and the present structure was built in 1877.

8.8 Turn LEFT at STOP sign onto Rt. 254 East with CAUTION. Maps from the late 1800s show a cluster of houses, but no post office, at this community called **Hermitage**. One of the more prominent is the elaborate Queen Anne style dwelling on the right. It was built by the Eustler Brothers of Grottoes as a home and office for a local physician.

9.4 Turn RIGHT onto Rt. 796.

11.4 Proceed STRAIGHT on Rt. 796 at intersection with Rt. 795.

12.3 The community of **Kiddsville** was a predominantly black settlement clustered around Mount Marine Baptist Church. It was built in the late 1800s. The small log structure on the left dates back to the 1800s. The original section was a one-room cabin which was expanded later by cinderblock additions.

13.0 Bear LEFT at STOP sign onto Rt. 608. The brick house at Spring Valley Farm, on the right, was built around 1850, but the spring house supposedly predates this. Notice the spring-fed pond emerging from underneath the springhouse.

13.5 Turn LEFT at STOP sign and proceed with CAUTION on Rt. 250 across from the Augusta County Library. Settlers began putting down roots around **Fishersville** as early as 1738. The community is named after Daniel and Nancy Fisher who settled here around 1788 and raised 17 children.

13.7 After riding under overpass, turn RIGHT at traffic light onto Rt. 608. ★ Food and drinks are available at this intersection. ★

14.9 Tinkling Spring Church is one of the oldest Presbyterian churches in Augusta County. Congregational meetings were first held here on April 14, 1745, when the church was half-finished according to Rev. John Craig's diary. Rev. Craig presided over this church and the Augusta Stone Church at Fort Defiance. By comparison to the parishioners at Fort Defiance, Craig found John Lewis and the other early community leaders who attended Tinkling Spring to be "a stiff-necked and perverse generation... their leaders close-handed about providing necessary things for pious and religious uses, and could not agree for several years upon a plan or manner where or how to build their meeting-house, which gave me very great trouble to hold them together, their disputes ran so high."

15.3   **Watch for traffic entering and exiting I-64.**

15.5   **Turn left onto Rt. 631 to take the 23-mile loop. Otherwise continue STRAIGHT on Rt. 608.**

19.7   Be sure to stop by The Cheese Shop on the left. This Amish-Mennonite family business carries dried fruits, nuts, snacks, and over 30 varieties of cheese. If you've worked up an appetite for some Mennonite baked goods, turn right onto Rt. 651 and check out the treats at Kinsingers Bakery.

20.3   **Proceed with CAUTION past the traffic light at the intersection of Rt. 340 heading into Stuarts Draft.** Before crossing Rt. 340, you may want to visit The Candy Shop on the right side of Rt. 608. In the absence of tours through the Hershey plant up ahead, you'll find a terrific selection of chocolate products at this store. The Stuarts Draft Post Office was established in this area in 1837, probably named for Robert Stuart who ran a nearby chopping mill. The post office was about one mile from the present village, both of which were moved in 1882 to the new railroad station. ★ **Food and drinks are widely available in Stuarts Draft.** ★

21.1   **Cross RR tracks with CAUTION.**

21.8   **Proceed STRAIGHT on Rt. 610, after passing the Hershey plant on the right. Rt. 608 goes right.**

22.0   **Bear LEFT on Rt. 610. Rt. 912 goes straight.**

22.3   A right turn onto Rt. 660 will take you to Shenandoah Acres. This resort offers food, camping, horseback riding, and a selection of water amusements that are guaranteed to bring the kid out in anyone. Before 1935 this was known as Dodge's Pond or Mountain Lake. ★ **Food and drinks are available at Shenandoah Acres.** ★

27.1 **Turn LEFT at STOP sign onto Rt. 664. Sherando** is an alternative spelling of *Shenandoah*. The Howardsville and Rockfish Turnpike ran through here in the 1800s between Greenville and Nelson County on the east side of the Blue Ridge. This area was heavily mined for manganese, iron ore, and sandstone. ★ **Food and drinks are available at the Sherando Grocery.** ★

30.4 ★ **Food and drinks are available at The Country Store.** ★

30.6 **Bear RIGHT at bend in road onto Rt. 624.** Nearby Lyndhurst was a rail stop on the Norfolk and Western line. It was named for Lord Lyndhurst by George C. Milne.

31.3 **Cross Back Creek before it joins the South River.**

31.9 **Enter Waynesboro.**

32.5 On the right is the future site of the Wildlife Center of Virginia. When completed this facility will offer veterinary and rehabilitation services to injured wildlife as well as a nature study center in conjunction with the George Washington National Forest.

33.2 **Watch for traffic entering and exiting I-64.**

34.1 **Turn LEFT onto Windsor Rd. before passing Wayne-Tex plant.**

34.2 **Cross RR tracks with CAUTION.**

34.4 **Turn RIGHT at four-way STOP onto Woodrow Ave.**

34.6 **Bear RIGHT at YIELD sign onto Wayne Ave. Pass YMCA on the right.**

34.9 **Turn LEFT onto 14th St.**

35.6 **Turn LEFT at four-way STOP onto Magnolia Ave.**

35.7 **End ride at starting point**

23-MILE LOOP

15.5   Turn LEFT onto Rt. 631 after crossing I-64.

18.3   Proceed STRAIGHT at traffic light across Rt. 340. The P. Buckley Moss Museum is **.3 mile** to the left on Rt. 340. The Waynesboro Outlet Mall is right next door. ★ **Food and drinks are available at the Outlet Mall.** ★

19.2   Bear LEFT on Rt. 664 with Rt. 664 also intersecting from the right.

19.6   Enter Waynesboro.

21.9   Bear LEFT at intersection with Woodrow Ave. on the right.

22.2   Turn LEFT onto 14th St.

22.8   Turn LEFT at four-way STOP onto Magnolia Ave.

23.0   End ride at starting point

Log Buildings

Early European settlers, particularly from Germany and Switzerland, brought the earliest log construction to the Shenandoah Valley. Recent studies have revealed a wide distribution and variety of log construction techniques across Europe. Variables include the shape of the logs, rounded or square; the amount of space between them; and the manner of fastening the logs at the corners, called corner notching.

Log construction was widely used in the Valley for all types of buildings during the 1700s and 1800s including smokehouses, wash houses, small barns, and dwellings. The majority of the frontier houses were made of wood, and many of these were probably log. Although the Germans and Swiss introduced the use of log building in the Valley, Scots-Irish and English settlers capitalized on this technique given the abundance of trees in the New World.

A typical German or Scots-Irish building would include squared logs, infilled with pieces of wood called chinking. Daubing, a mixture of clay, lime, horsehair, and straw, covered the chinking. Examples of this can be seen on the route of these early settlers from Pennsylvania southward into the Valley of Virginia.

The ends of the logs in Valley houses have squared corners as opposed to those whose corners project past the end of the building. The most common corner notch was the V-notch, which looks like an upside down *V*. A less common but older notch is the full dovetail, similar to the dovetails found in the joinery of furniture from the 1700s and 1800s. A simpler variation is the half-dovetail. Buildings using either of the dovetails will, more than likely, date back to the late 1700s or early 1800s.

Logs were widely used in emerging frontier towns like Staunton and Winchester as well as in turnpike villages in the 1800s. Tastes changed, and as the local residents became more refined, they did not want to give the appearance of living in a log home. It is often difficult to determine from the exterior of a home covered by weatherboard if the core is, in fact, log. If in doubt, one way to judge is to look at the thickness of the walls at the window and door openings. Log walls will be eight to twelve inches thick. Log construction was generally used in smaller homes, although it was common to begin a home in log and build on frame additions surrounding it. A typical plan was the simple two-room design, usually 1½ stories high with one or two stone chimneys at the ends of the building.

By the late 1800s, frame construction began to replace the use of logs throughout the Valley. However mountain folk continued to build log homes, barns, and outbuildings well into the 1900s. The farm at Humpback Rocks on the Blue Ridge Parkway (Milepost 6) is an excellent example of a simple mountain cabin. Lurking behind metal-sided barns and sheds as well as weatherboarded homes are some of the area's oldest log buildings.

COAST TO THE CAVERNS
Waynesboro • Route 14 • 36.2 miles

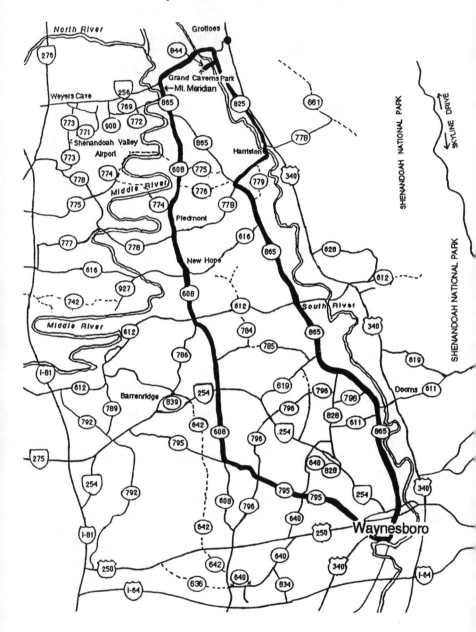

Coast to the Caverns

You may not coast all the way, but you'll find a good bit of flat cycling on this ride. Pedal past Trinity Lutheran Church and cemetery that served the Valley's earliest settlers in the 1700s. Plan to picnic and explore Grand Caverns as others have done since their discovery in 1804. Be sure to stop and admire André Viette's extensive perennial gardens on your way back into Waynesboro.

0.0 **Begin at the entrance to Ridgeview Park on Magnolia Ave. Proceed NORTH on Magnolia Ave. away from the park.**

0.3 **Turn RIGHT at four-way STOP onto 12th St.**

0.4 **Turn LEFT onto Poplar Ave.**

0.6 **Proceed with CAUTION on Poplar Ave. past traffic lights at Main St. and Broad St.**

0.8 **Cross RR tracks with CAUTION.**

0.9 **Poplar Ave. becomes King Ave. after crossing Ivy St.**

1.4 **Bear LEFT on King Ave. at the intersection with Hemlock Ave. and Dogwood St.**

2.1 **Turn RIGHT at STOP sign with CAUTION onto Hopeman Pkwy.**

2.4 **Turn LEFT onto Sherwood Ave./Rt. 865.** The South River, on the right, joins the North River at Port Republic and forms the South Fork of the Shenandoah River. Farther ahead this was the old Rockfish Gap Road. It was used throughout much of the 1800s to haul produce over the Blue Ridge Mts. to the port of Scottsville on the James River. Valley residents could exchange for goods arriving from Virginia's towns to the east.

2.6 Windmills like the one at the house on the left were once a familiar sight in the Shenandoah Valley. This particular one was used to pump water into the house for more than 50 years. It's no longer being used, although still in working condition.

3.7 Southwick Farm on the right was built in the 1800s and was a major breeding farm for Percheron draft horses around 1900.

4.9 Turk Mountain is the large peak to the right. It is part of the Blue Ridge Mts. and lies within Shenandoah National Park.

6.3 Col. Robert Porterfield settled along here after the Revolutionary War. He served with the Continental army at Valley Forge. He later became a General in the Virginia militia.

7.5 The log house at Sewell Farm on the left was built by German settlers around 1790.

8.2 Continue STRAIGHT at STOP sign on Rt. 865 at intersection with Rt. 612. This crossroads was once known as Koiner's Store. The Koiners were German and among the earliest settlers in this area. Many of their ancestors remain in the Shenandoah Valley with name variations including Koyner, Coiner, and Coyner. The community of Crimora, east of here on Rt. 612, flourished in the late 1800s because of the prolific manganese mines and their proximity to rail lines. The mines shut down in 1957.

9.0 Trinity Lutheran Church was founded in 1772. Parishioners first worshiped at (Rev. Adolph) Spindler's Meeting House, as it was then known, in a 36 X 40-foot log building. The present brick church was built in 1880. The cemetery includes some of Augusta County's oldest tombstones including sandstone markers of slaves and Revolutionary War veterans.

12.1 Turn RIGHT onto Rt. 778 toward the Blue Ridge Mts.

13.4 Cross the bridge over the South River and then turn LEFT onto Rt. 825. Willow Grove Farm, on the right before crossing the river, was originally the center of the **Harriston** community. William Patterson called his 200-acre farm Harriston in 1762 after his homeplace in England. Most likely the present house was built just after the Civil War. The property has remained in the family ever since. The actual village of Harriston was laid out in 1890 on the east side of the South River when the railroad came through.

15.9 The ridge to the left is Cave Hill. Madison's Cave, Fountain Cave, Grand Caverns (formerly Weyer's Cave), and a number of smaller grottoes are all contained in this mound. Grand Caverns is the only one that remains open to the public.

16.1 Cosby Mill, to the left on Rt. 770, has been in continuous operation on the South River since 1803. It has gone by a number of names over the years depending on the owner at any given time. These included Kennerly Mill, Mohler Mill, Davisson Mill, Patterson Mill, and Myers Mill.

16.5 **Turn LEFT onto Rt. 844 and cross South River to enter Grand Caverns Regional Park.** Picnic facilities make this an excellent lunch and rest stop. Thomas Jefferson wrote about nearby Madison Cave in his 1787 *Notes on the State of Virginia*. Bernard Weyer uncovered the additional caverns in 1804 while looking for a raccoon trap. They were opened to the public in 1806 as Weyer's Cave and are among the oldest publicly toured caves in the country. The name Grand Caverns was adopted in 1906, but the former nearby railroad stop, Weyer's Cave, has retained the old name. General Stonewall Jackson and his troops camped in the caves during the Valley campaign in 1862. The signatures of Confederate soldiers are still on the inner walls. **After a break at the park, turn LEFT onto Rt. 825 and enter Grottoes to continue on the route.**

16.9 **Turn LEFT at STOP sign and proceed with CAUTION on Rt. 256 West.** Grottoes was called Liola in 1882, and renamed Grottoes in 1888. Its name was then changed to Shendun (after the first syllable of *Shenandoah* and the Gaelic word *dun*, which means fort or town). It was finally changed back to Grottoes in 1893. Samuel Miller, owner of the Mossy Creek Ironworks, operated an iron forge near Grottoes in the early 1800s. His son, William, established the Mount Vernon Forge here in 1848. ★ **Food and drinks are available at Herby's Food Store and Deli at this intersection.** ★

17.4 The birthplace of painter George Caleb Bingham is on the right after crossing the South River. Bingham was born in 1811 in a house that was located behind the present brick home. He and his family moved to Missouri in 1819. He left behind a legacy of paintings of the American West when he died in 1879. The Old

Chaney House that you see now was built in 1856 and marks the Augusta-Rockingham County line.

18.6   Turn LEFT onto Rt. 865.

18.8   Mount Meridian was once located on the oldest section of the original Valley Road before it was resurveyed in the late 1700s so as to run west of here near the present Route 11 into Staunton. This was a small village until the late 1800s that included a mill, general store, wagonmaker, and blacksmith. The steel truss bridge to the right on Rt. 769 is the longest of the 14 that still remain in Augusta County. Built by the Champion Bridge Co. of Wilmington, Ohio in 1907, this 360-foot span crosses the Middle River near the Harnsberger Octagonal Barn. The barn was built by Robert Harnsberger around 1867, and the siding was replaced by the present owners in 1978. This is the only octagonal barn that was originally built in Augusta County and is listed on the Virginia Historic Landmarks register.

19.3   John Fulton III built the impressive neo-colonial house on the right at Meridian Farm in the early 1900s. It's said that he planned this 10-room mansion on such a grand scale to impress his new bride Olga Patterson Mohler and her former suitor John Will Carpenter.

19.7   Turn RIGHT at bend onto Rt. 608.

20.4   Bonnie Doon Farm on the right was part of an original land grant. It has remained in the Crawford family since the 1700s. Samuel Crawford, father of C.D. Crawford, inherited the farm from his father in 1848 and named it Bonnie Doon. The house that originally stood here was badly damaged by cannonballs during the Battle of Piedmont in 1864 and was later torn down in 1892. C.D. Crawford replaced it with the present 12-room Victorian home.

22.8   The plaque on the left pays tribute to the Civil War Battle of Piedmont. This strategic battle was fought along here on June 5, 1864. Gen. David Hunter's Union victory opened the Shenandoah Valley to subsequent destruction and conflagration from here to Lexington.

24.2   **New Hope.** James Kerr was one of the area's first settlers with some sources dating his arrival back to 1730, even before John Lewis, Staunton's founder. Much of the land along what is now Rt. 608 was Kerr land as part of the original Beverley Grant. Some of the earliest Kerr houses are still standing, including the old homeplace on Rt. 612 above the Middle River. One oft-repeated reason for New Hope's name arises from a desire on the part of John Kerr's wife to abandon their 400-acre farm. John, the oldest son of James Kerr, remained confident that the couple would gain "new hope" from sticking it out on their homestead.

25.7 ★ **Food and drinks are available at New Hope Grocery at Rt. 608 and Rt. 612.** ★

27.9 **Cross Rt. 254 at STOP sign with CAUTION.**

30.0 **Turn LEFT onto Rt. 795.** Just ahead on Rt. 608 is the home and gardens of horticulturist André Viette. He is widely known for his perennials, of which more than 1,000 varieties are grown and displayed here. The gardens are open to the public as are his scheduled tours and lectures.

33.4 **Enter Waynesboro.**

34.4 **Take a sharp left at apartment complex onto Guilford Lane.**

34.6 **Turn RIGHT at STOP sign onto Ivy St./Rt. 254 East.**

34.7 **Continue STRAIGHT at traffic light and cross Hopeman Pkwy. with CAUTION.**

35.2 **Turn RIGHT at STOP sign onto N. Poplar Ave.**

35.4 **Cross RR tracks with CAUTION.**

35.5 **Proceed past traffic lights at Broad St. and Main St. with CAUTION.**

35.8 **Turn RIGHT at STOP sign onto 12th St.**

35.9 **Turn LEFT at four-way STOP onto Magnolia Ave.**

36.2 **End ride at starting point.**

The Revolutionary War

When the flames of Revolution spread across the American colonies in the 1770s, Shenandoah Valley settlers found themselves wrapped up in their second major war in the New World, although they had barely been living here 50 years. Valley residents were agitating for independence and passing resolutions of freedom even before the Declaration of Independence was signed in 1776.

Although no battles were fought in the southern Valley during the Revolutionary War, some historians have compared the area during that time to an armed camp with men, munitions and rations all being supplied to the Continental Army. Valley men represented the region in all ranks of the American army and fought in campaigns from Quebec to Georgia. The Virginia troops were put under the command of Augusta County's Andrew Lewis, whose first task consisted of driving the royal governor from the state. The Valley supplied at least 500 commissioned officers to the American ranks, including four regimental commanders from Augusta County and one from Rockbridge.

Wagon trains and cattle drives from the Shenandoah Valley kept the Continental Army supplied throughout the war as loads of flour and grain, meat, butter, and beverages made their way to the battle front. One hundred thirty barrels of flour were transported by land to Boston after the port was closed as a result of the 1774 "tea party."

The war struck closer to home in 1781 when Shenandoah Valley residents feared a British invasion from the east. This concern was sparked by a British attempt to ensnare the fleeing Virginia legislature. Hoping to avoid capture at the hands of Gen. Charles Cornwallis, Virginia's revolutionary government fled westward, first to Richmond and then past Charlottesville before convening briefly in Staunton. As the legislators moved farther west from Staunton to Warm Springs, rumors of an invasion spread like wildfire through the region. Warnings were sounded from the pulpits and town centers. Some Stuarts Draft and Fishersville residents took their guns to church in anticipation of the impending attack. Men and boys, armed with everything from guns to rocks, strategically positioned themselves in every mountain pass from Massanutten to Lexington.

The Valley invasion never materialized since the Redcoats turned back before reaching Charlottesville. The Virginia legislature returned to Staunton where it met for two weeks at Trinity Church, making Staunton the state capital for that period in June 1781. Supposedly Patrick Henry fled with his fellow legislators so quickly on their first stop in Staunton, that he left one of his boots in the church. Although the Revolutionary church structure is no longer standing, the present building and cemetery on the same site in downtown Staunton have a great deal of history associated with them.

Other reminders that the Valley was once engaged in the fight for independence are evident in some of the local placenames. Lexington was named in honor of Lexington, Massachusetts, where the Revolutionary War began. Rockingham County was named for Lord Rockingham, a member of the British parliament who was sympathetic to the colonists' cause. Waynesboro and Greenville were named in honor of two American military heroes, Gen. Anthony Wayne and Gen. Nathanael Greene, both of whom led many soldiers from the Valley during the war.

PEDALING THE PARKWAY

Waynesboro • Route 15 • 39.3 miles

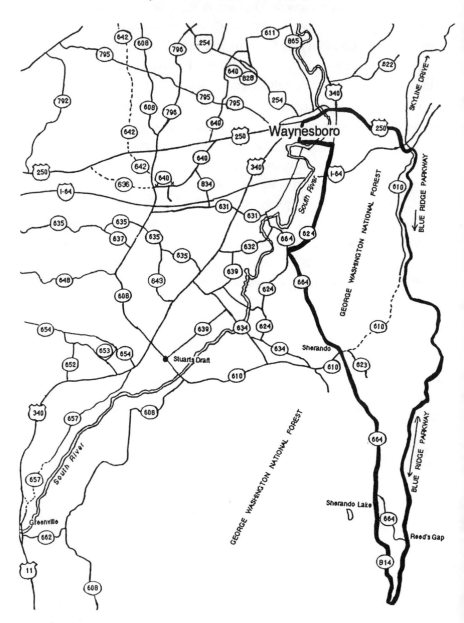

Pedaling the Parkway

After climbing up Afton Mountain to Rockfish Gap, you'll savor the views along the Blue Ridge Parkway, America's premier cycling road. Then plummet down from Love Gap on your way back. Stop off at Sherando Lake for a swim out to the island and to bask on the sandy beach.

0.0   **Begin at the entrance to Ridgeview Park on Magnolia Ave. Proceed NORTH on Magnolia Ave. away from the park.**

0.5   **Turn RIGHT at STOP sign onto Main St. Proceed with CAUTION through downtown Waynesboro.**

2.4   **Gear down and begin to ascend Afton Mt. on Rt. 250 East.** From the parking lot at Rockfish Gap Outfitters on the left, you'll climb 580 feet in the next three miles. Route 250 follows one of the earliest roads connecting the Shenandoah Valley and Richmond, 100 miles to the east. In the 1700s this was called Three Notch or Three Chopt Road. It was one of the few passes through the Blue Ridge Mountains.

5.1   **Watch for traffic entering and exiting I-64.**

5.3   **Turn RIGHT onto Rt. 610 in front of Howard Johnson.** A short sidetrip on Rt. 610 will take you to Swannanoa. This Italian Renaissance marble mansion was once home to Dr. Walter and Lao Russell, and it is now the University of Science and Philosophy. The palace and gardens are open year round for a small fee. There was a stagecoach stop at Afton in the early 1800s for travelers between Staunton and Charlottesville. ★ **Food and drinks are available at Howard Johnson and Afton Mt. Convenience Store.** ★

5.4   **Turn RIGHT at STOP sign onto Blue Ridge Parkway.** Arguably the finest cycling road in the world, the BRP stretches for 470 miles to its terminus at Cherokee, North Carolina. Under the beginning of this road is a 4,250-foot railroad tunnel that was designed by engineer, Claudius Crozet. It remained in use from 1858 until 1942. Riding south, you'll get outstanding views of the Shenandoah Valley on the right and Rockfish Valley on the left. Keep an eye out for wildflowers in bloom. Along the Blue Ridge Parkway there are over 1,250 vascular plants, equal to the number of varieties in all of Europe.

5.6 Afton Mt. Overlook, elev. 1,895 feet.

6.9 Rockfish Valley Overlook, elev. 2,148 feet.

8.4 Shenandoah Valley Overlook, elev. 2,354 feet.

11.3 The Visitor Center and Pioneer Farm at Humpback Rocks offer a re-creation of a typical turn-of-the-century mountain farm. Across the road is the start of a short trail to the crest of Humpback Rocks at 3,210 feet. Wagons once used the gap here to haul goods into the Shenandoah Valley. ★ **Food and drinks are available in season.** ★

11.7 The field on the left is called Coiner's Dead'nin. A *dead'nin* was a wooded area which early settlers turned into a corn field by girdling trees and then planting corn among them as they stood dying.

11.8 The stacked limestone and split rail fences along the BRP are typical of those found on early mountain farms. Rocks were gathered to clear the fields and rails were generally split from chestnut trees. Supposedly this fence was built by slaves from a plantation east of the mountain.

14.1 Picnic area and toilets on the left.

14.5 Greenstone Overlook, elev. 2,000 feet. Greenstone results from metamorphosed basalt or volcanic ash falls.

15.3 Dripping Rock Parking area and trail, elev. 2,440 feet.

16.1 Rock Point Overlook, elev. 3,115 feet.

16.5 Ravens Roost, elev. 3,200, offers a great view into the Shenandoah Valley. Adventurous hang gliders sometimes take off from here.

17.6 Hickory Spring Parking area and picnic table, elev. 2,940 feet.

19.0   Three Ridges Mt. Parking area, elev. 2,800 feet.

19.5   Intersection with Rt. 664 at Reed's Gap, elev. 2,637 feet. Winter-green Ski Resort is to the left on Rt. 664, and Sherando Lake is down the mountain to the right.

21.4   Love Gap, elev. 2,650 feet.

22.1   Turn RIGHT onto Rt. 814 and begin a 3.8 mile descent dropping 940 feet in elevation. Check your brakes before starting out. Nelson County was formed in 1807 and was named for Gen. Thomas Nelson Jr., the third governor of Virginia.

22.2   Mountain Top Christian Church moved into this white frame building around 1920 from a log church up the road. The cemetery has several homemade stones from the late 1800s.

25.7   The community of **Love** was founded by Scots-Irish settlers. Once called Meadow Mountain, this proved to be too long to fit on a postmark. The federal government pressured Postmaster Hugh Coffey to shorten it. His daughter Lovey had died of typhoid fever, so in 1894 he renamed it in her honor. Love was once a thriving community with several churches, schools, stores, and mills. *Backroads* is a local rural newspaper dedicated to keeping the mountain folkways alive. Stop by *A Mountain Place*, bed and breakfast and craft shop, on your way down the mountain. The old cabin was moved here from Goshen in Rockbridge County.

26.0   Rt. 814 becomes Rt. 664 at the intersection with Rt. 664 on the right. Proceed STRAIGHT on Rt. 664.

26.6   Sherando Lake Recreation Area is part of the George Washington National Forest. During the summer it offers swimming, fishing, and camping adjacent to the two lakes. The larger 24-acre lake was built by the Civilian Conservation Corps in the 1930s.

28.1   Mount Tory Furnace was built in 1804 by Englehard Yeiser. Like Miller's Iron Works at Mossy Creek and Buffalo Forge in Rock-bridge County, Mount Tory supplied pig iron during the Civil War to aid the Confederate cause. It was destroyed during Gen. David Hunter's march through the Valley in the summer of 1864. It was reopened after the war but closed down in 1884.

29.2   ★ Food and drinks are available at B&R Grocery. ★

30.4   ★ Food and drinks are available at Shirley's Store. ★

30.7   **Sherando** is an alternative spelling of *Shenandoah*. The Howardsville and Rockfish Turnpike ran through here in the 1800s between Greenville to the west and Nelson County on the east side of the Blue Ridge. This area was heavily mined for manganese, iron ore, and sandstone. ★ **Food and drinks are available at Sherando Grocery.** ★

34.0   ★ Food and drinks are available at The Country Store. ★

34.2   **Bear RIGHT at bend in road onto Rt. 624.** Nearby Lyndhurst was a rail stop along the Norfolk and Western line. It was named for Lord Lyndhurst by George C. Milne.

34.9   **Cross Back Creek before it joins the South River.**

35.5   **Enter Waynesboro.**

36.1   On the right is the future site of the Wildlife Center of Virginia. When completed this facility will offer veterinary and rehabilitation services to injured wildlife as well as a nature study center in conjunction with the George Washington National Forest.

36.8   **Watch for traffic entering and exiting I-64.**

37.7   **Turn LEFT onto Windsor Rd. before passing Wayne-Tex plant.**

37.8   **Cross RR tracks with CAUTION.**

38.0   **Turn RIGHT at four-way STOP onto Woodrow Ave.**

38.2   **Bear RIGHT at YIELD sign onto Wayne Ave. Pass YMCA on the right.**

38.5   **Turn LEFT onto 14th St.**

39.2   **Turn LEFT at four-way STOP onto Magnolia Ave.**

39.3   **End ride at starting point.**

Staunton

The Queen City

ROUTES

Staunton
The Queen City

Although the hills of downtown Staunton may pose a challenge to many cyclists, surprises at the crest of each rise will make it worth the effort. Well preserved Victorian architecture, frontier history, fine lodgings and dining, country music stars, and a presidential manse are just a few of the Queen City's treasures.

Staunton (pronounced Stanton) has many direct links to the early 1700s when Scots-Irish, German, and English settlers forged a trail southward from Pennsylvania into a new frontier called the Shenandoah Valley. John Lewis is considered Staunton's founder after establishing a homestead called Bellefonte in 1732 on Lewis Creek several miles east of town.

William Beverley, a wealthy Tidewater farmer, saw the opportunities west of the Blue Ridge Mountains in 1736. He obtained a 118,491-acre land grant from Virginia's Governor William Gooch. Beverley built a log mill along a stream in what is now Staunton, and settlers were soon putting down roots at *Beverley's Mill Place*, as it was first called. It was renamed Staunton in honor of Governor Gooch's wife, Lady Rebecca Staunton.

A crude log courthouse was erected in 1745 on the site where the Augusta County Courthouse presently sits, and streets were laid out near Beverley's Mill in 1749. Staunton soon became the heart of the frontier county known as Augusta after the Princess of Wales, daughter of King George III. Today it is Virginia's second largest county, but in the 1740s it extended west to the Mississippi River taking in what now encompasses 21 Virginia counties and all or part of the states of Kentucky, Ohio, Indiana, Illinois, Pennsylvania, and West Virginia.

You may want to take a self-guided walking tour through Staunton or absorb the sights on a relaxing horse-drawn carriage ride available from Red Velvet Carriage. Free historic guides are available from the Staunton Welcome Center located behind Woodrow Wilson's Birthplace or at the Staunton-Augusta Travel Information Center on Rt. 250 by Interstate 81.

No trip to Staunton would be complete without visiting the Birthplace

Staunton

City Map

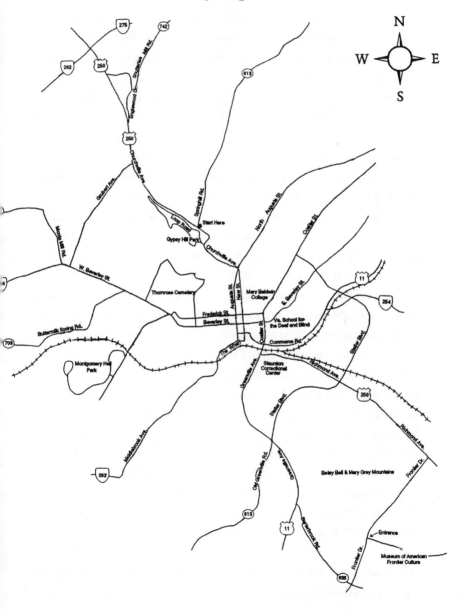

and Museum commemorating Woodrow Wilson, the city's favorite son and 28th President of the United States. This complex on North Coalter Street offers visitors an opportunity to see the influences that shaped the son of a Presbyterian minister into an international leader. In addition to guided tours of the Birthplace, the newly opened museum consists of seven exhibit galleries detailing Wilson's accomplishments as an author, scholar, educator, politician, and statesman.

Staunton's more contemporary favorite sons are country music's Statler Brothers. This celebrated group has organized and participated in a gala Fourth of July celebration since 1970. The event has included a parade, midway booths, non-stop country music, and an evening topped off by a free Statler concert and fireworks display. Although the Statlers' last Happy Birthday USA concert will take place in 1994, the festivities should continue to draw upwards of 75,000 people from all over the world to this city of 25,000. The Statler Brothers Museum, located in their old schoolhouse opposite Gypsy Hill Park, offers a daily tour during the week with extra tours scheduled during Happy Birthday USA.

Gypsy Hill Park was once a camping place for gypsies, thus the name. This tract of land was first acquired by the city in 1876 because of its springs. The former pumphouse at the entrance now houses the Staunton-Augusta Art Center. The Baldwin Augusta Fair Grounds adjoined the pumphouse tract, and the city purchased that in 1881. It officially became a park in 1889.

Those wanting to get a better idea of how the common man lived in earlier days will want to visit the Museum of American Frontier Culture located just off Interstates 81 and 64 on Rt. 250. This living history museum features four restored farms which were moved to this 178-acre site from England, Ireland, Germany, and the Valley of Virginia. The Shenandoah Valley farm represents the synthesis of these separate cultures. Costumed interpreters carry out the daily and seasonal activities typical of the 17th, 18th, and 19th century cultures left behind by America's immigrants.

All routes begin and end at the intersection of Churchville Ave. and Springhill Rd. across from Gypsy Hill Park. Vehicle parking is available along the park's loop road. Gates to the park are open daily 5AM - 11PM.

Oakdene *typifies the striking architectural forms in and around Staunton's historic downtown. This home on East Beverley Street was built in 1893 for Edward Echols who later became Virginia's Lt. Governor.*

SPRINGHILL SPRINT

Staunton • Route 16 • 18.2 or 28.3 miles

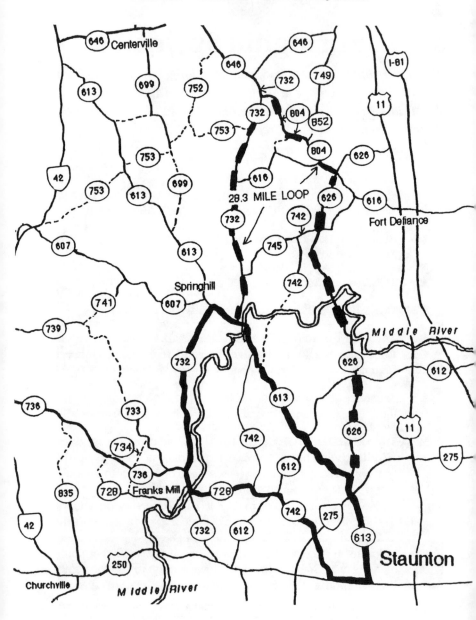

Springhill Sprint

The climb from Franks Mill to Springhill is long, but the views from this pre-Civil War village make it worthwhile. Take a break along the Middle River, and then cross smaller streams like Naked Creek, Byers Branch, and Goose Creek.

0.0 Begin at the intersection of Churchville Ave./Rt. 250 and Springhill Rd. on the north side of Gypsy Hill Park. Proceed WEST on Churchville Ave. with the park on your left.

1.1 Bear RIGHT onto Englewood Dr. just before passing Gene's Market on Rt. 250.

2.0 This area was once farmland called Sandy Hollow.

2.2 Cross Rt. 275 Bypass at STOP sign with CAUTION.

4.2 Turn LEFT onto Rt. 728 and begin 1.5 mile descent. Watch for dump trucks and gravel in road from Luck Quarry. Chimney Farm was settled here by Arnold Anderson in 1797.

5.5 Shutterlee cemetery on the hill to the right is the resting place for the Shutterlees, former operators of the mill known as Franks Mill.

5.7 Turn RIGHT at STOP sign onto Rt. 732 and cross bridge over Middle River. The tan house next to the old mill was built in 1812 by George Hanger, the original owner and operator of this Middle River mill. The Shutterlees purchased it later in the 1800s, and then the Franks took possession in 1912. It ceased operating on January 31, 1971. The Middle River is one of three rivers which eventually join to form the South Fork of the Shenandoah River. All three originate in Augusta County, with the Middle and the North merging near Grottoes, and then flowing north to join the South River at Port Republic in Rockingham County.

6.1 Turn RIGHT onto Rt. 732 at bend to the left.

7.5   Mount Pleasant on the hill to the left was built of local limestone in the late 1700s.

8.3   The brick house on the left was built in the 1800s and is unusual because of its brick molded cornice.

9.0   Notice the remains of at least two limestone outbuildings on the left. The one still standing is some type of barn with fine stonework in the arched window on the north side.

10.1   **Turn RIGHT at STOP sign onto Rt. 613.** The post office in **Springhill** was established before the Civil War and was known as Long Glade after the nearby creek of the same name that flows north into the North River at Bridgewater. The road through town was also known as Long Glade. Jacob Miller Crist and Jacob Crist Spitler mapped out this "planned town" in 1838, and water was piped from a spring uphill to the town, a likely rationale for the present name. An 1834 deed from the Crist family mentions this same spring. Area development moved eastward toward the Valley Road, and so the architecture of Springhill is well preserved from its early days.

10.8   **Pass Rt. 732 on the left and cross bridge over the Middle River.** The Federal brick I-house on the right is called the Gamble House after the name of early owners. It was built sometime between 1820 and 1840 and was associated with several mills nearby on the Middle River. For the time the house was quite lavish and indicative of the wealth of the owner. **If you'd like to stretch this 18.2-mile ride to 28.3 miles, follow directions on next page starting from this point.**

11.6   **Continue STRAIGHT on Rt. 742. Rt. 742 also goes right.**

13.9   Pleasant View Evangelical Church was established in 1879.

14.2   **Continue STRAIGHT on Rt. 613. Rt. 612 goes left and then right.**

15.5   **Turn RIGHT at YIELD sign onto Rt. 613. Rt. 626 turns left.**

15.9   **Cross Rt. 275 Bypass at STOP sign with CAUTION.**

18.2   **End ride at starting point.**

28.3 MILE OPTION

10.8   **Turn LEFT onto Rt. 732 before crossing bridge over Middle River.**

12.2   The brick home on the hill to the left was built in the 1780s.

13.2   The white house with two-story porch and green shutters, off the road to the left, was built by Capt. John Rimel about 1868. The Rimels were the primary residents of this hollow in the late 1800s. This siding and shutter color combination was so common among rural dwellings that national magazines mentioned the "boring white and green" of farmhouses everywhere. The driveway to this house is the site of the former Roman community bandstand.

14.1   **Roman** was a thriving community from 1885 to 1920. The village had a post office, school, church, stores, blacksmith shop as well as a town band that performed at parties and special events. Zachariah Taylor once ran the Roman General Store in the red building to the right.

15.2   The white house on the left was constructed using a technique that was developed locally in the late 1800s. After building wooden forms, native stone was tossed into the forms and covered by a cement-like slurry to form the walls. This is the home of renowned cornhusk artist, Pat Broyles. Her work is available for sale at the Woodrow Wilson Birthplace Gift Shop in Staunton.

15.9   **Turn RIGHT onto Rt. 804. Rt. 732 goes straight.**

16.3   The tan abandoned building on the right was built using the same poured slurry technique as the Broyles' house at Roman. Graves with German surnames and the twin doors in front are indications that this was once a Mennonite church.

17.1   **Cross Naked Creek (unmarked) and continue STRAIGHT on Rt. 804. Rt. 746 goes right.**

17.4   Old Salem Lutheran Church on the left was organized by German settlers around 1802. A sanctuary was built in 1805 with the older cemetery on the left before the crest of the hill. A newer brick church was built in the 1850s, and it was enlarged in 1928. A young woman named Ida Stover was a member of the congregation in the late 1800s. She later moved to Kansas where she married David

Eisenhower. Their son Dwight David Eisenhower became our 34th president.

18.0   Continue STRAIGHT on Rt. 616. Rt. 616 also goes right.

18.4   Turn RIGHT at 4-way STOP onto Rt. 626.

19.6   The Sheets family has been making apple cider here for more than 60 years. The press usually operates several days a week from September until January. Stop in for a taste of fresh cider if Roscoe Sheets and his family are at work. The ridge through here is called Pisgah Heights or Grindstone Ridge. It contains large deposits of flint and limestone making much of the soil untillable.

19.8   Continue STRAIGHT at four-way STOP at intersection with Rt. 742.

22.8   The Poage limestone house on the right was built around 1750, and has been occupied by seven generations of the same family. There is a mill across the road, hidden by trees, that was used until WWII to process marl for fertilizer. David Carroll, the present owner, has extended an invitation for cyclists to stop and see the mill, but it's best to ask first.

23.4   Continue STRAIGHT at STOP sign at intersection with Rt. 612. Two organizations that promote much of the area's dramatic entertainment are located just west on Rt. 612. ShenanArts is a non-profit performing arts company that produces plays, musicals, a touring company, as well as the Shenandoah Valley Playwrights Retreat from its base at Pennyroyal Farm, an early 1800s farm-house. The Oak Grove Players, next to Pennyroyal Farm, offer five summer plays in an outdoor setting. Although tickets are by subscription only, visitors may buy them at the door on a seats available basis.

23.6   The Mowry Link House on the left was built in 1830. Its design is typical of the Shenandoah Valley I-house design in the 1800s. The Mowrys were associated with a nearby mill known at different times as Quicks Mill and Mowrys Mill. Levi Fishburne ran the mill during the Civil War until 1875.

25.7   Continue STRAIGHT on Rt. 613 at intersection with Rt. 626 on the right.

26.0   Cross Rt. 275 Bypass with CAUTION.

28.3   End ride at starting point.

Early Valley Architecture

Riding along the Valley's rural routes today can be like a step back into the past. The older farmsteads reflect the settlement and development of the area, from its frontier days in the early 1700s through the continued agricultural prosperity of the present.

The Shenandoah Valley offered an abundance of wood and stone for building. Many of the earliest houses were built of log, including those dwellings found in towns along the early turnpikes like Greenville and Mount Sidney. However, by the late 1700s some of the wealthy farmers and residents began to build more substantial houses of stone, particularly local limestone that was found throughout the region. The Poage House west of Verona, and Grey Gables near Hebron typify the large, square stone houses built during this time.

A local tradition has developed identifying these limestone houses as *Hessian houses,* presumably because several were constructed by Hessian prisoners who had served as mercenary soldiers during the Revolutionary War. Although these prisoners were certainly held in this region, there is no proof that they ever helped build these houses. They were constructed using a great variety of floorplans throughout the Valley, and were residences for just as many Scots-Irish as German families.

The early architecture reflects the ethnic diversity that characterized the first white settlements. German, Swiss, Scots-Irish, and English immigrants not only brought their possessions; they also brought construction techniques that they had used in the Old Country. The ways in which these settlers organized household space and constructed their homes reflected the traditional customs of their European homelands. The most significant distinction is between the Central Europeans, the Germans and Swiss, and those from the British Isles, particularly the English and Irish.

The German-American houses are most clearly identified by a large central chimney. The first floor included the kitchen and living areas, the second floor bedrooms, and storage space in the attic. Many German houses have brick-arched vaulted cellars for cold food storage. Page, Rockingham, and Shenandoah counties had the heaviest German settle-

Turnpike towns such as Mount Sidney contain many examples of the Valley's early architecture.

ment, and it is here that you'll see many examples of the German design, particularly Fort Lynn near Greenmount just north of Harrisonburg.

The Irish and English houses, by comparison, had one or two end chimneys. Typically there were two rooms on the first floor. The main door was at the center of the house and led into the hall, an all-purpose cooking and living area. A parlor, or parents' bedroom, was located off to the side. The village of Middlebrook contains many examples of this two-room layout.

More formal English designs became popular in the early 1800s. In keeping with the new fashion, Valley residents began to abandon their traditional ethnic house designs in favor of more symmetrical houses. These were characterized by a central front door, balanced facade, two story elevation, and matching end chimneys. Inside the front door was a central hallway with one room on each side. Many of the antebellum houses were built of brick, often with ells off the back. These were called I-houses or sometimes Georgian houses. The name I-house comes from folklorists who first identified these structures in the Midwestern states whose names started with the letter *I*, such as Iowa, Illinois, and Indiana. From the side, these houses have a tall narrow silhouette that also resembles this letter.

Even though residents succumbed to more stylish brick exteriors, certain interior and exterior decorative elements retained their ethnic characteristics. Robustly carved mantels and woodwork with bright marbling and sponge work reveals a strong German influence. The outside often featured decorative brickwork, sometimes with molded bricks at the cornices or with glazed bricks creating herringbone or diamond-shaped patterns in the walls. Some folklorists claim that those houses with two front doors found from Pennsylvania through the Shenandoah Valley are linked to the old German plans.

HEBRON HOP
Staunton • Route 17 • 27.6 miles

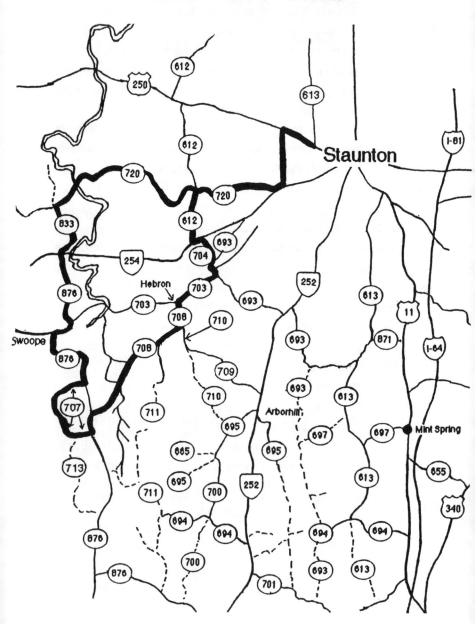

Hebron Hop

Although less has been sung about the Allegheny Mountains than the Blue Ridge, you'll marvel at this range on the western edge of the Shenandoah Valley. Vast open farm lands surround little traveled roads as you pedal past one of the Valley's oldest churches at Hebron and the Taylor-Boody Organ Factory where Valley craftsmen build pipe organs in the European tradition.

0.0   **Begin at intersection of Churchville Ave./Rt. 250 and Springhill Rd. on the north side of Gypsy Hill Park. Proceed WEST on Churchville Ave. with the park on your left.**

0.8   **Turn LEFT at traffic light onto Grubert Ave.**

1.8   **Turn RIGHT at traffic light onto West Beverley St.**

1.9   **Make quick RIGHT turn onto Morris Mill Rd.**

2.4   **Turn LEFT onto Morris Mill Rd./Rt. 720.** The apple orchards along this road are remnants of those that covered large sections of the Shenandoah Valley in the 1800s.

7.3   **Cross the Middle River.** This river snakes its way north through Augusta County, ultimately flowing into the North River near Grottoes. Together as the North River they join the South River to become the South Fork of the Shenandoah River at Port Republic. The headwaters of the Middle River are located southwest of here at the base of Little North Mt. Morris Mill was located in this vicinity along the Middle River. Also called Painter's Mill after a previous owner, it is one of many mills that are long since gone, but at one time were as close as a mile apart on the Middle River.

8.0   **Turn LEFT at crest of hill onto Rt. 833.** "Keller Fort" once stood **.9 mile** to the right on Rt. 833 where the road forded the Middle River at Trinity Point. Sturdy stone houses such as this one offered protection to area settlers in the event of Indian attacks. Alexander and Mary Crawford found refuge here in 1764, but were then killed by Shawnees in Augusta County's last massacre after leaving to tend to their nearby farm. The derivation of the name Trinity Point is somewhat vague. It's possible that it referred to the point on the Middle River where three roads converged at a well-used ford. On the other hand, the presence of a nearby Dunker church called Episcopal Trinity Chapel may have lent its name in some way.

8.8   The red barn on the left is a good example of a bank barn. The earthen ramp makes it easier to get farm equipment to the second floor.

9.2   Turn RIGHT at STOP sign onto Rt. 254 West and with CAUTION make a quick LEFT turn onto Rt. 876. The building on the left just before this intersection is the Lambsgate Bed and Breakfast. It was built around 1816, and family legend has it that Gen. Stonewall Jackson visited here during the Civil War. This road known as the Parkersburg Turnpike was constructed in 1838 as one of Virginia's "super highways." Parkersburg, West Virginia, 234 miles west of here, was an important city because of its location on the Ohio River. The brick building on the corner to the left was an early consolidated school built in 1898 and known as the Valley Mill School. This two-room school was sold to a doctor from Craigsville in 1948. The Valley Mill itself was located just to the east on the Middle River.

10.9   Turn RIGHT onto Rt. 703.

11.3   From the bridge over the Chesapeake and Ohio Railroad cyclists can get a good view of Little North Mountain, part of the Allegheny chain that forms the western edge of the Shenandoah Valley. Also visible is Elliots Knob which, at 4,463 feet, is the tallest peak in the George Washington National Forest. The C&O, originally called the Virginia Central Railroad, was the Valley's first railroad and began running from Richmond to Staunton in 1854.

11.6   Turn LEFT onto Rt. 876. This area is called **Swoope** (pronounced Swōpe) after Jacob Swoope, the first elected mayor of Staunton. He donated land for the railroad depot around which the community, Swoope's Depot, sprang up in the 1850s.

12.4   Wheatlands, the Swoope homeplace, is off to the left. This brick house was built in 1813 by George Washington Swoope and was used as winter headquarters by Confederate Gen. Fitzhugh Lee from 1864-65. The barns and mill were burned by Yankee troops.

12.8   Bear RIGHT on Rt. 876/707. Gravel Rt. 707 goes left.

13.4   Turn RIGHT onto Rt. 707.

13.7   Meadow View, the former home of John Trimble, is on the left. He settled this land on an original grant from Col. William Beverley in the 1730s. There was a mill built in the area as early as 1746. This is not the same John Trimble who was the last Augusta County settler killed by Native Americans in 1764.

13.9   The conical knob rising above the landscape to the left is Sugar Loaf Mountain. The area around it was settled by German Lutherans in the 1700s.

14.2   Cross the Middle River and bear LEFT on Rt. 707. Rt. 806 goes right to the Boy Scout Camp.

14.8   Bethlehem United Methodist Church was founded in 1852, and the present brick structure built in 1917. The graveyard has markers dating back to the mid-1800s. Augusta County Methodists began as the Methodist Episcopal Church in 1806 and grew slowly. By 1882, however, there were 20 such congregations in the county.

15.4   Turn LEFT at STOP sign onto Rt. 876.

15.8   Continue STRAIGHT on Rt. 708. Rt. 876 goes left.

16.3   Walnut Grove on the left was built about 1807 by Jacob Baylor. Interior woodwork is almost entirely made from walnut, including the dining room and kitchen floors. The doors and shutters are walnut as well. Bricks for the house were made here on the property. At one time the farm included an icehouse and its own school. Baylor used 28 slaves to maintain the 1,160 acre property. In the late 1800s, Walnut Grove passed into the Swoope family.

17.6   Bear LEFT at Y-intersection. Rt. 711 goes right.

18.4   On the left, Sunnyside, now known as Grey Gables, is one of several stone homes in the Staunton area. It was built by James Brown around 1780 presumably with the help of Hessian prisoners of war.

18.8   Bear LEFT at Y-intersection onto Rt. 708. Rt. 710 goes right.

19.8 **Turn RIGHT at Hebron onto Rt. 703.** The school building on the left was originally Hebron School, an early 1900s consolidated school. This building has been restored to its original 1923 appearance, and now is the home of Taylor & Boody Organ Builders where mechanical pipe organs are made in the old European style. Hebron Presbyterian Church, across the road, is one of the area's oldest churches. This congregation began in 1740 as part of the North Mountain Meeting House under Rev. John Craig. However, it split off as Brown's Meeting House under Maj. John Brown. The name was changed to Hebron Presbyterian Church in 1827 when the new sanctuary was built. That one burned down in 1900, and the present one was dedicated in 1901.

20.1 The small white outbuilding on the left used to be a Standard Oil service station.

20.3 The white brick house on the left was built in the 1850s. The Chesapeake and Ohio Railroad runs right behind here, and around 1900 this was a flag stop called **Snyder.** Passengers could board the train and ride into Staunton for 10¢.

21.2 **Turn LEFT at STOP sign onto Rt. 693.**

21.4 **Turn LEFT with CAUTION onto Rt. 704 at bend in road. Cedar Green** was a small community of black residents with its own church and school. Residents in this community provided a "laundry stop" for the C&O. Dirty linens were dropped off and clean ones picked up.

22.1 **Turn LEFT at STOP sign onto Rt. 254 West with CAUTION.** ★ **Food and drinks are available to the right on Rt. 254 East at Jodi's Place.** ★

22.2 **Turn RIGHT onto Rt. 612.**

23.3 **Turn RIGHT at STOP sign onto Rt. 720.**

24.7 **Turn RIGHT at STOP sign onto Morris Mill Rd.**

25.2 **Turn LEFT at STOP sign with CAUTION onto W. Beverley St.**

25.3 **Turn LEFT at traffic light onto Grubert Ave.**

26.3 **Turn RIGHT at traffic light onto Churchville Ave.**

27.6 **End ride at starting point.**

Cemeteries

Shenandoah Valley cemeteries are cultural markers of a time long past as well as a place to bury the dead. They have many interesting tales to tell those who are willing to stop and listen. Most of these graveyards were either part of a church or family plot. Although the village of Churchville had its own community plots at Green Hill Cemetery in 1880, this is the exception. Few other community burial grounds existed until the 1900s.

Many of the 1700s Valley cemeteries were established on church grounds whose religious buildings have long since disappeared. The Dayton cemetery was once the site of the Anglican Chapel of Ease, the oldest established church in Rockingham County. In Augusta County, the present-day Koiner's Church, also called Trinity Lutheran, stands just outside the graveyard, but the original building was inside the fenced burial grounds.

The type of tombstone marking the final resting place of the early settlers often says a lot. In the early 1700s, a grave was frequently marked with a long slabstone, headstone, and footstone. The Timber Ridge Cemetery, just off Rt. 11 in Rockbridge County, has examples of this style. The three stones together resembled a rock bed, a fitting metaphor since the word *cemetery* has roots in Greek meaning "to lull to sleep." Metaphors aside, the long slab also kept animals from destroying the gravesite.

Some early stones contain German inscriptions and/or folk-art like hearts and flowers. The Glebe Burying Ground in Augusta County near Hebron has examples of these. Stones from the 1700s until about 1830 were generally carved in the shape of a round-shouldered doorway, representing an entrance into heaven. Sandstone was used for these, but it tends to weather badly over time so old inscriptions are often difficult to read.

In the 1800s, grey stones became the dominant markers, and often included elaborate and sentimental carvings of funeral urns, willow trees, lambs, angels, and the Lord's hand. Mt. Vernon Cemetery in Grottoes contains unique cast iron markers, while many others have plots with wooden markers or rough, unshaped stones with the name of the deceased scratched on the rock's uneven surface.

ARBORHILL ARC
Staunton • Route 18 • 36.9 miles

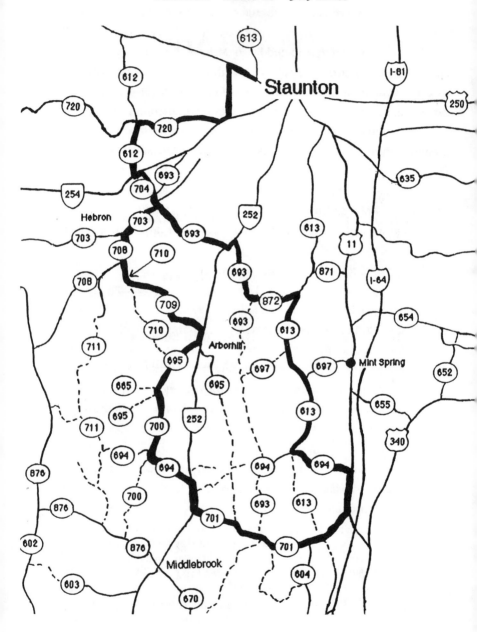

Arborhill Arc

Pedal through Hebron where Shenandoah Valley craftsmen build mechanical pipe organs in the European tradition. Browns Meeting House across the road served the religious needs of the earliest settlers in 1747. Then ride along the old Middlebrook-Brownsburg Turnpike past Arborhill, formerly the home of a Staunton silversmith and veteran of the War of 1812.

0.0 **Begin at the intersection of Churchville Ave./Rt. 250 and Springhill Rd. Proceed West on Churchville Ave./Rt. 250 West with the park on your left.**

0.8 **Turn LEFT at traffic light onto Grubert Ave.** This was once the end of the streetcar line at Plunkettville, a small village where the Plunkett family lived.

1.8 **Turn RIGHT at traffic light onto West Beverley St.**

1.9 **Make a quick RIGHT turn onto Morris Mill Rd.**

2.4 **Turn LEFT onto Morris Mill Rd./Rt. 720.** Morris Mill was located west of here near the intersection with the Middle River. Also called Painter's Mill after a previous owner, it is one of many mills that are long since gone but at one time were as close as a mile apart on the Middle River. Apple orchards along this road are remnants of those that once covered large sections of the Shenandoah Valley in the 1800s.

3.8 **Turn LEFT onto Rt. 612.**

5.0 **Turn LEFT at STOP sign and proceed with CAUTION on Rt. 254 East.** The Parkersburg Turnpike was once the main road through the Allegheny Mts. to Parkersburg, West Virginia.

5.1 **Turn RIGHT onto Rt. 704. Cedar Green** was a small community of black residents with its own church and school. Residents in this community provided a "laundry stop" for the C&O railroad. Dirty linens were dropped off and clean ones picked up.

5.8   **Turn RIGHT at STOP sign onto Rt. 693.**

6.0   **Turn RIGHT onto Rt. 703 after crossing RR overpass. Rt. 693 goes straight.**

6.6   The white brick house on the right was built in the 1850s. The Chesapeake and Ohio Railroad runs behind here, and around 1900 this was a flag stop called **Snyder.** Passengers could board the train and ride into Staunton for 10¢.

6.8   The small white outbuilding on the right was once a Standard Oil gas station.

7.1   **Turn LEFT onto Rt. 708 at Hebron Presbyterian Church.** This congregation began in 1740 as part of the North Mountain Meeting House under Rev. John Craig. However, it split off as Brown's Meeting House under Maj. John Brown. The name was changed to Hebron Presbyterian Church in 1827 when the new sanctuary was built. That one burned down in 1900, and the present one was dedicated in 1901. The school building across the road was originally Hebron School, an early 1900s consolidated school. It has been restored to its original 1923 appearance, and now is the home of the Taylor & Boody Organ Builders where mechanical pipe organs are made in the old European style.

7.5   On the right and behind you, Sunnyside, now known as Grey Gables, is one of several limestone homes in the Staunton area. It was built by James Brown around 1780, presumably with the help of Hessian prisoners of war.

7.6   **Bear LEFT on Rt. 710. Rt. 708 goes right.** Eidson Creek on the right is named for the Eidsons who were early settlers in this area. Some of them are interred at the Hebron Church cemetery. It was also called Smokey Row Creek in the 1880s.

8.1   **Turn LEFT at Smokey Row Baptist Church onto Rt. 709.** This church was formed in the 1920s to serve the small black community called **Smokey Row.** This community sprang up in the late 1800s along Eidson Creek. The Green-Harden House on the right is a typical I-style brick house from the Valley in the mid-1800s.

8.8 The gray house with a tin roof on the left was formerly the two-room Smokey Row School. The story goes that this building was dismantled and moved from Mint Spring to its present location where it provided schooling until the 1920s. The current resident said that she'd attended the school as a child.

10.3 **Turn RIGHT at STOP sign and proceed with CAUTION on Rt. 252 South.** This road was once part of a turnpike that linked Staunton and Lexington. The Middlebrook-Brownsburg Turnpike Company was established in 1851 and turned this road into a major transportation route. The word *turnpike* means a tollroad. The name comes from the device used to stop traffic so that the toll would be paid. The turnpike itself was usually a tall wooden box with a pike, or pole, resting on it. The pole stretched across the road with the opposite end supported by a forked post. The pike was raised or turned after the toll had been paid.

10.7 **Turn RIGHT onto Rt. 695 at Arborhill.** Just north of this turn, a toll booth once stood that collected 10¢ from wagons and Model Ts heading into Staunton. A second booth to the south collected fares from those headed to Middlebrook. The Arborhill community included a grange meeting hall for local farmers, a general store, and a school. The old general store sits at this intersection, a few hundred yards from its original location. The school has been converted into apartments at its location south of here on the right side of Rt. 252.

11.1 The Arborhill House, for which this community was named, was built in 1820 by Capt. William Young, a Staunton silversmith and veteran of the War of 1812. He named it for the large number of trees on the estate. Bricks for the house were made on the property.

11.7 Sugarloaf Mountain is off to the right. In the 1700s and 1800s sugar was sold in a large cone or loaf and early residents apparently saw some similarity between their sugar and this hill. Lone peaks such as this one are generally made of chert, a flint-like mineral that is slower to erode than the surrounding limestone.

12.2 **Continue STRAIGHT on Rt. 700 after bend in road. Rt. 695 goes right.**

12.4   The original part of the house at Flowing Spring Farm on the right was built in the early 1800s, and the land itself was part of the original Beverley Manor tract. The name comes from the ice cold spring that was forced into a reservoir and then piped through a stone trough in a "refrigerator" room off the kitchen. The spring is still fully functioning.

13.0   Kimton Farm was built in 1891 using walls poured into forms to a thickness of 16 inches. Lime for the mortar was burned from limestone across the road from the house, and the chestnut rafters were cut on the property. There was a leather tanning operation on the creek in front of the house in the 1800s.

13.6   Turn LEFT at STOP sign onto Rt. 694.

13.9   Mt. Tabor Lutheran Church was organized in 1804, and the present building constructed in 1886. Headstones in the cemetery date from 1830 and include several wooden markers. David Bittle founded the Virginia Institute near here in 1842. The school was later moved to its present site in Salem, Virginia and became Roanoke College.

14.8   Turn RIGHT at STOP sign and proceed with CAUTION on Rt. 252 South.

15.4   Turn LEFT onto Rt. 701. This road was an extension of the Howardsville Turnpike that crossed the Blue Ridge connecting Greenville with Martin's Mill in Nelson County.

17.0   Christian Bumgardner settled on this land in 1772. His son Jacob was not only a Revolutionary War veteran; but apparently participated in the Boston Tea Party while visiting New England with his father. The present house at Bethel Green Farm, on the right, was built in the 1850s by Christian's grandson, James Bumgardner. The family made "Old Bumgardner" using spring water at their distillery. Making spirits was not only legal, but also the second largest industry in Augusta County behind milling. It's ironic that, just across the road at Bethel Presbyterian Church, Rev. Francis McFarland preached temperance to his congregation. The teetotaling Presbyterians got the last laugh when the distillery was finally torn down, and many of the timbers were used to remodel Bethel's Sanctuary

17.1   Bethel Presbyterian Church on the left is one of the oldest area

17.1   Bethel Presbyterian Church on the left is one of the oldest area churches. It was established in 1740 along with the Presbyterian church at Hebron as the North Mountain Congregation. The present building was erected in 1888, although the first sanctuary was built on this site in 1779. The cemetery is the resting place for a number of Revolutionary War soldiers.

19.6   Turn LEFT at STOP sign and proceed with CAUTION on Rt. 11. Riverheads High School on the left is part of the Riverheads Magisterial District. The name is derived from fact that the headwaters of two rivers arise here. Many of the creeks flow north and become part of the Shenandoah, but just south of here the waters flow southward and then empty into the James River.

20.5   Turn LEFT onto Rt. 694.

21.2   The white house with columns on the left is typical of many old area houses which began as log structures and were subsequently expanded and covered with clapboard. The small log structure behind the main house is supposedly the former Gravelly Hill School that had been moved from its former site on the hill off the road to the right.

22.0   Turn RIGHT at STOP sign onto Rt. 613. This is the old Greenville Road that carried travelers between Staunton and Greenville in the 1800s.

23.7   Bear LEFT and follow Rt. 613 downhill. Rt. 697 goes uphill to the right.

24.6   The house at the end of the maple-lined drive on the left dates back to the 1800s. It was constructed in a number of stages that were not combined until well into the 1900s. Much of the landscaping was done by Elizabeth Seymour Rawlinson, a well known horticultural writer, who lived here during the 1920s. It was also home to South Carolina Congressman L. Mendel Rivers during the 1940s.

25.0   Hillside Farm on the left was the home and orchard for the Neff family. The house dates back to the 1830s. The apple orchard on both sides of the road remained in operation until 1980.

25.8   Turn LEFT onto Rt. 872 after crossing Folly Mills Creek (unmarked). The remains of Cochrans Mill are farther ahead on Rt. 613.

26.8 The house on the right is typical of area brick houses built between 1800 and 1850. The bricks were made locally and often right on the farm.

27.0 Turn RIGHT at STOP sign onto Rt. 693. The white house with green trim across the road is a two-story log structure that supposedly served as a stagecoach stop. It is called the Stingy Hollow House after a former owner. According to a local legend, this man was so thrifty that once, while feeding his hogs out back, he slipped and fell into the mud. Rather than just leave the spilled grain, he scraped it out of the mud and fed it to his animals just the same.

28.6 Turn LEFT at STOP sign and proceed with CAUTION on Rt. 252 West.

28.9 Turn RIGHT onto Rt. 693.

30.7 Continue STRAIGHT on Rt. 693 and cross RR overpass. Rt. 703 goes left.

31.1 Turn LEFT with CAUTION at bend onto Rt. 704.

31.8 Turn LEFT at STOP sign and proceed with CAUTION on Rt. 254 West. ★ Food and drinks are available at Jodi's Place to the right on Rt. 254 East. ★

31.9 Turn RIGHT onto Rt. 612.

33.1 Turn RIGHT at STOP sign onto Rt. 720/Morris Mill Rd.

34.1 Enter Staunton.

34.5 Turn RIGHT at STOP sign onto Morris Mill Rd.

35.0 Turn LEFT at STOP sign and proceed with CAUTION on West Beverley St. Stay in left turn lane.

35.1 Make quick LEFT turn at traffic light onto Grubert Ave.

36.1 Turn RIGHT at traffic light onto Churchville Ave.

36.9 End ride at starting point.

Later Victorian Architecture

As Shenandoah Valley farmers and village residents prospered in the 1800s, their houses became more substantial and decorative. Many builders incorporated stylish details around the front door, along the cornice, or on the front porch. One of the most ornate examples from the antebellum period is Bethel Green. Gothic arch chimneys and back porch, tall windows, and decorative cornice grace this house located across from Bethel Church near Middlebrook.

After the Civil War, many Valley residents remodeled their homes by adding elaborate gingerbread decoration. The availability of factory-made Victorian trim made this a popular style throughout the country as well. Older farm and village houses enjoyed "facelifts" in addition to those in the railtowns that were beginning to crop up. Middlebrook, Mt. Crawford, Mt. Sidney, Bridgewater, and Dayton contain good examples of this new style.

Although many farmers continued to build more traditional I-houses well into the early 1900s, others wanted to build entirely new and more stylish residences. The Eustler Brothers of Shendun, now called Grottoes, built many of the most elaborate Victorian houses in the central Shenandoah Valley. The company produced many of the building components at their workshop and then moved the pieces to the site for construction. The building supply company is still in business today.

The Eustler Brothers popularized a T-shaped house design which included an asymmetrical plan and more elaborate interior and exterior decoration. You'll see homes of this design along the railroad tracks in Grottoes, in the town of Weyers Cave, and along the Shenandoah River tributaries in northern Augusta County.

By the mid-1900s, local architecture began to lose much of its regional character. Residents began to build more bungalows and colonial designs that were found throughout the country. However, a considerable legacy of buildings has survived to preserve and document the cultural history of the Valley.

EASTERN LOOP
Staunton • Route 19 • 38.5 miles

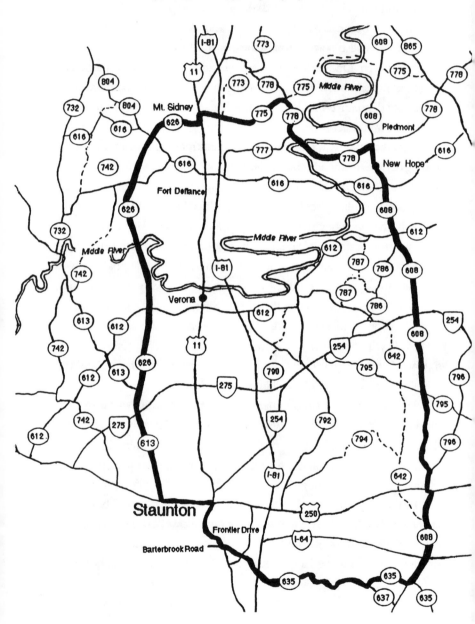

Eastern Loop

On your way out of Staunton, stop off at the Museum of American Frontier Culture and see how the first settlers lived. Then onto Tinkling Spring Church dating back to 1745. Be sure to visit the gardens of André Viette and see his extensive perennial collection. Farther on you'll pass through Mt. Sidney, a former stagecoach stop along the Valley Road. Today you'll find it's a great spot to go antiquing.

0.0   **Begin at intersection of Churchville Ave./Rt. 250 and Springhill Rd. on the north side of Gypsy Hill Park. Proceed east on Churchville Ave. toward downtown Staunton.**

0.1   **Bear RIGHT at traffic light and then LEFT at entrance to Gypsy Hill Park.** The old Lee High School, now the College of the Holy Child Jesus, will be on your right.

0.5   **Turn RIGHT at traffic light onto Augusta St.**

1.1   **Turn LEFT at traffic light onto Johnson St. by the Augusta County Courthouse.**

1.3   **Turn RIGHT onto Greenville Ave. at traffic light and ride under railroad overpass. CAUTION: Heavy traffic for the next 1.4 miles on Greenville Ave.** An alternative to riding on Greenville Ave. is to turn left after the overpass and ride for **1.7 miles** on Richmond Rd. Then turn right onto Frontier Dr. at the traffic light and ride **1.3 miles** to the intersection with Barterbrook Rd.

2.8   **Turn LEFT with CAUTION at traffic light on Barterbrook Rd. across from K-Mart.**

3.4   **Cross Frontier Drive at STOP sign staying STRAIGHT on Rt. 635.** Turn left here and ride for **.5 mile** to enter the Museum of American Frontier Culture. This living history museum is comprised of actual working farms that have been moved to this site from England, Ireland, Germany, and the southern Shenandoah Valley.

4.9 This quaint white frame church on the right side was built in the late 1800s as Hammond Chapel for Methodist worship. During the Depression, local Presbyterians held revivals here. It now serves as the Augusta Christian Church.

6.4 Cross Christians Creek named for Gilbert Christian, one of the area's early settlers. The former crossroads community of **Barterbrook** included a general store, post office, mill, and blacksmith near here.

7.5 Turn LEFT onto Rt. 635. Rt. 637 continues straight.

8.9 Turn LEFT at STOP sign onto Rt. 608.

9.7 CAUTION: Traffic entering and exiting I-64 and Augusta Expoland.

10.1 Tinkling Spring Church on the right is one of the oldest Presbyterian churches in Augusta County. When first organized in 1738, this congregation was known as "The Triple Forks of the Shenando." Meetings were first held here on April 14, 1745, when the church was half-finished according to Rev. John Craig's diary. Rev. Craig presided over this church and the Augusta Stone Church at Fort Defiance. By comparison to the parishioners at the Stone Church, Craig found John Lewis and the other early community leaders who attended Tinkling Spring to be "a stiff-necked and perverse generation... their leaders close-handed about providing necessary things for pious and religious uses, and could not agree for several years upon a plan or manner where or how to build their meeting-house, which gave me very great trouble to hold them together, their disputes ran so high." The present brick structure was built in 1850 and is on the National Register of Historic Places.

11.4 Turn LEFT at traffic light onto Rt. 250 East and proceed under overpass. Route 250 was one of the earliest roads connecting the Shenandoah Valley with Richmond. ★ **Food and drinks are available at the convenience store on the right.** ★

11.6 Turn RIGHT onto Rt. 608 at Fishersville. With additional residential development and the new hospital in Fishersville, traffic has increased on Rt. 608. Exercise CAUTION

especially on blind curves. Settlers began putting down roots here as early as 1738, but the community is named after Daniel and Nancy Fisher who settled here around 1788 and raised 17 children.

12.1   The brick house at Spring Valley Farm on the left was built around 1850, but the spring house supposedly predates this. Notice the spring-fed pond emerging from underneath the springhouse.

12.2   Bear LEFT on Rt. 608. Rt. 696 goes right.

12.8   Long Meadow Farm on the right was built around 1810 by John McCue, the third minister at Tinkling Spring Church. In early 1865, Gen. Jubal Early and half of the Confederate army camped here prior to the Battle of Waynesboro. It was after this engagement on March 2, 1865 that Early surrendered to Gen. Philip Sheridan.

14.1   Be sure to stop and look at the gardens of André Viette on the left. Viette is widely known for his perennials of which more than 1,000 are grown and displayed here. The gardens are open to the public as are his tours and lectures.

14.8   Long Meadow Run, the creek on the right, is said to drain some of the region's finest farmland even back in the 1700s.

16.4   Cross Rt. 254 at STOP sign with CAUTION.

18.6   ★ Food and drinks are available at the New Hope Grocery at the intersection with Rt. 612. ★

19.5   **New Hope.** James Kerr (pronounced Car) was one of the area's first settlers with some sources dating his arrival back to 1730, even before John Lewis, Staunton's founder. Much of the land along what is now Rt. 608 was Kerr land as part of the original Beverley Manor Grant. Some of the earliest Kerr houses are still standing, including the old homeplace on Rt. 612 above the Middle River. One oft-repeated reason for New Hope's name arises from a desire on the part of John Kerr's wife to abandon their 400-acre farm. John, the oldest son of James Kerr, remained confident that the couple would gain "new hope" from sticking it out on their homestead.

21.0   Turn LEFT onto Rt. 778. The Civil War Battle of Piedmont was fought just ahead on June 5, 1864. A Union victory here opened up the Valley, and the following day Yankee troops took Staunton.

23.1 **Cross Middle River.** This steel truss bridge was built by the Champion Bridge Co. of Wilmington, Ohio in 1915. Spans such as this one were much more numerous than the 14 that presently exist in Augusta County. Six of these cross the Middle River at various spots. The ruins of the former Knightly Mill are to the left just before crossing the river. This was first known as Allison Mill in the early 1800s, followed by Humbert's Mill, Hope Mill, and finally Knightly Mill. The mill ground wheat, corn, plaster, and sawed lumber in the mid-1800s. By the 1920s it was grinding flour as well as producing electricity as the Knightly Light and Power Co. Virginia Electric Power Company purchased it in 1931 and retains the property, although the buildings have been razed. The community at the top of the next hill is called **Knightly** as well.

23.4 **Continue STRAIGHT on Rt. 778. Rt. 777 goes left.**

24.5 **Turn LEFT onto Rt. 775.**

26.5 **Cross over I-81.**

26.8 **Cross RR tracks with CAUTION.**

27.0 **Turn LEFT at STOP sign onto Rt. 11. Mt. Sidney** was previously a stage coach stop known as Ten Mile Stage along the Valley Road. This name came from the fact that it was the only stop between Staunton and Keezletown, a distance then of ten miles along the existing road. The town grew up when the Valley Road was resurveyed in the late 1700s so that it now ran through here. It once included a tavern, blacksmith, shoemaker, and pottery. Town lots were laid out in 1822. There are two possible explanations for the town's present name. Samuel Curry, an Augusta County resident with a strong interest in the classics, may have named it after a nearby hill and Sir Phillip Sidney, an English gentleman. The second explanation is a bit more fanciful. Supposedly, two men, Sidney and Crawford, were traveling south on the Valley Road. They only had one horse between them, and so they alternated riding it. Farther north, Sidney got off and said to his comrade, "Mount, Crawford" at what is now Mount Crawford. When they reached Ten Mile Stage, Crawford got down, and said, "Mount, Sidney." Whatever the real source, be sure to take some time to browse through the town's antique shops. Ida Stover, the mother of President Dwight David Eisenhower, was born here and raised on a farm west of the village. ★ **Food and drinks are available at the convenience store at this intersection.** ★

27.2 **Turn RIGHT and begin uphill climb on Rt. 626.** This road is also known as Seawright Springs Road after the former medicinal springs. "Curative" waters were sold from the site several miles west of this route from the 1790s until a few years ago.

28.0 **Bear LEFT at 90 degree bend. Rt. 748 goes right.**

28.2 **Bear LEFT at second 90 degree bend.**

28.7 **Continue STRAIGHT at four-way STOP at intersection with Rt. 616.**

30.1 **Continue STRAIGHT on Rt. 626 at STOP sign at intersection with Rt. 742.** Just before this intersection on the right, the Sheets family has been making apple cider here for more than 60 years. The press usually operates several days a week from September until January. Stop in for a taste of fresh cider if Roscoe Sheets and his family are at work. The ridge through here is called Pisgah Heights or Grindstone Ridge. It contains large deposits of flint and limestone making much of the soil untillable.

31.7 **Cross Middle River.**

33.1 The Poage limestone house on the right was built around 1750 and has been occupied by seven generations of the same family. There is a mill across the road, hidden by trees, that was used until WWII to process marl for fertilizer. David Carroll, the present owner, has extended an invitation for cyclists to stop and see the mill, but it's best to ask first.

33.6 **Continue STRAIGHT on Rt. 626 at STOP sign at intersection with Rt. 612.** Two organizations that promote much of the area's dramatic entertainment are located just west on Rt. 612. Shenan-Arts is a non-profit performing arts company that produces plays, musicals, a touring company, as well as the Shenandoah Valley Playwrights Retreat from its base at Pennyroyal Farm, an early 1800s farmhouse. The Oak Grove Players, next to Pennyroyal Farm, offer five summer plays in an outdoor setting. Although tickets are by subscription only, visitors may buy them at the door on a seats-available basis.

33.8 The Mowry Link House on the left was built in 1830. Its design is typical of the Shenandoah Valley I-house design in the 1800s. The Mowrys were associated with a nearby mill known at different times as Quicks Mill and Mowrys Mill. Levi Fishburne ran the mill during the Civil War until 1875.

36.2   **Continue STRAIGHT on Rt. 613 at STOP sign after crossing intersection of Rt. 275 Bypass with CAUTION.**

36.3   **Enter Staunton.**

38.5   **End ride at starting point.**

Wildflowers

While cycling through the Shenandoah Valley, you'll see many flowering plants which were once travelers themselves. They came from Europe and Asia where, for thousands of years, they'd adapted to soils that had been disturbed by farming and road-building. These floral immigrants reached our shores in a variety of ways. Some were intentionally brought for New World farms and gardens, while others came as stowaways among hay and feed for cattle. When the early settlers cut the forests and tilled the soil to grow crops, they created a rich environment for a number of seeds. As the roads stretched south and west, Old World plants colonized the roadsides where you may still see them today. John Bartram, America's earliest and best known naturalist, collected many plants from the Shenandoah Valley for shipment to Europe but kept its location a secret to protect this special place.

Two key factors as to what may be in bloom are time of year and specific habitat. There are many varieties of clover growing along our rural routes. Birds-Foot Trefoil is low growing and bright yellow. Sweet clovers may be white or yellow with a tall lacy appearance. Mid-summer brings Chicory's inch-wide blue blossoms as well as the bristly blue blossoms and protruding red stamens of Blueweed.

Roadside ditches, marshes, and stream banks can be especially fruitful for those native wildflowers that thrive in a moist habitat. In late summer, look for the unmistakable red spike of the Cardinal-flower and the more subdued pink of Swamp Milkweed and Joe-Pye Weed.

Unused pastures come alive with the flat-topped purple blooms of Ironweed on towering six-foot stems. The profusion of Goldenrods, of which there are some 60 species in North America, marks the end of summer. But it's the deep, shady woods that hold our most popular native wildflowers including Bloodroot, Trillium, Hepatica (also called Liverwort), Virginia Bluebells, and Dutchmans Breeches. These deep woods plants bloom early in spring before the trees leaf out and block out the sunlight. Canada Lilies and Asters are in their glory in late summer primarily on wooded slopes.

FLY THROUGH MOSSY CREEK

Staunton • Route 20 • 40.1 miles

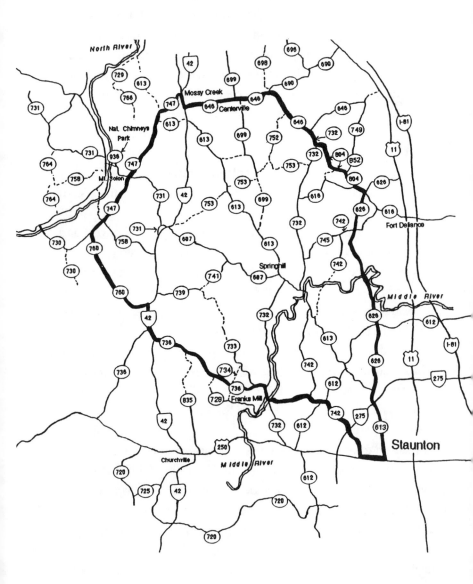

Fly Through Mossy Creek

Mossy Creek is best known to anglers as one of the state's premier trout streams for flyfishing, but its history and topography make it equally appealing to cyclists on their way to explore the limestone formations at Natural Chimneys and the former rail-road boomtowns of Mt. Solon and Stokesville.

0.0 **Start at the intersection of Churchville Ave./Rt. 250 West and Springhill Rd. on the north side of Gypsy Hill Park. Ride NORTH on Springhill Rd./Rt. 613 away from Gypsy Hill Park.**

2.3 **Continue STRAIGHT on Rt. 613 at STOP sign after crossing Rt. 275 with CAUTION.**

4.8 The Mowry Link House on the right was built in 1830. Its design is typical of the Shenandoah Valley I-house. The Mowrys were associated with a nearby mill known at different times as Quicks Mill and Mowrys Mill. Levi Fishburne ran the mill during the Civil War until 1875.

4.9 **Continue STRAIGHT at STOP sign on Rt. 626 at intersection with Rt. 612.** Two organizations that promote much of the area's dramatic entertainment are located just west on Rt. 612. Shenan-Arts is a non-profit performing arts company that produces plays, musicals, a touring company, as well as the Shenandoah Valley Playwrights Retreat from its base at Pennyroyal Farm, an early 1800s farmhouse. The Oak Grove Players, next to Pennyroyal Farm, offer five summer plays in an outdoor setting. Although tickets are by subscription only, visitors may buy them at the door on a seats-available basis.

5.4 The limestone Poage House on the left was built around 1750, and has been occupied by seven generations of the same family. There is a mill across the road, hidden by trees, that was used until World War II to process marl for fertilizer. David Carroll, the present owner, has extended an invitation for cyclists to stop and visit the mill, but it's best to ask first.

6.8 **Cross the Middle River.** This river snakes its way north through Augusta County, flowing into the North River near Grottoes, and then merging with the South River to form the South Fork of the Shenandoah River at Port Republic.

8.4 **Continue STRAIGHT on Rt. 626 at four-way STOP and intersection with Rt. 742.** The ridge through here is called Pisgah Heights or Grindstone Ridge. It contains large deposits of flint and limestone making much of the soil untillable.

8.6 On the left, the Sheets family has been making apple cider here for more than 60 years. The press usually operates several days a week from September until January. Stop in for a taste of fresh cider if Roscoe Sheets and his family are at work.

9.8 **Turn LEFT at four-way STOP onto Rt. 616.**

10.2 **Continue STRAIGHT on Rt. 804. Rt. 616 goes left.**

10.9 Old Salem Lutheran Church on the right was organized by German settlers around 1802. A sanctuary was built in 1805 with the older cemetery on the left before the crest of the hill. A newer brick church was built in the 1850s, and it was enlarged in 1928. A young woman named Ida Stover was a member of the congregation in the late 1800s. She later moved to Kansas and married David Eisenhower. Their son, Dwight David Eisenhower, became our 34th president.

11.2 **Continue STRAIGHT on Rt. 804. Rt. 746 goes left.**

12.0 The tan plaster church on the left is no longer in use, but descendants of early German settlers are buried in the sideyard. The twin doors indicate that this could have been a Mennonite church.

12.4 **Turn RIGHT at T-intersection onto Rt. 732.**

12.9 **Continue STRAIGHT at STOP sign onto Rt. 646. Rt. 646 also goes right.**

15.0 **Bear LEFT staying on Rt. 646. Rt. 690/698 goes right.**

15.9 **Centerville.** The old school building on the right is one of the area's first consolidated schools. The Centerville United Methodist Church on the left was built in 1880. In 1885 the post office here was known as Milnesville.

16.9 Torry Farm is on the left. The house was built in the 1880s, but its name comes from the present owners, Vic **tor** and Ma **ry.** The white building behind the house served as a granary on one side and a corn crib on the other. The red springhouse is just below the main house and was used by the family in the early 1900s for canning vegetables. The rolling hills between Mossy Creek Church and the Augusta Stone Church at Fort Defiance were called the "Hills of Judea" by Rev. Conrad Speece, minister at the old Augusta Stone Presbyterian Church from 1813 to 1836. This is a reference to the difficulty in growing crops on the hard, erosion-resistant chert hills.

17.1 **Cross Long Glade Creek.** This stream flows into the North River at Bridgewater. It originates near Springhill and was so-named by early settlers because it flowed through an open passage in the woods. Springhill's post office was called Long Glade as well.

18.0 **Turn RIGHT at STOP sign and proceed with CAUTION onto Rt. 42 North.** Route 42 was once part of the Harrisonburg-Warm Springs Turnpike. The oldest part of the road is the 11 miles from here north to Harrisonburg. This road was laid out in 1779 to give Mossy Creek residents access to the county court system in Harrisonburg. In the 1830s a company was chartered to connect this section and the Warm Springs-Staunton part of the road and complete the entire turnpike.

18.5 **Turn LEFT with CAUTION at sharp bend onto Rt. 809 at Mossy Creek.** A section of Mossy Creek has been specially managed by the landowners, the Virginia Department of Game and Inland Fisheries, and the Massanutten Chapter of Trout Unlimited to produce one of Virginia's finest trout streams for fly fishermen. Written permission is required to fish as is adherence to special regulations. Just north on Rt. 42 past the bend is the Henry Miller House, called Greystone Farm by the present owners. Miller built this home, one of the oldest in Augusta County, in 1784. The community of Mossy Creek grew up around Miller's Iron Works as well as his gristmill, sawmill, and papermill, all powered by the creek. His wife Hannah, was the niece of Daniel Boone, and it is said that he learned the iron trade from the famous woodsman's father, Squire Boone.

18.6   Continue STRAIGHT on Rt. 747.

18.8   In 1903 the C&W Railroad flooded the bottomland on the left and created a large pond. There was a pavilion and dance hall extending out into the pond. Wooden pilings from the structures are still visible in the creekbed. People from as far as Harrisonburg would ride the train out here, especially on holidays such as the Fourth of July. Closing the rail line put an end to this mini-resort. The dam was dynamited in 1969, draining the land.

19.5   Bear LEFT on Rt. 747.

19.8   Mossy Creek Presbyterian Church is to the left on Rt. 613. This is one of the oldest congregations in the area. The first Scots-Irish settlers began meeting here in 1768. The present building was constructed in 1882 by a local contractor, Col. William Pifer. It was near here that Jed Hotchkiss, Stonewall Jackson's famed mapmaker, founded the Mossy Creek Academy in 1850.

22.0   Continue STRAIGHT on Rt. 747 at 4-way STOP in Mt. Solon.
The naturally-formed limestone towers at Natural Chimneys have also been referred to as the "Cyclopean Towers," "Towers of Solon," and "Pillars of Hercules." The seven peaks range in height from 65 to 120 feet. They are the remnants of what was once a cavern whose roof collapsed and filled in the grotto long ago. Before that, however, the cavern would have been large enough to contain a 40-story building. In addition to facilities for swimming, picnicking, and camping, this park is host to the Oldest Continuous Sporting Event in America. The Natural Chimneys Jousting Tournament started in 1821 over competition for a local girl. Every year on the third Saturday in August, 20th century "knights" gallop on horseback attempting to spear small rings from a crossbar. The town of Mt. Solon grew up around the Chesapeake & Western Railroad, although there was an established settlement here in the late 1700s. The town had its own post office in 1836 as well as several mills, distilleries, and a tannery. The town was supposedly named by Samuel Curry, an Augusta resident with an interest in the classics, after Solon, a Greek statesman. ★ **Food and drinks are available at Natural Chimneys Regional Park, .5 mile to the right on Rt. 731.** ★

23.6   The log house on your right has inverted V-notching and was typical of homes built by the early settlers.

23.9   Freemason Run is the creek on the left.

24.2   Mt. Olivet United Brethren Church was founded in 1893 by residents of German descent. Notice the stained glass panes inserted in regular window frames.

24.4   **Turn LEFT at 3-way STOP onto Rt. 760 by Mt. Zion United Methodist Church.**

28.0   **Turn RIGHT onto Rt. 42 South and ride with CAUTION for the next 1.3 miles. Cross Moffett Creek.**

29.3   **Turn LEFT onto Rt. 736 after passing Elk Run Church of the Brethren.**

30.6   The Union Presbyterian Church on the left was founded in 1817.

32.7   **Bear RIGHT onto Rt. 734. Rt. 734 also goes left.**

32.8   **Bear LEFT onto Rt. 736. Gravel Rt. 734 goes straight.** If you can handle a **.4 mile** downhill on gravel, go straight on Rt. 734. Then turn left onto Rt. 728 and enjoy a beautiful **1.8 mile** flat stretch along the Middle River. Rejoin the route at the **34.3 mile** point.

33.6   **Stay STRAIGHT on Rt. 736. Rt. 733 goes left.**

34.0   **Bear RIGHT on Rt. 732. Rt. 732 also goes left to Springhill.**

34.3   **Cross Middle River with Franks Mill on the right.** The tan house next to the mill was built in 1812 by George Hanger, the original owner and operator of this Middle River mill. The Shutterlees purchased it later in the 1800s; and the Franks, for whom it is still called, took possession in 1912. It ceased operation on January 31, 1971.

34.4   **Turn LEFT onto Rt. 728 and begin 1.5 mile climb. CAUTION: Watch for dump trucks and gravel in road from Luck Quarry.** The Shutterlee cemetery, on the left near the beginning of the climb, is the resting place of the family of the previous owners of Franks Mill.

36.0   **Turn RIGHT at STOP sign onto Rt. 742.** Chimney Farm was settled by Arnold Anderson in 1797.

37.7   **Enter Staunton.**

37.9   **Cross Rt. 275 bypass at STOP sign with CAUTION.**

39.0   **Turn LEFT at STOP sign and proceed with CAUTION on Rt. 250/Churchville Ave.**

40.1   **End ride at starting point.**

Ironworks

Beginning with the first settlement at Jamestown, obtaining iron ore was of great concern to colonists in the New World. Domestic production of iron products took on an even greater importance when England banned the importation of Swedish iron to the colonies in the early 1700s. The Colonial governments encouraged English and German settlers to build forges and furnaces for iron production in response to this sudden shortage.

Pig iron was the primary type of metal produced. The name itself comes from the practice of pouring the molten substance into a central trough with smaller troughs off to the side at right angles giving the appearance of a pig suckling its young. When hardened, it could again be heated and hammered into bar iron with large trip hammers. Blacksmiths used bar iron to make an assortment of household and farm implements. Molten iron could also be cast from the furnace into kettles and stove plates.

All the Valley ironworks were charcoal blast furnaces through the end of the Civil War. They were fired with charcoal made from the slow, controlled burning of wooden planks cut from thousands of acres of timber.

The Mossy Creek Iron Works was established in northern Augusta County about 1774. Early western Virginia iron communities such as this one consisted of saw mills, grist mills, and agricultural production as supporting industries. Labor was supplied by skilled and unskilled slaves as well as indentured servants, hired hands, and members of the ironmaster's family.

Post-Revolutionary War operations concentrated on the domestic needs of early pioneers. Local facilities included Union Forge near Waynesboro (c.1800), Gibraltor Forge north of Lexington (c.1800), Buffalo Forge north of Lexington (c.1800), and Mount Vernon Furnace at Grottoes (c.1848).

The demand for iron again increased with the outbreak of the Civil War. The Tredegar Iron Works in Richmond contracted with some Shenandoah Valley forges, like Mount Torry near Sherando Lake, to supply the raw materials for munitions. These were frequent targets of Union troops as they moved southward through the Valley in an attempt to cripple the Confederate war effort.

SOUTHERN AUGUSTA AMBLER

Staunton • Route 21 • 52 miles

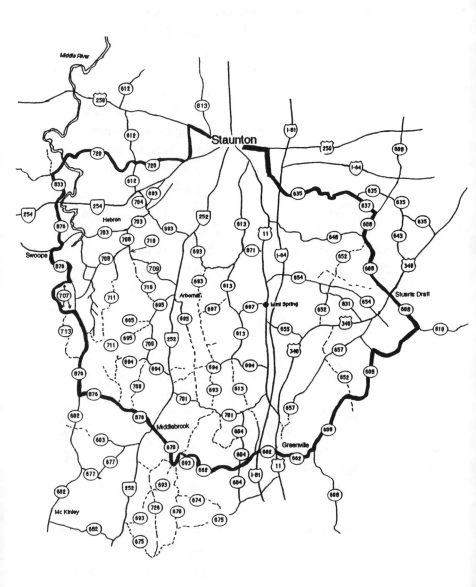

Southern Augusta Ambler

Pedal toward the Allegheny Mountains through open farm lands. Walk around the village of Middlebrook whose preserved architecture has it listed on the National Register of Historic Places. By the time you reach Stuarts Draft, you'll be ready for some chocolate treats from The Candy Store or Mennonite goodies from the Cheese Shop and Kinsingers Bakery. Before finishing your ride, stop off at the Museum of American Frontier Culture for a look at the lifestyle of the Valley's earliest settlers.

0.0 **Begin at intersection of Churchville Ave./Rt. 250 and Springhill Rd. on the north side of Gypsy Hill Park. Proceed WEST on Churchville Ave. with the park on your left.**

0.8 **Turn LEFT at traffic light onto Grubert Ave.**

1.8 **Turn RIGHT at traffic light onto West Beverley St.**

1.9 **Make quick RIGHT turn onto Morris Mill Rd.**

2.4 **Turn LEFT onto Morris Mill Rd./Rt. 720.** The apple orchards along this road are remnants of those that once covered large sections of the Shenandoah Valley in the 1800s.

7.3 **Cross the Middle River.** This river snakes its way north through Augusta County, ultimately flowing into the North River near Grottoes. Together as the North River they join the South River to become the South Fork of the Shenandoah River at Port Republic. The headwaters of the Middle River are located near here at the base of Little North Mt. Morris Mill was once located on the river near this spot. Also called Painter's Mill after a previous owner, it is one of many mills that are long since gone but at one time were as close as a mile apart on the Middle River.

8.0 **Turn LEFT at crest of hill onto Rt. 833.** "Keller Fort" once stood **.9 mile** to the right on Rt. 833 where the road forded the Middle

River at Trinity Point. Sturdy stone houses such as this one offered protection to area settlers in the event of Indian attacks. Alexander and Mary Crawford found refuge here in 1764, but were then killed by Shawnees in Augusta County's last massacre after leaving to tend to their nearby farm. The derivation of the name Trinity Point is somewhat vague. It's possible that it referred to the point on the Middle River where three roads converged at a well-used ford. On the other hand, the presence of a nearby Dunker church called Episcopal Trinity Chapel may have lent its name in some way.

8.8　　The red barn on the left is a good example of a bank barn. The earthen ramp makes it a lot easier to get farm equipment to the second floor.

9.2　　**Turn RIGHT at STOP sign onto Rt. 254 West and with CAUTION make a quick LEFT turn onto Rt. 876.** The building on the left just before this intersection is the Lambsgate Bed and Breakfast. It was built around 1816, and family legend has it that Gen. Stonewall Jackson visited here during the Civil War. This road, known as the Parkersburg Turnpike, was constructed in 1838 as one of Virginia's "super highways." Parkersburg, West Virginia, 234 miles west of here, was an important city because of its location on the Ohio River. The brick building on the corner to the left was an early consolidated school built in 1898 and known as the Valley Mill School. This two-room school was sold to a doctor from Craigsville in 1948. The Valley Mill was located just east of here on the Middle River.

10.9　　**Turn RIGHT onto Rt. 703.**

11.3　　From the bridge over the Chesapeake and Ohio Railroad, cyclists can get a good view of Little North Mountain, part of the Allegheny chain that forms the western edge of the Shenandoah Valley. Also visible is Elliots Knob which at 4,463 feet is the tallest peak in the George Washington National Forest. The C&O, originally called the Virginia Central Railroad, was the Valley's first railroad and began running to Staunton in 1854.

11.6　　**Turn LEFT onto Rt. 876.** This area is called **Swoope** (pronounced Swōpe) after Jacob Swoope, the first elected mayor of Staunton. He donated land for the railroad depot around which the community, Swoope's Depot, sprang up in the 1850s.

12.4　　Wheatlands, the Swoope homeplace, is off to the left. This brick house was built in 1813 by George Washington Swoope and was used as winter headquarters by Confederate Gen. Fitzhugh Lee from 1864-65. The barns and mill were burned by Yankee troops.

12.8 Bear RIGHT on Rt. 876/707. Gravel Rt. 707 goes left.

13.4 Turn RIGHT onto Rt. 707.

13.7 Meadow View, the former home of John Trimble, is on the left. He settled this land on an original grant from Col. William Beverley in the 1730s. There was a mill built in the area as early as 1746. This is not the same John Trimble who was the last Augusta County settler killed by Native Americans in 1764.

13.9 The conical knob rising above the landscape to the left is Sugar Loaf Mountain. The area around it was settled by German Lutherans in the 1700s.

14.1 Bear LEFT on Rt. 707 at bend in road. Gravel Rt. 705 goes right. Watch for loose gravel in the road.

14.2 Cross the Middle River and bear LEFT on Rt. 707. Rt. 806 goes right to the Boy Scout Camp.

14.8 Bethlehem United Methodist Church was founded in 1852, and the present brick structure was built in 1917. The graveyard has markers dating back to the mid-1800s. Augusta County Methodists began as the Methodist Episcopal Church in 1806 and grew slowly. By 1882 there were 20 such congregations in the county.

15.4 Turn RIGHT at STOP sign onto Rt. 876.

16.4 The Glebe Farm is on the left. Glebe lands were those properties set aside before the Revolutionary War for the use of the minister of the Episcopal Church, the official church of England. However, the Church disassociated itself from this 200-acre farm around 1800. The current farm buildings were built long after that.

16.7 In the hollow off to the right stands the old Glebe Schoolhouse. It was built before the Civil War as a private school for a few area children, but was later integrated into the public school system as Glebe House #9. It ceased operating shortly after the turn of the century. The Glebe cemetery, located behind the school, contains some of the oldest stone markers in Augusta County including victims of early Indian skirmishes as well as Revolutionary War soldiers. These include the grave of Col. John Willson, a member of the House of Burgesses from 1746-1773.

19.7 **Turn LEFT onto Rt. 876 by the large three-story brick house on the left.** This home was built in the 1950s on the site of the original manor house for the 1,000-acre Harper Farm.

20.2 Brookside, the yellow house across the field on the right, was built in the 1880s. Its walls were formed by pouring a mortar mix over stacked fieldstones, a method called rubble construction, and cost $150 in 1880.

20.8 Heritage Hill, with its two-story portico, sits on top of the hill to the right. George Mish built it in 1832 on a 1,000-acre tract that was part of the Borden Grant, a 92,000-acre grant that extended south from Beverley's Grant. The Pennsylvania-style barn behind the house was built in 1814 from bricks and 50 x 100 foot oak framing. The barn is one of two brick barns in Augusta County and is on the National Register of Historic Places. Bricks for both the house and barn were made from clay along the banks of the creek in front of the house.

21.1 **Turn RIGHT at STOP sign onto Rt. 252 and make a quick LEFT turn onto Rt. 670 at Middlebrook.** Its name comes from the branch of Back Creek that passes through the middle of town. This is one of the oldest and best preserved villages in Augusta County and is definitely worth a look around. Town lots were first sold in 1799, and Middlebrook's location on the Staunton-Brownsburg Turnpike between Staunton and Lexington as well as its proximity to railroad lines fostered its growth into the 1880s. The entire village is on the National Register of Historic Places. Be sure to stop in on stained glass artisans, Karen and Mike Holson, who operate *A Cut Above* out of their home in the center of town. If they're not at work in this former church parsonage dating back to 1866, they may be on the road playing bluegrass music with their group The Original Blend. Speaking of good homegrown music, Robin and Linda Williams, featured performers on Garrison Keiler's Prairie Home Companion, are local residents as well. ★ **Food and drinks are available at the Middlebrook General Store.** ★ After turning onto Rt. 670, you'll notice the pair of brick buildings on the left that once served as the Middlebrook School. Both were built in the early 1900s and were closed in the early 1970s.

23.5   The gray house in the hollow to the right is known as the Wiseman Place. It may be obscured by vegetation. This two-story log house was built in the early 1800s.

23.8   Bear LEFT on Rt. 693. Several gravel roads intersect here—just stay on the hard surface road.

24.3   Bear RIGHT on Rt. 662. Gravel Rt. 693 goes straight.

25.8   The limestone outcroppings on the left are indicative of karst topography. Another characteristic is the presence of caverns. There is at least one of these known to exist in this hill.

26.3   The creek that runs under Rt. 662 is the beginning of the South River which flows north through Augusta County before meeting the Middle and North Rivers at Port Republic. The three rivers combine there to become the South Fork of the Shenandoah River. This section of the county is called the Riverheads District because the headwaters of two rivers arise here. Many of the creeks flow north and become part of the Shenandoah, but just south of here the waters flow southward and then empty into the James River. For an interesting **1.4 mile** sidetrip, turn right onto gravel Rt. 673 past an old quarry site. Springdale Water Gardens is at the end of the road. The owners have constructed more than 16 ponds and water gardens for customers to browse around. It's an especially nice stop when the water lilies are in bloom. They also have a number of large pond goldfish for sale.

28.6   Cross Rt. 11 at STOP sign with CAUTION and then turn RIGHT on Rt. 1205. Proceed through Greenville. Before turning right onto Rt. 1205, look to the left at the large brick house on the north bank of the South River. This is Greenville's oldest building and was built in the 1700s. It was once a tavern, and legend has it that singer Kate Smith, famous for her renditions of *America the Beautiful* and often called the "Songbird of the South," was born in this tavern when her family was visiting relatives in Greenville.

28.8   Turn LEFT onto Rt. 662 or ★ proceed straight on Rt. 1205 .4 mile for food and drinks at Greenville Grocery. ★ Greenville was the first Augusta County town platted after Staunton and Waynesboro. Thomas and Jane Steele laid out the town in 1794. It was named after Gen. Nathanael Greene, who commanded many local residents during the Revolutionary War. The town prospered because of its location on the Valley Road as well as proximity to nearby Baltimore and Ohio, and Norfolk and Western Railroads. Stage coaches stopped here as early as 1800. Greenville eventually replaced Middlebrook as a transportation crossroads. The old Greenville School on the right was built in 1913 and closed in the early 1970s.

29.0   The Blue Ridge Mts. loom straight ahead. Almost all of this mountainland is part of the George Washington National Forest which encompasses over one million acres. The white scarred areas at the base of the range are the remains of kaolin mines. This white, yellow and red clay was used for pottery and camouflage paint during WWII. The mines operated from the turn of the century until 1951 when a fire destroyed the plant.

30.3   **Caution: RR crossing after steep downhill.** This was formerly a post office and rail stop called **Ellard.** The Shenandoah Valley Railroad Co., later the Norfolk and Western, first came through here in the 1880s. Watch for large trucks and debris in road from the lumber curing yard.

31.3   **Turn LEFT at STOP sign onto Rt. 608 after crossing Pine Run.**

32.2   The Spring Valley Church of the Living God was built in the 1900s, and its cemetery contains several handmade stones from the turn of the century.

34.9   Hatton Pond Baptist Church on the left has continued to serve its black congregations since 1882. Its name comes from Hatton Pond, just over the hill. According to local folklore, it was customary for single men to toss their hats onto the pond. Interested women would then choose the hat of the man they wanted to date.

35.2   **Bear RIGHT at Y-intersection staying on Rt. 608.**

37.5   **Turn LEFT at STOP sign staying on Rt. 608.** The Howardsville and Rockfish Turnpike crossed the Blue Ridge Mts. and was an important link to the James River and cities to the east. In 1848 the turnpike ran from Nelson County to Greenville. It was later extended to meet the Middlebrook-Brownsburg Turnpike.

37.7   **Cross the South River.**

38.2   **Cross RR tracks with CAUTION.** The **Stuarts Draft** Post Office was established here in 1837, probably named for Robert Stuart who ran a nearby chopping mill. The post office was about one mile from the present village, both of which were moved in 1882 to the new railroad station. Before you see it on the left, a good breeze will alert you to the presence of the Hershey Chocolate plant. Hard-core chocoholics may actually be able to pick out the individual scents of the Reese's Pieces, Whatchamacallits, Reese's Cups, and Bar Nones that are produced here. Although there are no provisions for sampling the wares at the factory itself, The Candy Shop, located ahead at the intersection of Rt. 608 and Rt. 340, carries a complete line of Hershey products. ★ **Food and drinks are widely available.** ★

39.0 **Cross Rt. 340 at traffic light with CAUTION.** Reid's Chapel, on the right, has served black United Methodist congregations since the late 1800s. The Candy Shop is on the left side of Rt. 608.

39.7 The Cheese Shop on the right is an Amish-Mennonite run business and carries an ample selection of dried fruits, nuts, breads, cheeses as well as other on and off the bike snacks. If your appetite runs to baked goods, turn left onto Rt. 651 and check out Kinsinger's Kountry Kitchen "where everything is made from scratch."

42.5 **Turn LEFT onto Rt. 637.**

44.6 **Cross Christians Creek.** Gilbert Christian and his family settled along this creek bearing their name about 1732.

47.0 This quaint white frame church on the left side was built in the late 1800s as Hammond Chapel for Methodist worship. During the Depression, local Presbyterians held revivals here. It now serves as the Augusta Christian Church.

47.6 **Turn right onto Frontier Dr.** To enter the Museum of American Frontier Culture, turn at the entrance **.5 mile** on the right. This living history museum is comprised of actual working farms that have been moved to this site from England, Ireland, Germany, and the southern Shenandoah Valley. Betsy Bell and Mary Gray Mt., on the left, were named by early Scots-Irish settlers as a remembrance to similar twin peaks in the old country. The two Scottish peaks were said to have been named after sisters who perished from the plague in 1645. A 50-acre tract of Betsy Bell was deeded to the City of Staunton in 1941 with several stipulations. These included the land's use as a public park with the timber cut so as to exhibit a cross, and that a majority of the members of city council visit the peak every spring.

47.9   Enter Staunton.

48.9   Turn LEFT at traffic light onto Richmond Rd. and proceed with CAUTION.

50.6   Pass the Staunton Correctional Center on the left and turn RIGHT at traffic light. Ride under RR overpass and continue uphill on Coalter St.

50.9   Turn LEFT onto Frederick St. by Woodrow Wilson Birthplace and Museum. Stop by the Staunton Welcome Center on the left for area information.

51.1   Turn RIGHT onto New St. at traffic light with Mary Baldwin College on the right. Follow signs for Churchville Ave./Rt. 250 West.

51.5   Cross Augusta St. at traffic light with the newly renovated Staunton Library on the right in the old school building.

51.8   Bear RIGHT on Churchville Ave./Rt. 250 West at entrance to Gypsy Hill Park.

51.9   Bear LEFT at traffic light staying on Rt. Churchville Ave./Rt. 250 West.

52.0   End ride at starting point.

Historic Lexington

Home of Robert E. Lee and Stonewall Jackson

ROUTES

Historic Lexington
Home of Robert E. Lee and Stonewall Jackson

It's only natural that a town named after the site of the first battle of the Revolutionary War would also have its share of military history. In 1778 the people of this Virginia town decided to call their home Lexington after the historic Massachusetts community of the same name. Over the next 100 years or so, four generals and a renowned scientist would be linked with the city.

Visitors will notice Lexington's two colleges that sit side by side next to the historic downtown area. Washington and Lee University was founded in 1777 as Liberty Hall Academy at a site several miles north. George Washington saved the financially floundering school in 1796 with a gift of $50,000 in stock from the James River Canal Company. It was subsequently renamed to honor his generosity. Confederate General Robert E. Lee became the school's president after the Civil War and spent his remaining years there. His role in reviving the educational quality of the war-torn campus was considerable, and in 1871 the name was formally changed to Washington and Lee. Lee's shadow still lingers among the older buildings, particularly Lee Chapel where he is buried, and his office remains on display just as he left it when he died in 1870.

Up on the hill next door is the Virginia Military Institute. VMI was founded in 1839 as the nation's first state-supported military college. Its austere, tan buildings on the "post" stand in contrast to W&L's stately columns and covered porticos. General Stonewall Jackson taught "Natural Philosophy" at VMI from 1851 until the outbreak of the Civil War in 1861. A visit to the Stonewall Jackson House, a few doors from the Lexington Visitor Center on East Washington Street, will answer many questions about this enigmatic man. This modest brick home is the only residence he ever owned. Daily guided tours provide visitors with a complete picture of the life of this distinguished Civil War tactician as well as the period in which he lived here.

The George C. Marshall Museum, located at the south end of the VMI

Historic Lexington

City Map

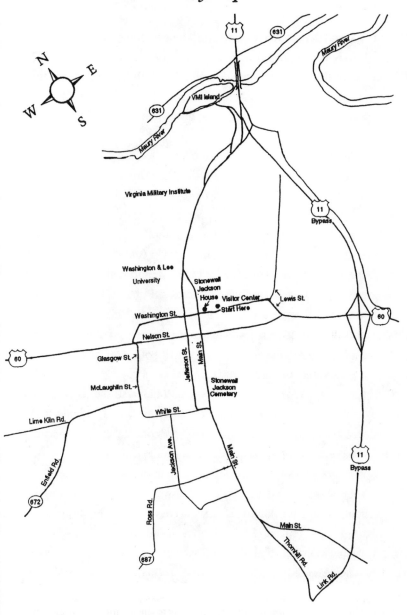

The statue of Stonewall Jackson stands in front of the arch at the Barracks bearing his name at VMI. He used the cannons in the foreground to teach military strategy during his tenure at the school from 1851 to 1861.

parade ground, will spark some interest in those more interested in contemporary military history. Subsequent to graduating from VMI in 1901, Marshall went on to lead a distinguished career. In addition to earning the rank of general during World War II, he is the only military person to have ever won the Nobel Prize for Peace. He received this honor for his European Recovery Plan.

Commodore Matthew Fontaine Maury, a professor of meteorology at VMI, also left his mark on history. Maury was known as "The Pathfinder of the Seas" and helped organize the National Weather Service. The river flowing through Lexington bears his name.

Visitors to Lexington will find unique shops tucked into the same 19th century buildings that have brought Hollywood moviemakers here to film scenes from bygone days. Most recently, these streets provided a backdrop for Richard Gere and Jodie Foster during the filming of *Sommersby* in the fall of 1992. Pick up the Walking Tours guide to the downtown area from the Visitor Center or hop into one of the horse-drawn carriages to get a taste of the city's history and charm. The Rockbridge Historical Society, open Monday-Friday 9AM - 4PM, is located across the street from the Visitor Center

Rockbridge County surrounds the town and is named for Natural Bridge, one of the Seven Natural Wonders of the World, which stands at the southern end of the county. The county was formed in 1778 from Augusta County. Although largely agricultural, the county saw an influx of industries with the arrival of the North River Navigation System in the 1850s and the railroads in the 1880s. In addition to its historic past and natural beauty, this area has attractions which draw an increasing number of visitors each year. These include competitive events at the Virginia Horse Center, outdoor drama at the Theater at Lime Kiln, the Rockbridge Community Festival in August, and the Lexington Road and River Relay in early May.

All routes begin and end at the Lexington Visitor Center at 102 East Washington Street. The center is open 9AM - 5PM daily.

OUT AND BACK
Lexington • Route 22 • 20.2 miles

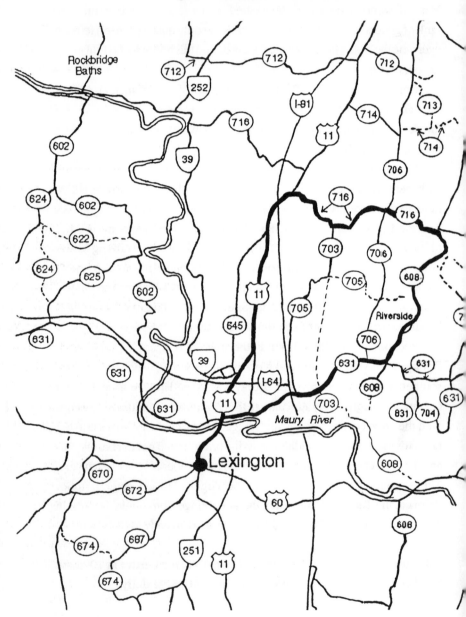

Out and Back

Try this ride for a short one, a warm-up, or just a chance to stretch the legs a little. Head out on the Valley Road, a trail used by Native Americans and bison, which early settlers followed on their migration from Pennsylvania. Return along the South River and be back in time for lunch at Spankys.

0.0   **Turn RIGHT from Visitor Center parking lot heading WEST on E. Washington St.**

0.1   **Turn RIGHT at traffic light onto Main St. Follow Main St./Rt. 11 past VMI.**

0.9   **Follow Rt. 11 North across overpass.**

1.1   **Bear RIGHT at STOP sign onto Rt. 11 North. Cross bridge over Maury River with CAUTION.** Once called the North River, the Maury was renamed for Commodore Matthew Fontaine Maury, who taught meteorology at VMI. Route 11 roughly parallels the Great Wagon Road here.

1.2   **Proceed on Rt. 11 after traffic light with CAUTION for the next 5.6 miles.** The hill after the bridge is Hunter Hill. Maj. Gen. David Hunter commanded the Union troops that topped this hill in June 1864 on their way into Lexington. They ransacked and burned homes, mills, iron foundries, and buildings on the VMI campus. Hunter was driven out by Confederate Gen. Jubal Early.

1.9   **CAUTION: Traffic entering and exiting I-64.**

5.9   **CAUTION: Traffic entering and exiting I-81.** Edge Hill, on the left across from the convenience store, was built in the early 1800s and had extensive renovation done in 1866. It's been a homeplace to the Campbell, Alexander, and Lyle families. ★ **Food and drinks are available at the convenience store on the right.** ★

6.3 Maple Hall, on the left, was built in 1850 by John Gibson. Apparently Gibson's intent in building this elaborate Greek Revival-style home was to outdo his neighbors. Maple Hall now operates as an inn and restaurant.

6.6 **Turn RIGHT onto Rt. 716/785 at Sam Houston Wayside.** Houston is primarily associated with Tennessee where he was a congressman and governor; and then Texas, where he led the army in its fight against Mexico, and later served as President of the Republic of Texas, and governor and senator from the state of Texas. However, he was actually a native Virginian, born nearby in a log cabin in 1793.

6.7 **Continue STRAIGHT on Rt. 716. Rt. 716 also goes left.** Washington and Lee University had its roots near this site when Rev. William Graham, a Presbyterian minister, moved his family and the school, then Liberty Hall, here in the 1770s. Twelve men were the school's first graduates in 1785. Even Sam Houston attended sporadically between 1801 and 1807. Timber Ridge Presbyterian Church was organized in 1746, and the building erected in 1756. It is the only pre-Revolutionary War Presbyterian church still being used in Rockbridge County. The mansion behind the cemetery is known as Church Hill. It was built in 1866 by Rev. Horatio Thompson, pastor at the Associate Reformed Presbyterian Church across the road. It is a Registered Virginia Landmark.

6.9 **Begin climbing Timber Ridge.** Timber Ridge was one of the first areas settled and farmed in Rockbridge County in the 1700s.

7.9 Williams Dairy is in the hollow to the left. This farm was established by John Mackey who also built the Timber Ridge Presbyterian Church. His farm dates back to 1724 when he received a land grant from the British Crown. This property has never been sold. Mackey's original stone house is out of sight at the rear of the property. Mackey's gravesite in the Timber Ridge cemetery is notable for its use of three stones as well as the prophetic, although misspelled, epitaph.

8.1 **Bear LEFT on Rt. 716. Rt. 703 goes right.**

8.3 Rising Zion Baptist Church was built in 1752.

9.7 **Continue STRAIGHT at STOP sign on Rt. 716.**

11.7   **Turn RIGHT at STOP sign onto Rt. 608. Cornwall** was first named Crowder after Robert Crowder's store. It was later renamed after Cornwall, England, because of the tinworks common to both places. It has been the site of various industries, going back to the 1700s, which produced iron cannonballs, tin, and lumber. ★ **Food and drinks are available at Harvell's Country Store.** ★

12.2   Twin Falls is on the right where Marl Creek flows into the South River. Although tempting, this is on private property.

14.5   **Turn RIGHT at STOP sign onto Rt. 631.** This crossroads is also called **Old Buena Vista.** The remains of a former iron-works stand in the field across Rt. 631. It was built in 1840, and later destroyed by Northern troops during their occupation of Lexington in 1864. This area was seriously affected by flooding after Hurricane Camile in 1969 when waters reached to Neriah Baptist Church. ★ **Food and drinks are available at the South River Market on the left.** ★

15.0   **Turn LEFT onto Rt. 631 at bend in road. Rt. 706 goes right.**

17.4   **Ride under I-81.**

18.3   The Chessie Nature Trail to the left is a seven-mile former railbed. Trains used this route from the late 1800s until 1969. This scenic path along the Maury River is now open to runners, hikers, and equestrians, but not cyclists.

18.5   The stately brick home on the right is called Clifton. It was built in the 1880s by Maj. John Alexander. Its name comes from the views of the cliffs along the Maury River which are visible from the house.

19.0   **Turn LEFT at traffic light onto Rt. 11 and cross bridge over Maury River with CAUTION. Follow signs for Visitor Center.**

19.8   **Bear RIGHT at Y-intersection onto Jefferson St. past W&L.**

20.0   **Turn LEFT at traffic light onto Washington St.**

20.2   **End ride at starting point.**

LAKE ROBERTSON ROUNDUP
Lexington • Route 23 • 25.6 miles

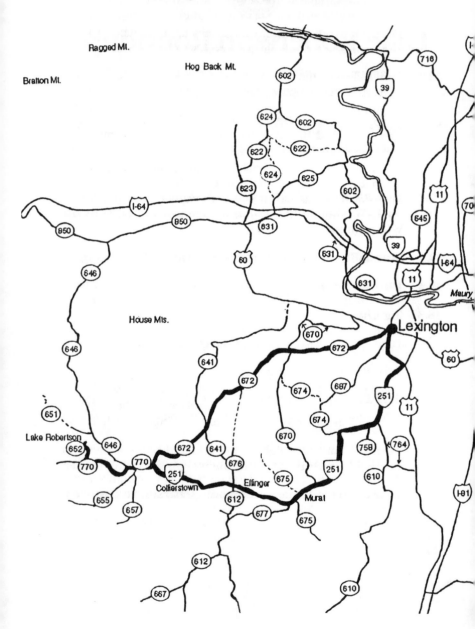

Lake Robertson Roundup

Pedal the same roads that Gen. Robert E. Lee and his horse Traveller used on your way to Lake Robertson. Stop off for a dip in the pool or a paddle around the 31-acre lake in the shadow of House Mountain. You may not be ready to head back at day's end, so plan on spending the night at the campground.

0.0   **Turn RIGHT from Visitor Center parking lot heading WEST on E. Washington St. Continue across Main St. through W&L campus.**

0.3   **Bear LEFT in front of Warner Center at W&L.**

0.4   **Turn LEFT onto Nelson St. and make a quick RIGHT turn onto Glasgow St. in front of Lenfest Center for the Performing Arts.**

0.5   **Turn RIGHT at STOP sign onto McGlaughin St.**

0.7   **Turn RIGHT onto Lime Kiln Rd.**

1.0   **Bear LEFT onto Enfield Rd./ Rt. 672.** Continue straight on Lime Kiln Rd. to go to the Lime Kiln Theater. Rt. 672, also known as Collierstown Road, is a series of ascents and descents including Brushy Hill which crests at 1,550 feet. Union soldiers used this road as an invasion route into Lexington in 1864. After the war, Robert E. Lee used to ride out this way on his horse, Traveller, during breaks from his responsibilities as President at Washington College.

3.6   **Continue on Rt. 672 at intersection with Rt. 670 on the left.**

3.7   **Bear LEFT at STOP sign onto Rt. 672. Rt. 670 is on the right.**

4.4   The large mesa-like rise to the right is actually the twin peaks of Little House and Big House Mountains. Their resistant sandstone composition has left them towering above the largely limestone and dolomite Valley floor.

5.2 The creek bordering the road is Toad Run. Its name comes from that of the German settlers named Todd (pronounced with a long *o*) who lived and established at least one mill in this area.

5.4 Mackey's Tavern, now a private residence, was built in the late 1700s as a tavern and toll stop along the Lexington-Covington Turnpike. The word *turnpike* means a tollroad. The name comes from the device used to stop traffic so that the toll would be paid. The turnpike itself was usually a tall wooden box with a pike, or pole, resting on it. The pole stretched across the road with the opposite end supported by a forked post. The pike was raised or turned after the toll had been paid.

5.6 Bear RIGHT and climb uphill by grassy traffic island. Rt. 676 and Toad Run are on the left.

7.6 Sugarfoot Farm, on the right at the curve in the road, is an example of a typical 1800s farm in one the local hollows. Notice the numerous outbuildings, each with a specific purpose, and the considerable use of local limestone in their construction.

7.8 The House Mts. are straight ahead, and Hogback and Ragged Mts. are off to the right.

9.7 Continue STRAIGHT onto Rt. 770 at STOP sign by Colliers Creek Grocery Store on the left. Rt. 251 is on the left. Across from the store is a set of steps leading up the hill to where an inn and toll collection stop once stood. ★ **Food and drinks are available.** ★

10.1 **Collierstown** is most likely named for John Collier and his family who settled along the nearby creek in the 1700s and built a mill in 1779. However, it's also possible that the name comes from the colliers, or charcoal makers, who operated nearby. The Collierstown Presbyterian Church was organized in 1842. The red brick Greek Revival building was constructed in 1856 and the cemetery at the top of the hill has also been in use since then. If you're into old cemeteries or great vistas, the climb to the top of the hill will be worth it.

10.3 Turn LEFT onto Rt. 770 and cross Herbert Chittum Bridge over Colliers Creek. Rt. 646 goes straight.

11.3   The house on the left with the swinging bridge is the home of Lois Brown, owner and operator of North Mountain Knitters. She makes wool socks, mittens, leg warmers, and scarves on a hand-operated sock loom. This machine is a reproduction of the type originally made and distributed by hosiery companies for home-makers running small cottage industries in the early 1900s. She welcomes visitors into her home to browse through her products.

11.7   **Turn RIGHT at entrance to Lake Robertson and proceed .3 mile to the office.** This 581-acre recreation area is operated by the Virginia Department of Game and Inland Fisheries. It includes a 31-acre lake for fishing and boating, a swimming pool, camp-sites, and 12 miles of hiking trails. The complex is named for A. Willis Robertson who was a former Congressman and Senator from Lexington as well as the father of TV evangelist Pat Robertson.

After an enjoyable stop at Lake Robertson, backtrack down the driveway and road to the intersection of Rt. 770 and Rt. 652. Turn LEFT onto Rt. 770.

13.6   **Turn RIGHT onto Rt. 770 after crossing Herbert Chittum Bridge.**

14.2   **Bear RIGHT on Rt. 251 after passing the Colliers Creek Grocery Store. Rt. 672 goes uphill to the left. Ride with CAUTION on Rt. 251/Harry B. Wright Memorial Highway.**

14.5   Collierstown United Methodist Church was founded in 1840.

15.6   **Bear LEFT on Rt. 251.** The Wade-McCaleb Mill on the right side of Colliers Creek is a private residence built in the 1920s. It sits on the site of the original Colliers Mill that was built in 1779.

16.2   The log houses on the right across the high water bridge were made from handhewn logs. The first house was built from logs salvaged from another log structure that stood on this site as well as timbers from a second location. The second house was built of logs salvaged from another location.

16.5   Clemmer's Store on the right was originally Painters Mill. ★ **Food and drinks are available.** ★

16.8   **Turn RIGHT on Rt. 251 and cross Colliers Creek at Effinger. Rt. 676 and Toad Run go straight.** The large white building across the bridge is a private residence, but was formerly a high school. This community is named for George W. Effinger, who served in Rockbridge County as a teacher, school superintendent, and schoolboard chairman over a span of 26 years.

17.4   Buffalo Creek joins Colliers Creek at this point.

18.6   **Turn LEFT at STOP sign on Rt. 251. Rt. 677 goes right.** The community of **Murat** once included a mill, general store, and post office. Supposedly this village was named by the postmaster after his cat, who in turn was named after Napoleon's general of the same name.

18.8   **Cross the Thomas S. Dixon Bridge over Buffalo Creek.** Buffalo once roamed much of this region; however, it's the trout in this special regulation stream that now attract attention. This creek drains much of southwestern Rockbridge County before emptying into the Maury River.

20.3   The farm on the left utilizes a lot of local limestone in the construction of its walls, chimney, and foundations just as the early settlers did.

21.8   Cyclists can pedal a little easier on what amounts to an excellent bike shoulder on the edge of Rt. 251.

22.8   Spring Meadow Farm on the left was built in 1859.

23.4   Thorn Hill , a red brick Greek Revival mansion, sits up on the hill on the left behind the newer tan house. After its construction around 1792, it was home to Col. John Bowyer, a veteran of the American Revolution. It was later the home of Gen. E.F. Paxton, a commander in the Stonewall Brigade. He was killed in the May 1863 Battle of Chancellorsville which also claimed the life of Stonewall Jackson.

23.8   **Enter Lexington. Rt. 251 becomes Thornhill Rd.**

24.2   **Turn LEFT onto Thornhill Rd. at intersection with Link Rd.**

24.6   **Bear LEFT at STOP sign onto Main St./ Rt. 11 North.**

25.1   Take some time to wander around the Stonewall Jackson Memorial Cemetery where Jackson and other Civil War veterans are buried.

25.5   **Turn RIGHT at traffic light onto Washington St.**

25.6   **End ride at starting point.**

Agriculture

Settlers started trickling into the Shenandoah Valley in the 1720s. The Scots-Irish and Germans trekked southward from Pennsylvania, and the English entered the Valley through Blue Ridge Mountain passes such as Rockfish Gap and Swift Run Gap. For the most part, these early pioneers were farmers who were drawn to the Valley because fertile land was plentiful and cheap, literally pennies an acre.

They grew subsistence crops and raised livestock for their own needs, but many farmers also grew hemp. This material was sold for making sailcloth, ropes, tents, and clothing in the Colonies as well as in England. Valley farmers led the state in hemp production in the 1760s, but it died out after the American Revolution. Cattle were also vital to the Valley's growing agricultural base. These were raised on the range and sold at markets that were miles away. Main thoroughfares like the Great Wagon Road, or Valley Turnpike, were the scene of fall cattle drives in the 1700s and 1800s as drovers walked alongside their herds and moved them from their summer pastures to market in Lexington, Staunton, Harrisonburg, or points north and east of the Valley.

Tobacco was another important crop in some localities. The fact that Colonial taxes and government salaries were paid in quantities of this crop attests to its accepted value. Although tobacco was grown in Rockingham, Augusta, and Rockbridge Counties, it was in Rockbridge that its production was most successful, primarily because of the transportation network with eastern Virginia cities. Thousands of tons of tobacco, wheat, and corn floated down the newly completed North River Navigation System on huge canalboats headed for Richmond in the 1850s. The North River, now known as the Maury River, connected with the James River and Kanawha Canal.

The cultivation of tobacco dwindled to almost nothing after the Civil War. By far, however, the most important Shenandoah Valley crop around the time of the Civil War was wheat. Corn, rye, and hay were also grown in large quantities, but it was wheat for which the Valley was known. Rockingham County produced more wheat and hay in 1850 than any other Virginia county with neighboring Augusta close behind. The area became

Mills such as this one at the McCormick Farm helped the Shenandoah Valley earn the distinction of being the "Breadbasket of the Country." It was at this farm near Raphine that Cyrus McCormick invented the reaper in 1831 causing an agricultural revolution.

known as the "Breadbasket of the Country" for its exportation of grain and flour throughout the United States as well as the rest of the world. In fact, a great deal of local flour was shipped from the east coast, around the tip of South America, and north to California to feed the California 49ers during the gold rush. The Valley also was the "Breadbasket of the Confederacy," and local grain mills were a frequent target of Northern conflagration in an attempt to end the Civil War.

Farmers in the late 1800s moved toward mixed agricultural practices, growing a variety of crops including wheat, corn, and rye in addition to raising cattle, sheep, and hogs. Improved pasteurization processes and shipping on railroads caused an increase in the number of dairy farms as well. Many turn-of-the-century stone milking parlors still stand alongside more modern facilities. Fruit production, particularly peaches and apples, also increased at this time. Be sure to stop by commercial orchards such as Roscoe Sheets' in Augusta County and Osceola and Burkholder's in Rockingham County to sample some just-picked fruit or fresh cider in the fall.

Modern poultry production has joined these other endeavors in the Shenandoah Valley where nearly 50 percent of the land in Augusta, Rockingham, and Rockbridge Counties is still zoned agricultural. Late summer and fall visits will offer the opportunity to enjoy area agricultural fairs that feature a variety of local livestock, produce, and crafts as well as the usual assortment of midway attractions.

GOSHEN GALLOP
Lexington • Route 24 • 35.1 miles

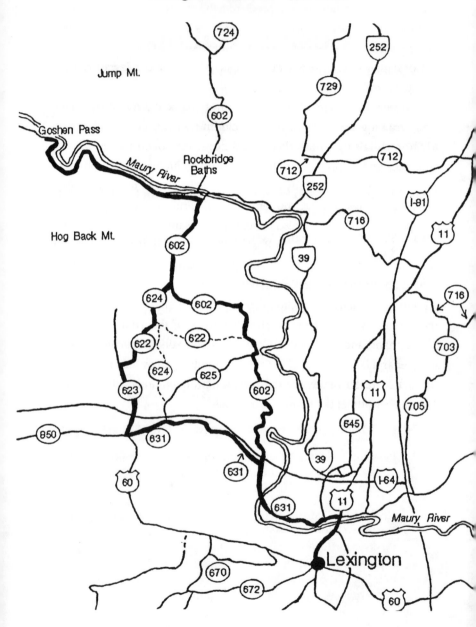

Goshen Gallop

Pedal along the Maury River and enjoy the splendor of Goshen Pass where the river crashes through the Alleghenies. Along the way you can enjoy views of Little House and Big House Mountains. Travelers in the 1800s flocked to Wilson Springs and nearby Rockbridge Baths for their curative properties.

0.0   **Turn RIGHT from Visitor Center parking lot heading WEST on E. Washington St.**

0.1   **Turn RIGHT at traffic light onto Main St. Follow Main St./Rt. 11 past VMI.**

0.9   **Follow Rt. 11 North across overpass.**

1.1   **Bear RIGHT at STOP sign onto Rt. 11 North. Cross bridge over Maury River with CAUTION.** Once called the North River, the Maury was renamed for Commodore Matthew Fontaine Maury, who taught meteorolgy at VMI.

1.2   **Turn LEFT at traffic light immediately after crossing bridge onto Rt. 631.**

1.7   **Bear LEFT at three-way STOP on Rt. 631. Rt. 681 goes right.**

2.2   Pass Furr's Mill on the left. Alfred Leyburn built the first mill here around 1830. D.D. Furr bought it in 1901 and expanded it in 1924. Flour milling ceased in 1962.

3.6   **Cross J.H.C. Mann Bridge over the Maury River at Beans Bottom.** Col. Mann taught Civil and Structural Engineering at VMI for 46 years. Beans Bottom marks the spot in the annual Lexington Road and River Relay where the initial 3.3-mile run ends, the 10-mile bike loop begins and ends, and the 2-mile canoe leg begins. The event takes place on the first Saturday in May.

3.7   The limestone outcroppings on the left are common indicants of karst topography.

4.6   Turn RIGHT onto Rt. 602 and ride under I-64.

4.7   Turn LEFT onto Rt. 602. Rt. 835 goes straight. Begin to ascend Turkey Hill.

6.0   Crest Turkey Hill.

7.3   Bear RIGHT on Rt. 602 at Bethany Evangelical Lutheran Church. Rt. 625 goes left.

7.6   Alone Mill bustled with activity during the 1800s. Alone Mill Creek flows into the Maury River.

8.9   The large mesa-like rise to the left is actually the twin peaks of Little House and Big House Mountains. Their resistant sandstone composition has left them towering above the largely limestone and dolomite Valley floor.

13.3   Turn LEFT at STOP sign and ride with CAUTION on Rt. 39 West. The magnesia springs at **Rockbridge Baths** were one of the many popular 1800s resorts in western Virginia. Although no longer open to the public, they are located within a beige cement block wall across from the Maury River Mercantile. The building housing the store across the street was once part of the dance hall for the resort which included a large hotel before burning in 1926. These baths tended to attract city people including Robert E. Lee, during his tenure as President at Washington College after the Civil War. ★ **The Maury River Mercantile has food and drinks available.** ★

14.5   The former Wilson Springs Hotel is on your left. Construction of this former resort began in 1775 in conjunction with a sulfur spring that flowed out of an island in the Maury River. The hotel was first owned by the Porters (no relation to the author), then the Stricklers, and finally the Wilsons who allowed almost anyone to build a cabin on the property and partake of the medicinal waters. Compared to Rockbridge Baths, this spring tended to attract the rougher, rural folks. During the Civil War, Confederate soldiers camped here to defend Goshen Pass.

16.3   **Goshen Pass Overlook.** During the infamous November 1985 Flood, the Maury River obliterated this overlook and parts of Rt. 39.

It was two years before traffic could once more pass through here. Goshen Pass was first known as Dunlap's Pass and then Strickler's Pass. Later its name was associated with the nearby town of Goshen. This sandstone gap, etched by time, has served as a passage for elk, buffalo, stagecoaches, and the railroad. The body of Commodore Matthew Fontaine Maury, the renowned VMI professor known as the "Pathfinder of the Seas," was carried at his request by a VMI honor guard. His procession went through the pass in May with the rhododendron in bloom. The use of a temporary vault in Lexington solved the dilemma of storing the body after his death in February until May.

16.7   Picnic and bathroom facilities are available at Goshen Pass Wayside. This is also a great wading spot, although don't expect much privacy on any nice weekend from May through September. ★ **Food and drinks are available five miles west on Rt. 39 in the town of Goshen.** ★ The Maury River begins above the western end of the pass with the confluence of the Calfpasture and Little Calfpasture Rivers. **To continue on the route, backtrack from Goshen Pass Wayside, heading east on Rt. 39 toward Rockbridge Baths.**

20.1   **Turn RIGHT onto Rt. 602 just before crossing the Maury River.**

22.0   **Pass Rt. 621 on the right.**

22.8   **Turn RIGHT onto Rt. 624.**

23.8   **Bear RIGHT at curve on Rt. 622. Pass Rts. 624 and 622 on the left.**

25.3   **Turn LEFT at STOP sign onto Rt. 623. Watch for large trucks and debris in road from lumber mill.**

26.5   **Cross over I-64. CAUTION: Traffic entering and exiting interstate.**

27.0   **Turn LEFT at STOP sign onto Rt. 60 East.**

27.1   **Turn LEFT with CAUTION onto Rt. 631.** A stone marker on the left serves as a reminder of the area's last Indian raid. On October 10, 1764, a party of Shawnees came over the mountain and killed 50-60 settlers near the Big Spring. ★ **Food and drinks are** available just ahead on Rt. 60 East at Kerrs Creek Store on the left. ★

28.5 Cross bridge over Kerrs (pronounced *Cars*) Creek. James Kerr and his offspring were among Augusta County's first settlers. Other Kerrs moved south and were putting down roots in Rockbridge County by the early 1740s.

29.3 The gravel road to your left on the other side of Kerrs Creek is the old roadbed. The houses on that side of the creek are older than those on the right. The white house at the top of the hill on the left is the McCowen Place, dating back about 200 years. The spring at the bottom of the hill once supplied water to the house and barns. However, when I-64 was built through here, the Virginia Department of Transportation broke through several caverns above the house and spring. As a result, the spring turned muddy, so VDOT drilled a well for additional water. The problem of cavern collapse is not uncommon in a karst region.

30.3 Continue STRAIGHT on Rt. 631 at intersection with Rt. 602 on the left.

31.2 Cross J.H.C. Mann Bridge over the Maury River at Beans Bottom.

33.3 Continue STRAIGHT at STOP sign on Rt. 631. Rt. 681 goes to the left.

33.6 Turn RIGHT at traffic light and proceed with CAUTION on bridge over Maury River.

33.9 Bear RIGHT on Rt. 11 North.

34.7 Bear RIGHT at Y-intersection onto Jefferson St. past W&L.

34.9 Turn LEFT at traffic light onto Washington St.

35.1 End ride at starting point.

Resort Springs

The Shenandoah Valley falls into the "springs region of Virginia" or "America's Sanitarium" according to the 1870 guide *The Virginia Tourist* by Edward Pollard. For both health and social reasons, visitors flocked to these resorts to drink or bathe in mineral waters that promised curative properties unknown to medical science at the time. Matthew F. Maury, renowned Professor of Meteorology at Virginia Military Institute, is quoted in the 1878 *Physical Survey of Virginia* as saying that Rockbridge County is within "the famous region of mineral waters of Virginia, in, perhaps, the most remarkable region of the world. With a radius of 100 miles, a circle may be drawn, lying chiefly in Virginia, which will include varieties of all the mineral waters of Europe..."

It is questionable as to whether their waters did actually possess the ingredients to combat the devastating diseases of the era including yellow fever and cholera. However, the fact that people did not succumb to these in the mountains gave some credence to the medicinal value of saline, sulfur, chalybeate, alkaline, calcic, and thermal waters.

Let it not be said that the migration to the springs was merely a health craze. Ballroom dancing, bowling alleys, billiards, and carriage rides were just a few of the activities that also attracted guests. Visiting the springs was primarily a summer activity, and it was common for those of sufficient means to spend the hot months at a succession of these resorts in Virginia's western mountains. The rapid growth of the rail system was a key factor in allowing people to travel to relatively inaccessible places.

The springs peaked in popularity in the mid-1800s, declined during the Civil War, regained favor in the late 1800s, and then steadily declined after World War I. Important factors leading to their waning popularity were the automobile and advances in modern medicine. The automobile offered more flexibility in vacation planning so people were no longer limited to resorts simply because they were on a particular railroad line. As doctors were better able to combat certain maladies, the medicinal properties of the springs became less necessary.

The former splendor of many of these spots now exists only as a name on a map, a road sign, or the remnants of a foundation in an overgrown field. Warm, Hot, and Healing Springs in nearby Bath County are the only Virginia spas still open to the public of the dozens listed in Stan Cohen's *Historic Springs of the Virginias*. While pedaling through the Shenandoah Valley, you'll notice various names that refer back to these bygone resorts including Massanetta, Rawley, and Sparkling Springs in Rockingham County; Stribling, Seawright, and Variety Springs in Augusta County; Rockbridge Baths, Wilson, and Rockbridge Alum Springs in Rockbridge County; and Loth and Basic City Lithia Springs in the city of Waynesboro.

This swinging bridge across the Maury River at Rockbridge Baths is fun for the young and the young at heart.

NATURAL BRIDGE LOOP
Lexington • Route 25 • 36.1 miles

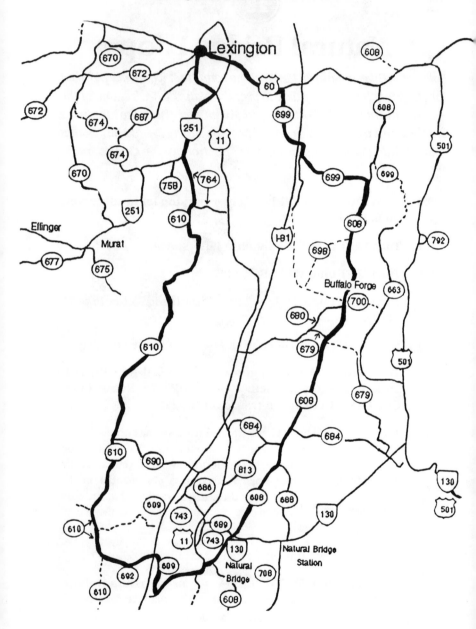

Natural Bridge Loop

Follow the Bikecentennial Route along roads that were once planked for stagecoaches on your way to visit the Natural Bridge, one of the Seven Natural Wonders of the World. Allow enough time to take in the caverns and wax museum. Pedal past the stately Seven Hills Homes and Buffalo Forge, a major source of pig iron for the Confederacy.

0.0   Turn RIGHT from Visitor Center parking lot heading west on E. Washington St.

0.1   Turn LEFT at traffic light onto Jefferson St.

0.5   Turn LEFT onto White St.

0.6   Turn RIGHT onto Main St./ Rt. 11 South and follow *Bike* 76 Route.

1.1   Bear RIGHT onto Thornhill Rd. *Bike* 76 Route goes left.

1.5   Turn RIGHT at STOP sign onto Thornhill Rd./ Rt. 251. Link Rd. is on the left. Rejoin *Bike* 76 Route here. CAUTION: High speed traffic on Rt. 251.

2.2   Thorn Hill, a red brick Greek Revival mansion, sits up on the hill on the right behind the newer tan house. After its construction around 1792, it was home to Col. John Bowyer, a veteran of the American Revolution. Gen. E.F. Paxton, a commander in the Stonewall Brigade, later resided here. He was killed in the May 1863 Battle of Chancellorsville, which also claimed the life of Stonewall Jackson.

2.8   Spring Meadow Farm, on the right, was built in 1859.

3.0   Turn LEFT onto Rt. 764 and ride through Possum Hollow. Follow *Bike* 76 Route. Possum Run is the small creek to the left of the road.

4.1   Bear RIGHT onto Rt. 610. Follow *Bike 76* Route.

5.0   Turn LEFT onto Rt. 610. Rt. 753 goes right. Follow *Bike 76* Route. Cross small bridge and Buffalo Creek is on the right. Note limestone cliffs along the road. Possum Run empties into Buffalo Creek here.

6.3   Cross Buffalo Creek and then bear RIGHT on Rt. 610. Rt. 678 goes left. Notice the large limestone abutments to the right on either side of the creek. These and others along this road are remnants of the ill-fated Valley Railroad project that was planned to run through this area in the late 1800s. It would have connected Staunton, Lexington, and Salem; but went bust during the depression in 1893. The bonds cost Rockbridge County millions of dollars and were finally paid off in 1922. All that remains are intermittent stacks of limestone and masonry culverts throughout the county.

7.2   The brick house on the right was built around 1800 and reflects the significance of this small valley which was, at the time, in the midst of a transportation network consisting of the Plank Road, proposed Valley Railroad, and the nearby Valley Road.

8.5   Cross Broad Creek across from the cement block telephone substation.

13.9   Cross Cedar Creek which runs south through Natural Bridge.

14.2   Longwood stands on the right with its green roof and pillared portico as it has since 1845. The house has remained in the same family since 1868 and now operates as a bed and breakfast inn.

14.6   Turn LEFT onto Rt. 692 at *Plank Road* sign. Follow *Bike 76* Route. Plank, or corduroy, roads were common in the first half of the 1800s. Planks laid across the road provided a smoother surface for wagons.

16.2   Continue STRAIGHT on Rt. 609 and pass under I-81. A left turn onto Rt. 609 will take you to Stone Tavern, **.5 mile** away. This late 1700s inn was a popular stopover point on the Valley Road. It is said that Thomas Jefferson and Daniel Boone signed their names on the building's walls.

16.3 **Turn RIGHT on Rt. 609 and cross bridge at Red Mill. Follow** *Bike 76* **Route.** This was the nucleus of a community on the Valley Road and Cedar Creek that included a late 1700s inn and a mill built around 1865.

17.3 **Turn LEFT at STOP sign onto Rt. 11 North.** *Bike 76* **Route goes right. CAUTION: High speed traffic on Rt. 11.**

19.0 **Turn RIGHT onto Rt. 130. Watch for fast moving traffic on Rt. 130.** The Natural Bridge Complex includes a wax museum, caverns, restaurant, and hotel, all centered around the 215-foot limestone arch that is one of the Seven Natural Wonders of the World. The limestone bridge is actually the remains of an underground cavern that collapsed millions of years ago. George Washington surveyed Natural Bridge in the early 1700s, and Thomas Jefferson purchased it for 20 shillings (about $2.40) in 1774. Information regarding recreational opportunities in the Jefferson National Forest is available across Rt. 130. ★ **Food and drinks are available.** ★

20.2 **Turn LEFT with CAUTION onto Rt. 608 at bend by Natural Bridge Animal Hospital. Stay on Rt. 608 for the next 9.6 miles.** ★ **Food and drinks are available at Natural Bridge General Store just ahead on Rt. 130.** ★

22.0 On the hill to the right stands Marlbrook. The oldest part of this red brick house was built in the 1770s by David Greenlee Sr. He called the mansion Cherry Hill because of the cherry orchard he'd planted on the grounds. In the late 1700s and early 1800s members of the Grigsby and Greenlee families built seven large homes atop various hills in this vicinity. Reminiscent of the Seven Hills of Rome, Cherry Hill and the others are known as the Seven Hills Homes.

22.3 **Bear LEFT on Rt. 608. Rt. 688 goes right.**

22.5 This area is often referred to as **Tinkerville** for "Tink" McCullough who built the first cabin here.

22.8 **Continue STRAIGHT at STOP sign on Rt. 608. Rt. 684 goes to the left.**

23.3 **Continue STRAIGHT on Rt. 608. Rt. 684 goes to the right toward Glasgow.**

23.7   Hickory Hill on the left is another of the Seven Hills Homes. Reuben Grigsby built it in the 1820s.

24.4   Be sure to pull over at the crest of the hill at Mt. Zion United Methodist Church for a grand view of the Blue Ridge Mountains. This particular section ahead is Rocky Row Mountain and is located in the George Washington National Forest.

25.5   The fields to the left provide a clear view down to Falling Spring Presbyterian Church in the distance. This congregation first met in a log structure in 1746, and built the present one in 1862. Confederate troops camped in these fields during the Civil War.

26.3   Vineyard Hill, the stone house on the left, was built by Alexander Beggs in the late 1700s.

26.8   **Cross Buffalo Creek. Buffalo Forge** was a major producer of iron from 1800 through the Civil War. The community was centered on this stretch of Buffalo Creek and included a gristmill, general store, sawmill, blacksmith shop, leather shop, carpenter, post office, and ice house. Pig iron was produced from iron ore and shipped to Richmond for the manufacture of cook stoves, farm machinery, and, during the Civil War, Confederate munitions.

29.8   **Turn LEFT onto Rt. 699 at Y-intersection.**

30.4   **Bear RIGHT on Rt. 699 by Wesley United Methodist Church, built in 1873. Rt. 697 goes left.**

32.2   **Bear LEFT on Rt. 699 and cross over I-81. Gravel Rt. 700 goes right. CAUTION: Steep, curvy downhill road ahead.**

33.8   **Cross eastbound lanes of Rt. 60 at STOP sign with CAUTION and turn LEFT onto Rt. 60 West. CAUTION: High speed traffic on Rt. 60.**

35.8   **Turn RIGHT onto Lewis St. after entering Lexington.**

35.9   **Bear LEFT onto Washington St.**

36.1   **End ride at starting point.**

Civil War Destruction

The Battle of New Market on May 15, 1864, broke a two-year peace that had existed in most of the Shenandoah Valley since Stonewall Jackson's successful campaign. This engagement is probably best remembered for the gallant efforts of 247 teenage cadets from VMI who marched from Lexington to join Gen. John Breckinridge's 5,000 regular army soldiers in their defense of the Valley against 6,500 Northern troops. Despite the loss of 10 cadets, this was a great victory and the only time in history that a battle flag was captured by college students.

Unfortunately for the Confederacy and the Shenandoah Valley, this victory was short-lived. The total devastation that followed far overshadowed this temporary bit of solace. Gen. Robert E. Lee recalled Breckinridge and his two brigades to reinforce the troops to the east at Cold Harbor. With the way clear, Gen. David Hunter, a native Virginian, moved his Union forces through the Shenandoah Valley with a rage and a penchant to not only destroy, but to totally devastate the Confederate forces and the citizens in the Valley.

Hunter and his men moved south and took Staunton after a victory at the Battle of Piedmont near Weyers Cave on June 5, 1864. For the next five days, the Queen City was the target of Northern burning and looting, with damages amounting to about $1,000,000. Although Grant had given orders to head toward Charlottesville to cut off the rail line there, Hunter opted to continue south through the Valley to Lexington. Burning mills along the way, the Union troops entered Lexington after some minor resistance from Confederate soldiers and VMI cadets. The hill along Rt. 11 that descends to the Maury River at East Lexington, still carries the name Hunter Hill to mark the point at which Hunter was temporarily delayed on his way into town.

Hunter vented an even greater wrath for two days in Lexington, probably because it was the home of Virginia Military Institute, the West Point of the South. His wave of destruction far exceeded the military value of the operation. The buildings at VMI were destroyed and lecture halls at Washington College were used for stables. Even the libraries at both schools and the residences of VMI professors were targets of his seemingly vindictive torch. Despite the overwhelming mob mentality that Gen. Hunter promoted among his troops, it seems that a great many Yankee soldiers stopped to pay homage at the grave of Stonewall Jackson, who had died May 10, 1863 at the Battle of Chancellorsville. His home was protected by an armed Northern guard.

Hunter then moved his army toward Lynchburg, but was driven back into West Virginia by Gen. Jubal Early. Given the rampant destruction that had taken place, it seemed amazing that after just three weeks, Early's men, including the Stonewall Brigade, returned to their hometown; and Staunton once again resumed its role as an important Confederate supply depot. Continuing north, Early cleared the Shenandoah Valley of remaining Union troops and advanced to the outskirts of the Northern capital in Washington, D.C. in July 1864.

In August 1864, Gen. Ulysses S. Grant transferred Gen. Philip Sheridan from Petersburg to take on Early. Three brigades of "the best of cavalry, numbering at least five thousand men and horses" were ordered to push southward through the Valley and "take all provisions, forage, and stock needed and such as cannot be consumed, destroy... Do all the damage to railroads and crops you can... If the war is to last another year, we want the Shenandoah Valley to remain a barren waste."

The Union cavalry carried out its assignment well, and Sheridan informed his superiors that "a crow would perish in the Valley." Upon learning, erroneously, that one of his officers had been killed, Sheridan ordered all homes within a five-mile radius to be burned. In all, over 2,000 barns and 70 mills were torched. His men destroyed 435,800 bushels of wheat, 3,800 horses, 10,900 cattle, 12,000 sheep, 77,000 bushels of corn, 12,000 pounds of bacon, and 20,400 tons of hay according to James Robertson's *Civil War Virginia-Battleground for a Nation.*

Union troops under General David Hunter and later Philip Sheridan laid the Shenandoah Valley to waste in 1864.

BRATTON'S RUN
Lexington • Route 26 • 45.7 miles

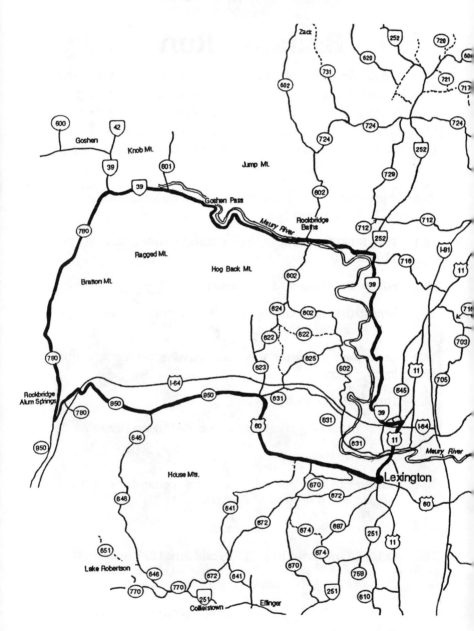

Bratton's Run

This ride is not for the faint of heart or body. Olympic hopefuls and Tour Du Pont wannabes will be at home on this ride that offers no historical info but a good workout on more heavily traveled roads. If your idea of a good ride is spinning big gears and not taking your feet off the pedals 'til the end, try this one. Armchair racers need not apply.

0.0 **Turn RIGHT from Visitor Center parking lot heading WEST on E. Washington St.**

0.1 **Turn RIGHT at traffic light onto Main St. Follow Main St./ Rt. 11 past VMI.**

0.9 **Follow Rt. 11 North across overpass.**

1.1 **Bear RIGHT at STOP sign onto Rt. 11 North. Cross bridge over Maury River with CAUTION.**

1.2 **Continue up Hunter Hill after crossing bridge at traffic light.**

2.3 **Turn LEFT onto Rt. 39 West.**

3.4 Watch for trucks and horse trailers from the Virginia Horse Center.

12.2 Rockbridge Baths.

16.4 Goshen Pass Overlook. With views this spectacular, even Greg Lamond would stop and take a peak.

16.8 Goshen Pass Wayside is on the right.

21.7 **Cross RR tracks with CAUTION and turn LEFT onto Rt. 780.**

30.4 **Turn LEFT at STOP sign onto Rt. 850.**

31.2 **Continue STRAIGHT on Rt. 850 at intersection with Rt. 780 on the right.**

31.8   Bear RIGHT on Rt. 850 at intersection with Rt. 633 on the left. CAUTION: Steep downhill with hairpin curves ahead.

39.3   Continue STRAIGHT on Rt. 60 East at intersection with Rt. 631 on the left.

39.4   ★ Food and drinks are available at Kerr's Creek Store on the left. ★ You don't have to admit to needing a break–blame it on some mechanical problem.

43.0   ★ If you breezed past the last store at 35 mph, Kellys Corner Store on the left is a good place to stop and get that stone out of your shoe. ★

44.3   ★ Maybe it's time to admit that Power Bars® and Gatorade® just aren't cutting it. The Shell station and convenience store on the right may even have some good old Mountain Dew® and a Moon Pie. ★

44.7   **Enter Lexington.** You may want to slow it down through town.

45.5   **Turn LEFT at traffic light onto Main St.**

45.6   **Turn RIGHT at traffic light onto Washington St.**

45.7   **End ride at starting point.** Check your time and pulse and then collapse. You earned it.

Co-author Randy Porter marvels at the spectacular Goshen Pass no matter how many times he travels through there.

BLUE RIDGE RAMBLE

Lexington • Route 27 • 53.7 miles

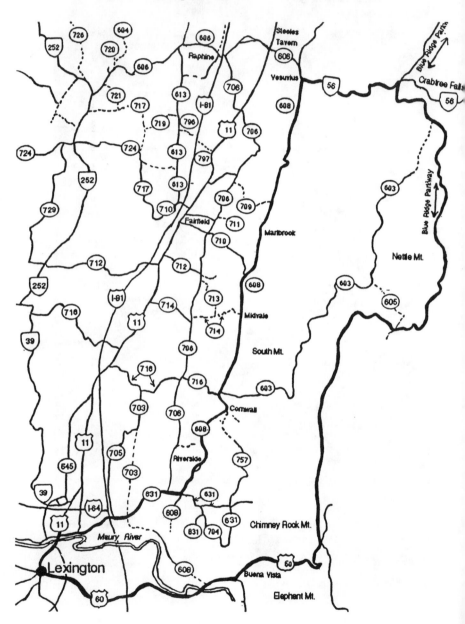

Blue Ridge Ramble

Start out with a few healthy ups and downs before coasting along the South River. Then climb one of the Bikecentennial Route's toughest hills up to the Blue Ridge Parkway. Views of the Valley are enhanced from atop these 200-million-year-old peaks. For an added adventure, take a sidetrip to Crabtree Falls, the tallest waterfall east of the Mississippi.

0.0   Turn RIGHT from Visitor Center parking lot heading WEST on E. Washington St.

0.1   Turn RIGHT at traffic light onto Main St. Follow Main St./Rt. 11 past VMI.

0.9   Follow Rt. 11 North across overpass.

1.1   Bear RIGHT at STOP sign onto Rt. 11 North. Cross bridge over Maury River with CAUTION. Once called the North River, the Maury was named for Commodore Matthew Fontaine Maury, who taught meteorology at VMI.

1.2   Turn RIGHT at traffic light onto Rt. 631 immediately after crossing bridge.

1.7   The stately brick home on the left is called Clifton. It was built in the 1880s by Maj. John Alexander. Its name comes from the views of the cliffs along the Maury River which are visible from the house.

1.9   The Chessie Nature Trail to the right is a seven-mile former railbed. Trains used this route from the late 1800s until 1969. This scenic path along the Maury River is now open to runners, hikers, and equestrians, but not cyclists.

2.8   Ride under I-81.

5.1   Neriah Baptist Church, on the left, was built in 1816.

5.2 Turn RIGHT at STOP sign onto Rt. 631. Rt. 706 goes left.

5.7 **Cross bridge over the South River and immediately turn left onto Rt. 608 at South River Market.** This crossroads is also called **Old Buena Vista.** The remains of a former ironworks stand in the field across Rt. 631. It was built in 1840, and was destroyed by Northern troops during their occupation of Lexington in 1864. This area was seriously affected by flooding after Hurricane Camile in 1969 when waters reached to Neriah Baptist Church. ★ **Food and drinks are available.** ★

6.8 **Riverside.**

7.3 The swinging foot bridge, on the left by the green dumpsters, is one of many accessing the opposite banks of the South River along this road.

8.0 Twin Falls is on the left where Marl Creek flows into the South River. Although tempting, this is on private property.

8.6 **Cornwall** was first named Crowder after Robert Crowder's store. It was later renamed after Cornwall, England, because of the tinworks common to both places. Going back to the 1700s, it has been the site of various industries which produced iron cannonballs, tin, and lumber. ★ **Food and drinks are available at Harvell's Country Store.** ★

10.2 Mallard Duck Campground is on the left.

12.0 **Midvale**.

13.2 For a good view of South Mountain, turn left onto Rt. 710, cross the RR tracks, and look back toward the Blue Ridge.

14.4 The town of **Marlbrook** and Marl Creek are named for the area's abundance of marl. This substance is similar to limestone and formed as a product of ocean sediment in the area millions of years ago. Farmers used marl as a fertilizer through the early 1900s.

16.8 Virginia Federation of Garden Clubs Nature Camp is on the right.

17.6 **CAUTION: RR tracks at the bottom of the hill.**

19.5 **Vesuvius** was once the site of an ironworks, an industry marked by intense heat, molten rock, and smoke. The similarities to volcanic action are the reason for the name of this village. ★ **Food and drinks are available at CT Cash Store.** ★ **Cross RR tracks onto Rt. 56 East. This is the start of a 3.8 mile twisty climb with a change in elevation of 1,500 feet. It's one of the toughest climbs on the 4,250-mile TransAmerica Trail. Proceed with extreme caution, stay as far to the right as possible, and yield to vehicular traffic behind you.**

20.3 Enter George Washington National Forest.

21.9 Blue Ridge Parkway Campground is on the right.

23.3 Ride under Blue Ridge Parkway and turn LEFT to enter BRP. For an interesting sidetrip and more hill work, continue straight for 7 miles on Rt. 56 East to Crabtree Falls. This series of seven cascades drops 1,200 feet and is the tallest waterfall east of the Mississippi.

23.4 Turn LEFT at STOP sign onto BRP South. Tye River Gap, elev. 2,969 feet, was named after Allen Tye, an early settler and mountain guide from the area.

25.5 Whetstone Ridge Restaurant and Gift Shop. ★ **Food and drinks are available in-season.** ★ Whetstone is used for sharpening tools.

28.1 Stillhouse Hollow Spring-parking area, spring, and picnic table. Elev. 3,000 feet. This spring was once used to provide water for a local distillery. Although legal in the 1700s and 1800s, many such stills continued production well into the 1900s.

30.8 Yankee Horse Ridge, elev. 3,140 feet. On the left is a 100-foot section of an old logging rail line that brought timber down from the mountains for milling in the valley below. Tracks often wound 50 miles in a circuitous route. The original rails on this site were laid out in 1919 and carried 100 million feet of lumber before being dismantled. The name of this ridge reportedly comes from an incident during the Civil War in which a Northern soldier shot his horse after it had collapsed from exhaustion.

34.1 Irish Gap, elev. 2,279 feet, is named for Irish Creek which flows down the west side of the Blue Ridge. Undoubtedly, both the Creek and Gap were named for the large number of Irish immigrants who settled the area in the 1700s. In fact, the land grant in Rockbridge County was often referred to as "The Irish Tract."

35.5 Boston Knob Overlook, elev. 2,523, and picnic table.

36.8 Clarks Gap, elev. 2,177 feet, may have been named for Joe Clark, subject of a well-known traditional mountain song. Whether it was associated with Old Joe Clark is open to question; however, there are quite a few Clarks residing in the hills and hollows on either side of the BRP in this area. They trace their roots to a pair of brothers who moved here after acquiring land grants based on their service in the War of 1812.

39.2 Irish Creek Valley Overlook, elev. 2,660.

41.2 Whites Gap Overlook, elev. 2,567 feet. The Jordan Toll Road once crossed the mountains at this point.

41.7 Chimney Rock Mountain Overlook, elev. 2,485 feet.

42.4 Turn LEFT for Rt. 60 and exit BRP.

42.6 Check your brakes and turn RIGHT at STOP onto Rt. 60 West beginning a 3.2 mile descent with a 1,240 foot drop in elevation. Route 60 runs from the Atlantic Coast to West Virginia along the old Midland Trail. Early settlers used this road to travel from Williamsburg to points west.

45.8 **Buena Vista** has also been known as Green Valley and Hart's Bottom. It experienced overnight industrial growth after its formation in 1892 based on the manufacture of iron ore, bricks, glass, wagons, and saddles. Its location on the Maury River and proximity to the James River facilitated transportation of products to the east. This boom prosperity died out several years later during the depression of that era. Its present name comes from a former iron works of the same name which produced cannonballs for the Mexican Battle of Buena Vista. ★ **Food and drinks are widely available.** ★

46.5 Continue STRAIGHT on Rt. 60 West/ 29th St. Watch out for heavy vehicular traffic on Rt. 60.

47.1 Continue STRAIGHT at traffic light on Rt. 60 West. Southern Virginia College for Women, a two-year college, is housed in what was one of the area's grand hotels built after the Civil War during the town's boom period.

47.6   Moomaws Landing, on the left, is at the start of an uphill climb. D.C. Moomaw owned a 370-acre estate here. This particular landing was part of the North River Navigation System.

48.5   ★ Food and drinks are available at the convenience store on the right. ★

49.2   Canoeists may want to stop at the James River Basin Canoe Livery on the left in the coffeepot building.

49.6   Before returning to Lexington, rest awhile at the Ben Salem Wayside on the Maury River to the right. This was one of nine locks on the North River Navigation System that connected boat traffic from the North River (now the Maury) to the James River during and just after the Civil War.

50.6   CAUTION: Interstate traffic entering and exiting Rt. 60.

53.1   Enter Lexington.

53.4   Turn RIGHT onto Lewis St.

53.5   Turn LEFT onto Washington St.

53.7   End ride at starting point.

NORTH ROCKBRIDGE TOUR
Lexington • Route 28 • 72.1 miles

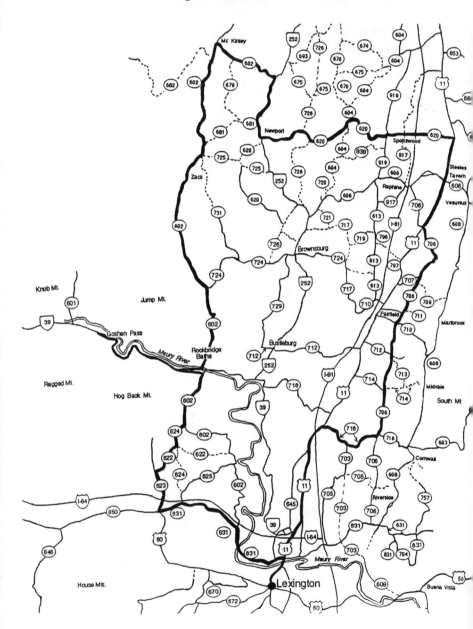

North Rockbridge Tour

Sample a wide variety of sights and terrain on this long loop. Begin with views of the Blue Ridge and finish up in the Alleghenies. Along the way, you'll pass the site of Sam Houston's birth, see the McCormick Farm where the reaper was born, and later enjoy an eight-mile downhill into Rockbridge Baths, once a public resort spring frequented by Gen. Robert E. Lee.

0.0 **Turn RIGHT from Visitor Center parking lot heading WEST on E. Washington St.**

0.1 **Turn RIGHT at traffic light onto Main St. Follow Main St./ Rt. 11 past VMI.**

0.9 **Follow Rt. 11 North across overpass.**

1.1 **Bear RIGHT at STOP sign onto Rt. 11 North. Cross bridge over Maury River with CAUTION.** Once called the North River, the Maury was named for Commodore Matthew Fontaine Maury, who taught meteorolgy at VMI. Route 11 roughly parallels the Great Wagon Road here.

1.2 **Proceed on Rt. 11 with CAUTION for the next 5.6 miles after traffic light.** The hill after the bridge is Hunter Hill. Maj. Gen. David Hunter commanded the Union troops that topped this hill in June 1864 on their way into Lexington. They ransacked and burned homes, mills, iron foundries, and buildings on the VMI campus. Hunter was driven out by Confederate Gen. Jubal Early.

1.9 **CAUTION: Traffic entering and exiting I-64.**

5.9 **CAUTION: Traffic entering and exiting I-81.** Edge Hill, on the left across from the convenience store, was built in the early 1800s and had extensive renovation done in 1866. It's been a homeplace to the Campbell, Alexander, and Lyle families. ★ **Food and drinks are available at the convenience store on the right.** ★

6.3   Maple Hall, on the left, was built in 1850 by John Gibson. Apparently, Gibson's intent in building this elaborate Greek Revival-style home was to outdo his neighbors. Maple Hall now operates as an inn and restaurant.

6.6   Turn RIGHT onto Rt. 716/785 at Sam Houston Wayside. Houston is primarily associated with Tennessee where he was a congressman and governor; and then Texas, where he led the army in its fight against Mexico, and later served as President of the Republic of Texas, and governor and senator of the state of Texas once it entered the union. However, he was actually a native Virginian, born nearby in a log cabin in 1793.

6.7   Continue STRAIGHT on Rt. 716. Rt. 716 also goes left. Washington and Lee University had its roots near this site when Rev. William Graham, a Presbyterian minister, moved his family and the school, then known as Liberty Hall, here in the 1770s. Twelve men were the school's first graduates in 1785. Even Sam Houston attended sporadically between 1801 and 1807. Timber Ridge Presbyterian Church was organized in 1746, and the building erected in 1756. It is the only pre-Revolutionary War Presbyterian church still being used in Rockbridge County. The mansion behind the cemetery is known as Church Hill. It was built in 1866 by Rev. Horatio Thompson, pastor at the Associate Reformed Presbyterian Church across the road. It is a Registered Virginia Landmark.

6.9   Begin climbing Timber Ridge. Timber Ridge was one of the first areas settled and farmed in Rockbridge County in the early 1700s.

7.9   Williams Dairy is in the hollow to the left. This farm was established by John Mackey, who also built the Timber Ridge Presbyterian Church. His farm dates back to 1724, when he received a land grant from the British Crown. This property has never been sold. Mackey's original stone house is out of sight at the rear of the property. Mackey's gravesite in the Timber Ridge cemetery is notable for its use of three stones as well as the prophetic, although misspelled, epitaph.

8.1   Bear LEFT on Rt. 716. Rt. 703 goes right.

8.3   Rising Zion Baptist Church was built in 1752.

9.7   **Turn LEFT at STOP sign onto Rt. 706. Stay on Rt. 706 for the next 8.8 miles.**

11.2   Rockbridge County's Commissioner of Revenue built Whispering Pines, the large frame house on the left, in 1865. The front of the house was added in the 1930s.

11.3   **Continue STRAIGHT on Rt. 706. Rt. 714 goes right.** This stretch of Rt. 706 is called **Donaldsburg**, although the actual village is over the hill to the east.

14.1   **Continue STRAIGHT on Rt. 706. Rt. 710 goes left and then bears right.**

14.5   **Continue STRAIGHT on Rt. 706. Rt. 711 bears left.**

16.9   Thomas Wilson, one of the area's first settlers, built Cyprus Falls Farm on the right at the bend in the road. He settled here along the banks of Moore's Creek in 1752. The main portion of this home was built in 1752 using bricks made on the property. The farm's name is derived from the cascading waterfalls located 100 feet downstream. Only three of the four cascades remain; the fourth was eliminated by Hurricane Camile in 1969. A grist mill and saw mill once utilized power from this waterfall, and the farm was prominent enough at one time to have its own post office.

17.2   **Bear LEFT on Rt. 706. Gravel Rt. 707 bears right.**

18.4   Oak Spring Farm and Vineyard, on the left, is currently operated as a bed and breakfast. The Fultz family built this house in 1826. Native American artifacts dating back 5,000 years have been found across the road. Pat and Jim Tichenor have furnished the inn with items collected during 26 years of military service. In addition to a five-acre vineyard, the grounds provide grazing for some of the animals from the Natural Bridge Petting Zoo, so don't be too surprised by what critters you may see.

18.5   **Turn RIGHT at STOP sign onto Rt. 11 North.**

20.4   **Steeles Tavern** was named after a late 1700s inn owned by David Steele. Apparently Steele had a disfiguring facial scar and a plate in his head from his service in the Revolutionary War. This village was also known as Midway because of its location as a stagecoach stop on the Valley Road, halfway between Staunton and Lexington. To visit the McCormick Farm, turn left onto Rt. 606 and ride **.5 mile.** At the age of 22, Cyrus McCormick successfully demonstrated his mechanical reaper in the fields near his farm, Walnut Grove. His invention's ability to harvest five times faster than a grain cradle began an agricultural revolution in 1831. He moved to Chicago with his business which became International Harvester. ★ **Food and drinks available at Stacy's Store on the right.** ★

21.1 **Continue STRAIGHT on Rt. 11 North past Mt. Carmel Presbyterian Church on the right.** The church was organized in 1837 on land donated by David Steele. The present brick building was erected in 1916.

22.1 **Veer LEFT with CAUTION onto Rt. 620. Road cuts diagonally across median strip, then crosses southbound lanes of Rt. 11.**

23.6 **Cross over I-81.**

23.7 **Spottswood** was possibly named for the Spotts family who lived nearby. It grew up along the Baltimore and Ohio Railroad line in the late 1800s. The old rail bed runs across Rt. 620 between the post office in the old depot and the building that housed the general store.

24.8 **Turn LEFT at STOP sign onto Rt. 620 at Old Providence Presbyterian Church. Rt. 919 goes right.** This was originally the site of the South Mountain Meeting House. The congregation broke off and formed its own Presbyterian sect in the mid-1700s. The disagreement was over several issues including the use of music in the church. The Old Providence Meeting House with the cemetery behind it was first built in 1793 and rebuilt in 1975.

25.0 **Turn RIGHT onto Rt. 620. Rt. 619 goes straight.**

25.4 **Bear RIGHT on Rt. 620. Rt. 850 goes left.**

25.6 The brick farmhouse on the left was built in 1826 and is now part of Fravel Farm, a modern dairy operation.

28.8 The large brick house in the hollow on the left is called Dutch Hollow Farm. It was built in the mid-1800s by Enos Ott. Ott Creek runs in front of the house, and the Ott family ran a mill about one mile away.

30.9   **Cross Moffetts Creek and turn RIGHT at STOP sign onto Rt. 252.** The old Middlebrook-Brownsburg Turnpike was a major thoroughfare from Staunton to Lexington after the 1850s.

31.4   **Newport** flourished in the 1800s because of its location on the turnpike. It was known in the 1800s as Moffett's Creek Post Office after the stream that runs through town. At that time there were 100 residents, two saw mills, a grist mill, two churches, and a public scale for weighing cattle for sale.

32.0   Oak Hill Baptist Church, down the gravel road on the left, was built shortly after the Civil War and has served black congregations since then.

33.5   **Turn LEFT onto Rt. 682 toward McKinley. CAUTION: Narrow road with gravel shoulders.**

34.4   The large brick house on the right at the bend is Airy Mount. It was built in 1857 by James Martin. Although the land was purchased by an ancestor who came to the Shenandoah Valley from Pennsylvania in 1742, the first record of someone living on the tract is from 1792. In the 1800s the Martins appear to have had a sawmill and gristmill across the road and grew tobacco to be shipped to Richmond for sale. The owner has offered water and a picnic spot to cyclists but be sure to ask first.

35.7   **McKinley** was named in 1896 to honor President William McKinley because of his efforts to establish small rural post offices across Virginia. This one, however, closed shortly thereafter in 1908. Before 1896 the village was known as Gravel Hill because of the area's rocky soil.

35.9   Redeemer Lutheran Church was established in 1872 as St. Mark's Evangelical Lutheran Church and then changed to its present name in the 1930s.

36.0   Irvin Rosen runs a fascinating operation at his "It's About Time" clock shop. Visitors are welcome to knock on the door to see if he's open for business. He was born and raised here in McKinley, so he's a wealth of knowledge about local history. Mr. Rosen splits his time between his shop here and Monticello, where he looks after the clocks at Thomas Jefferson's mountaintop home outside Charlottesville.

36.1   McKinley United Methodist Church began in a log building on this site in 1842. It was then known as Union Church because it combined Brethren, Lutheran, and Reformed congregations. After that building burned in 1871, the Lutherans moved up the road and built St. Mark's. A frame church was built here in 1873 and subsequently moved. The present structure was built in 1903 at a cost of $750.

36.3   Turn LEFT at STOP sign onto Rt. 602. Check your brakes!!! You've climbed Dividing Ridge to get to this spot. Technically, this is the southern boundary of the Shenandoah Valley since any precipitation falling south of here will end up in the James River. Any moisture to the north goes into the Shenandoah River. What this means to you as a cyclist is that you've got an eight-mile or so downhill to enjoy.

39.5   Walkers Creek runs along either side of the road. The Little North Mountain section of the Alleghenies is to the right, and you'll start to catch glimpses of Jump Mt. and Knob Mt. in the distance ahead.

40.4   Turn RIGHT at STOP sign onto Rt. 602/Rt. 681. Rt. 681 also goes left.

42.0   The community of **Zack** was presumably named after President Zachary Taylor. Immanuel Presbyterian Church, on the right, was founded in 1879, but the present building was erected in 1904.

43.8   The McCray Hunter Access Trail on the right offers a rough road into the Little North Mountain Wildlife Management Area. Mountain bikers looking for a little off-road action may want to take a detour onto this road. However, first be sure that it's not hunting season!!!

46.0   Bear LEFT on concrete bridge over Walkers Creek. Gravel Rt. 724 goes right. There was once a Jump Post Office in this area, but it no longer exists. It was named for Jump Mt., visible to the west. There's a local story that a Native American woman stood atop this peak watching a battle take place below. When her warrior died, she took her own life by plummeting off what became known as Jump Rock. Look back over your right shoulder at the old log cabin on the hill. Its inverted V-notching is typical of most log houses in the Valley.

46.2   The brick mansion on the right is Camp Maxwelton. It was built in

1815 by Hugh Stuart, who incorporated a two-story portico with brick pillars into the design. The farm has operated as a summer camp since 1953.

46.6 Bear RIGHT on Rt. 602. Rt. 724 goes left to Brownsburg. In 1901 almost 400 skeletons and a variety of artifacts were exhumed from a Native American burial mound in this area. Walkers Creek empties into Hays Creek nearby. Hays Creek was named for John Hays, a major in the Revolutionary War. He is buried on a hill overlooking the mound. It was his request that he be interred there so he could see their spirits rise when the world ended.

47.6 Cross Graham McCray Bridge over Hays Creek.

47.7 Bear RIGHT on Rt. 602. Rt. 731 goes left. Ragged and Hog Back Mts. are off to the right adjacent to Goshen Pass.

50.0 Turn RIGHT at STOP sign onto Rt. 39 West. The magnesia springs resort at **Rockbridge Baths,** to the left on Rt. 39, was one of the many popular 1800s springs in western Virginia. Although no longer open to the public, they are located within the beige cement block wall across from the ★ **Maury River Mercantile — where food and drinks are available.** ★ The building housing the store across the street was once part of the dance hall for the resort, which included a large hotel before burning in 1926. These baths tended to attract city people, including Robert E. Lee who visited during his tenure as President at Washington College after the Civil War.

50.3 Cross bridge over Maury River.

51.7 The former Wilson Springs Hotel is on your left. Construction of this resort began in 1775 in conjunction with a sulfur spring that flowed out of an island in the Maury River. The hotel was first owned by the Porters (no relation to the author), then the Stricklers, and finally the Wilsons who allowed almost anyone to build a cabin on the property and partake of the medicinal waters. Compared to Rockbridge Baths, this spring tended to attract the rougher, rural folks. During the Civil War, Confederate soldiers camped here to defend Goshen Pass.

53.4 Goshen Pass Overlook. During the infamous November 1985 Flood, the Maury River obliterated this overlook and parts of Rt. 39 through this sandstone gap. It was two years before traffic could once more pass through here. Goshen Pass was first known as Dunlap's Pass and then Strickler's Pass. Later its name was associated with the nearby town of Goshen. This trail that has been etched by time has served as a passage for elk, buffalo, stagecoaches, and the railroad. It was through here that Commodore Matthew Fontaine Maury, the renowned VMI professor also known as the "Pathfinder of the Seas," was carried after death by a VMI honor guard. He'd stipulated in his will that he be carried through the pass when the rhododendron was in bloom, but it created somewhat of a logistical problem since he died in early February. The use of a temporary vault in Lexington solved the dilemma of storing the body after his death in February until May.

53.8   Picnic and bathroom facilities are available at Goshen Pass Wayside. This is also a great wading spot, although don't expect much privacy on any nice weekend from May through September. ★ **Food and drinks are available five miles west on Rt. 39 in the town of Goshen.** ★ The Maury River begins above the western end of the pass with the confluence of the Calfpasture and Little Calfpasture Rivers. **To continue on route, backtrack from Goshen Pass Wayside, heading east on Rt. 39 toward Rockbridge Baths.**

57.2   **Turn RIGHT onto Rt. 602 before crossing the Maury River.**

59.9   **Turn RIGHT onto Rt. 624.**

60.9   **Bear RIGHT at curve and continue on Rt. 622. Gravel Rts. 622 and 624 go left.**

62.5   **Turn LEFT at STOP sign onto Rt. 623. Watch for large trucks and debris in road.**

63.7   **Cross over I-64. CAUTION: Traffic entering and exiting interstate.**

64.1   **Turn LEFT onto Rt. 60 East. CAUTION: High speed traffic.**

64.2   **Turn LEFT onto Rt. 631.** A stone marker on the left serves as a reminder of the area's last Indian raid. On October 10, 1764, a party of Shawnees came over the mountain and killed 50-60 settlers near the Big Spring. ★ **Food and drinks are available at Kerrs Creek General Store, .1 mile ahead on Rt. 60.** ★

65.6 **Cross bridge over Kerrs** (pronounced *Cars)* **Creek.** James Kerr and his offspring were among Augusta County's first settlers. Other Kerrs moved south and were putting down roots in Rockbridge County by the early 1740s.

66.4 The gravel road to your left on the other side of Kerrs Creek is the old roadbed. The houses on that side of the creek are older than those on the right. The white house at the top of the hill on the left is the McCowen Place, dating back about 200 years. The spring at the bottom of the hill once supplied water to the house and barns. However, when I-64 was built through here, the Virginia Department of Transportation broke through several caverns above the house and spring. As a result, the spring turned muddy, so VDOT drilled a well for additional water. The problem of cavern collapse is not uncommon in a karst region.

68.0 The limestone outcroppings on the right are also common indicants of karst topography.

68.4 Cross J.H.C. Mann Bridge over the Maury River at Beans Bottom. Col. Mann taught Civil and Structural Engineering at VMI for 46 years. Beans Bottom marks the spot in the annual Lexington Road and River Relay where the initial 3.3-mile run ends, the 10-mile bike loop begins and ends, and the 2-mile canoe leg begins. The event takes place on the first Saturday in May.

69.8 Pass Furr's Mill on the right. Alfred Leyburn built the first mill here around 1830. D.D. Furr bought it in 1901 and expanded it in 1924. Flour milling ceased in 1962.

70.4 **Continue STRAIGHT at STOP sign on Rt. 631. Rt. 681 goes left.**

70.8 **Turn RIGHT at traffic light onto Rt. 11 South and proceed with CAUTION across bridge over Maury River. Continue on Rt. 11 and follow signs for Visitor Center.**

71.7 **Bear RIGHT at Y-intersection onto Jefferson St. past W&L.**

71.9 **Turn LEFT at traffic light onto Washington St.**

72.1 **End ride at starting point.**

Native Americans

The first humans migrated into the Shenandoah Valley over 11,000 years ago. They were descendants of Asians who had crossed a Siberian landbridge that no longer exists. These early Native Americans hunted deer, elk, and moose which were in abundance. By 900 A.D., people living in the Valley had developed an agrarian lifestyle based on the cultivation of corn, beans, squash, and sunflowers. The invention of the bow and arrow helped add wild game and fish to their diet. Their villages consisted of circular houses constructed with sharpened posts driven into the ground closely against each other to form walls. The Thunderbird Site, near the Shenandoah River at Front Royal, has revealed many clues about prehistoric Native American life.

The native population of the Valley began to decline after 1500 for a number of reasons including inter-tribal warfare, pressure from European settlers, and the spread of European diseases from which the natives had no immunities. The idea of land ownership was foreign to the natives while Europeans practiced the doctrine of private property through legal title. As new settlers cultivated fields, built dwellings, and constructed fences for livestock, there was a steadily dwindling amount of land available to people whose tradition and lifestyle had been bound with it for 11,000 years. Although it may never be certain, it's thought that the most recent Native Americans in the Valley were linked to the Tutelo and Saponi tribes.

By 1700, the Valley was a hunting ground for the Iroquois nation with no Native American tribes actually living here. The only contact with natives was through chance encounters with small hunting parties. Initially this was friendly, but the years 1750-1765, encompassing the French and Indian War, saw a period of considerable hostility.

Although the tribes are gone, physical evidence such as pottery shards and names like Shenandoah and Massanutten keep 10,000 years worth of tradition from disappearing altogether.

Appendix A

Flat Routes

INTRODUCTION

While it is the hills that, in part, give the Shenandoah Valley its unique character, all too often would-be cyclists forsake any attempts to get out and ride because of the exertion that such climbs demand. For those who really would enjoy some time in the saddle given a less strenuous route, here is a sampling of several that are relatively flat. These are segments of other rides from each of the five localities. Refer to the respective larger route from which they are derived for maps, descriptive information, and specific mileage.

HARRISONBURG
Where's the Cave?

This ride begins at Port Republic (Mile 18.8) where the North and South Rivers merge to form the South Fork of the Shenandoah River. This town has a lot of interesting architecture and was the site of the Battle of Port Republic where Confederate General Stonewall Jackson scored a major victory in his Valley Campaign. Follow Route 825 to Grottoes whose name comes from its proximity to Grand Caverns (Mile 21.9), Fountain Cave, and Madison's Cave. Explore the cave uncovered in 1804 by Bernard Weyer that remains one of the nation's oldest open to the public and then enjoy a picnic lunch on the grounds.

BRIDGEWATER
Springhill Sojourn

The towering limestone pinnacles at Natural Chimneys (Mile 32.5) and accompanying swimming pool and picnic area make this a great place to begin your ride on the way to the former railroad boomtown of Stokesville (Mile 28.3). If camping is your thing, there are excellent facilities at both Natural Chimneys Regional Park and Stokesville Park where a computerized telescope and observatory will make this truly an out-of-this-world experience. Route 730 joins these two points and follows the North River after it leaves the Allegheny Mountains and the George Washington National Forest.

WAYNESBORO
Coast to the Caverns

William Patterson settled Harriston (Mile 13.4) in 1762. Follow the South River along Route 825 past Cave Hill to Grand Caverns Regional Park (Mile 16.5). Thomas Jefferson rode his horse over the Blue Ridge from Monticello to visit Madison's Cave, and Stonewall Jackson's troops camped in the cave during the Civil War. See the signatures of Confederate soldiers on the walls and have a picnic lunch.

STAUNTON
Springhill Sprint

Turn left onto Route 728 after passing Franks Mill (Mile 5.7) and pedal along the Middle River for 1.8 miles until the road turns from hardsurface to gravel. Tall cliffs make this short ride a memorable stretch. Little evidence remains of the extensive damage that was caused from the flood of November 1985.

LEXINGTON
Blue Ridge Ramble

Pack a lunch from the South River Market (Mile 5.7) and head north along Route 608. You'll crisscross the South River for the next 8.7 miles before reaching the village of Marlbrook (Mile 14.4) Pick a nice spot where wading is allowed and enjoy your meal *alfresco* in the shadow of the Blue Ridge Mountains. This is one of the longest flat stretches of secondary road that you're likely to find in the Shenandoah Valley.

Appendix B

Shenandoah Valley Information

BICYCLE ORGANIZATIONS AND AREA TOURS

Backroads ....(800) GO-ACTIVE
Bikecentennial ....(406) 721-1776
Bike Virginia ....(804) 229-0507
Blue Ridge Bicycle Club ....(703) 943-6911
East Coast Bicycle Academy ....(703) 433-3222
Freewheelin' Bike Tours ....(703) 289-9588
League of American Wheelmen ....(410) 539-3399
Shenandoah Valley Bicycle Club ....(703) 434-1878
Shenandoah Valley Bicycle Festival ....(703) 434-3862
VCC Four Seasons Cycling ....(802) 244-5135

Blue Ridge Parkway ....(704) 259-0769

CAVERNS

Endless Caverns ....(800) 544-CAVE
Grand Caverns Regional Park ....(703) 249-5705
Natural Bridge Village ....(703) 291-2121
Natural Chimneys Regional Park ....(703) 350-2510
Shenandoah Caverns ....(703) 477-3115

DAYTON

Daniel Harrison House ....(703) 879-2280
Harrisonburg-Rockingham Historical Society .(703) 879-2616
Mole Hill Bikes ....(703) 879-2011

George Washington National Forest ....(703) 433-2491

HARRISONBURG

Blueridge Cycle Works ....(703) 432-0280
Cool Breeze Cyclery ....(703) 433-0323
Marks Bike Shop ....(703) 434-5151
Harrisonburg-Rockingham Chamber
   of Commerce and Visitor Center ....(703) 434-2319
Wilderness Voyagers ....(703) 434-7234

LEXINGTON

Backroads Tour of Northern Rockbridge Co. Va. ....(703) 377-2604
Carriage Tours of Historic Lexington, Virginia ....(703) 463-5647
George C. Marshall Museum and Library ....(703) 463-7103

Lexington Bike Shop . . . . (703) 463-7969
Lexington Visitor Center . . . . (703) 463-3777
Rockbridge Historical Society . . . . (703) 464-1058
Stonewall Jackson House . . . . (703) 463-2552
Theater at Lime Kiln . . . . (703) 463-3074
Virginia Horse Center . . . . (703) 463-4300
VMI Museum . . . . (703) 464-7232

McCormick Farm . . . . (703) 377-2255
Mount Jackson Area Chamber of Commerce . . . . (703) 477-3275

NEW MARKET
New Market Area Chamber of Commerce . . . . (703) 740-3212
New Market Battlefield Historical Park . . . . (703) 740-3101

PLANTS
André Viette Farm and Nursery . . . . (703) 943-2315
Virginia Native Plant Society, Dr. Michael Hill
    c/o Bridgewater College . . . . (703) 828-2501

Shenandoah National Park and Skyline Drive . . . . (703) 999-2243
Shenandoah Valley Travel Association . . . . (703) 740-3132

STAUNTON
Augusta Historical Society — Richard Hamrick . . . . (703) 886-2363
Historic Staunton Foundation . . . . (703) 885-7676
Museum of American Frontier Culture . . . . (703) 332-7850
Oak Grove Theatre . . . . (703) 248-5005
Red Velvet Carriage . . . . (703) 377-6704
ShenanArts . . . . (703) 248-1868
Statler Brothers Complex . . . . (703) 885-7297
Staunton-Augusta Chamber of Commerce . . . . (703) 886-2351
Staunton-Augusta Travel Information Center . . . . (703) 332-3972
Staunton Office of Tourism . . . . (703) 885-2839
Staunton Welcome Center . . . . (703) 886-1466
Wilderness Adventure . . . . (703) 886-0320
Woodrow Wilson Birthplace and Museum . . . . (703) 885-0897

WAYNESBORO
Cycle Recycle . . . . (703) 949-8973
P. Buckley Moss Museum . . . . (703) 949-6473
Rockfish Gap Outfitters . . . . (703) 943-1461
Waynesboro-East Augusta Chamber of Commerce . . . . . (703) 949-8203
Wildlife Center of Virginia . . . . (703) 234-WILD

Appendix C

Further Reading

Bicycling the Blue Ridge by Elizabeth and Charlie Skinner

Blue Ridge Parkway Guide: Rockfish Gap to Roanoke by William G. Lord

Blue Ridge Parkway: The Story Behind the Scenery by Margaret Rose Reeves

Country Roads Rockbridge County, Virginia by Katherine Tennery and Shirley Scott

Forest Trees of Virginia published by the Virginia Department of Forestry

Historic Springs of the Virginias by Stan Cohen

Pictorial History of Staunton published by Historic Staunton Foundation.

Roadside Geology of Virginia by Keith Frye

Signposts & Settlers: The History of Place Names in the Middle Atlantic States by Robert I. Alotta

The Insider's Guide to Virginia's Blue Ridge by Margaret Camlin and Lin Chaff

Virginia's Shenandoah Valley by Greg Mock and Tom Dietrich

Wildflowers of the Shenandoah Valley and Blue Ridge Mountains by Oscar W. Gupton and Fred C. Swope

Appendix D

Biographies

RANDY PORTER'S cycling roots go back to Williamsburg where he parlayed a B.S. in Psychology from the College of William and Mary into a partnership known as The Freewheeler Bike Shop. He was one of the founders of Bike Virginia and in that capacity set up and led bike tours through the Shenandoah Valley where he has lived since 1979. In addition to his love of the outdoors, Randy holds an M.Ed. from Virginia Commonwealth University and has taught various levels of children and adolescents with disabilities. This book is the first of many regional guides to outdoor recreation that will be published by him under the Shenandoah Odysseys logo.

A Southerner at heart and a long-time resident of the Shenandoah Valley, co-author **NANCY SORRELLS** combines her interest in history and knowledge of the area to provide a unique insight to *A Cyclist's Guide to the Shenandoah Valley.* She has a B.A. in history from Bridgewater College and is pursuing an M.A. in state, regional, and local history at James Madison University. Nancy works at the Museum of American Frontier Culture as a research historian and does freelance writing as well. Prior to joining the museum, her seven years as a staff member of the sports department of the *Daily News Leader* in Staunton helped her launch her outdoor writing career. Her interests in cycling and Shenandoah Valley history have enabled her to combine her first loves onto these pages.

Index

S

T

V

W

Y

Z

A cyclist takes a water break at the railroad crossing formerly known as Ellard near the turnpike town of Greenville.